D0921081

I Was Young And Now I Am Old, Yet I have Never Seen the Righteous Forsaken or Their Children Begging Bread

Psalm 37:25

I Was Young And Now I Am Old

Psalm 37:25

The Adventurous and Blessed Life of Pastor Tui

Tui D. Pitman

I Was Young And Now I Am Old

The Adventurous and Blessed Life of Pastor Tui

Pitman Publishing

Requests for information should be addressed to:

Tui D. Pitman
Wetumpka, AL 36093
TuiPitman38@gmail.com

ISBN 978-0692828755

Paperback edition 2017

Printed in the United States of America

Tui's Stories

I didn't think much about a family legacy until I had grandchildren. My mother told me some wonderful stories, and she promised to write a book so that her grandchildren would also benefit from the treasure of experiences that molded her into one of the most impressive ladies I have known.

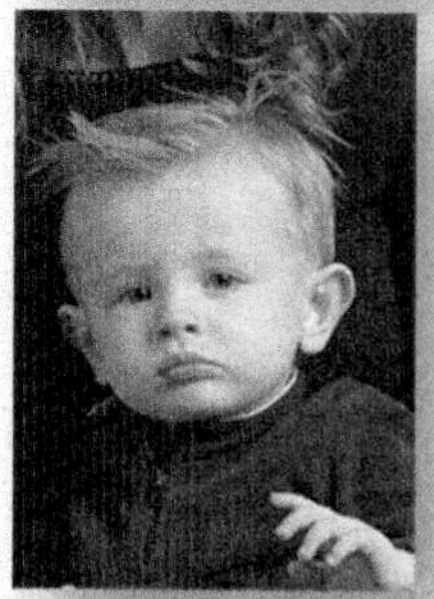

History helps us to realize that we are connected to something larger than ourselves. Each generation influences future generations either in positive or negative ways. Our family has had the privilege of some very positive personalities to pattern our lives after. To be honest, a few nut cases have rattled around the family closet as well.

I wrote these stories so that my grandchildren will understand how God has worked in the lives of our family. I want them to realize that God can be trusted. Not everything in life is positive, but somehow God manages to bring blessing out of disasters. At times He intervenes to pull us out of the fire. Along the way some humor and adventure is added to the mixture.

I am reminded of the story of Joshua who at the end of his life gathers the tribes of Israel together and reviews with them their family history and reminds them of the benefit of serving the Lord.

I hope that you will find these stories entertaining and spiritually enlightening as well. I dedicate this book to my grandsons with the prayer that they will grow and live their lives for God.

Wesley, Bradley, Daniel, Isaac and Caleb

Table of Contents

Family Background

Family Background

John Alexander Mooney

Most family trees are pretty colorful and filled with interesting characters and stories. Mine is no exception. My own blood line is primarily Irish, Dutch and German – all immigrants to the United States. And, most of my great or great-great grandfathers fought in the Civil War.

Having spent my early years growing up in the "South", I originally thought that the true name of the Civil War was, "The War of Independence from Northern Aggression". Once when I was just a young school boy I came home from a history lesson on the Civil War and announced to my mother, "Mom! We would have won that there war if we had just had enough men!"

John Alexander Mooney

Of course, not all of my ancestors would have agreed, as some fought on both sides of the conflict.

In any case, one notable character (my mother's maternal grandfather) was John Alexander Mooney, a short and irascible Irish Catholic with green piercing eyes and a dark complexion. He ran away from home at the age of fourteen and enlisted in the Union army (perhaps my excuse for running away from home when I was a boy – a story later in this book). Of course, his parents nullified his enlistment and took him back home, much to his dismay.

Predictably, he ran away again the following year with his close friend William Bendon and enlisted in the army under the pseudonym of John J. Cook. He wanted some action and he soon got it. At just 16 years of age he fought in the Battle of the Wilderness and received a saber wound to his head, but survived. His friend William wasn't so lucky and died of his wounds. These events frightened John so much that he immediately deserted the army. However, he soon built up his courage and rejoined the army, yet again, but under yet another pseudonym, Philip Cook (He didn't want to be discovered for deserting his post the first time).

Somehow he survived the Civil War and, in 1870, while stationed in Ohio, he married Catherine McCarty. Still, in the army he was then assigned to a series of posts in the west. As a military man, he was constantly moving his large family, with ten children, all around the country (One of these ten children was my grandmother Cora Lee. She was born on an army base in Louisiana). Unfortunately, military life also came with a few bad habits for my great grandfather. He took up drinking with a bit too much passion. This habit would eventually catch up with him. My mother remembers her grandfather as a real gentleman when sober, but difficult to manage when drunk.

When John was in his seventies he was traveling on a train and got drunk and became involved in a fight. He was pushed off the train while it was steaming rather rapidly down the track, and was instantly killed when his head hit a rock by the side of the track.

It took his wife, Catherine, several years to obtain a military pension because John had changed his name several times while enlisted. However, she was finally granted a pension of $12 a month for my great grandfather's service in the Indian Wars. This doesn't sound like much, but $12 in the late 1800s was equivalent to around $350 in today's money – still not a lot, but enough to live on.

On my father's side, my great-great grandfather Martin Pitman (of Dutch descent), married Mary Boone. Mary was a cousin to none other than the famous Daniel Boone. Unfortunately, this kinship did not include a great deal of natural beauty. She was not what you would call "easy on the eyes." And, her prominent nose has been passed down through the generations as a fairly distinctive Pitman trait. It is important to note, however, that those who knew her well said that she did, in fact, have a very sweet disposition – which has been, on occasion, a bit more difficult to trace through the Pitman line.

In any case, my great-great grandfather Martin also fought in the Civil War. He fought for the North under the leadership of William Tecumseh Sherman. On Sherman's infamous march across Georgia, Martin, along with a group of Union soldiers, stopped to "buy" (or more likely steal) berry pies. The pies were full of arsenic. Several of the men died. Martin, however, just managed to survive - but was affected the rest of his life with stomach problems. He also maintained and never overcame his extreme hatred for the South. My grandfather, Elmer, often said, "My grandfather Martin could smell a 'Johnny reb' a mile off!" He also maintained his devotion to General Sherman. That is why, when my great grandfather was born, he was given the name William Tecumseh Sherman Pitman.

Another of my great grandfathers, Wilson Kime on my mother's side, joined the Confederate army at the age of thirty-five, left his young family behind (my grandfather Samuel Henderson Kime was only five years old at the time), and became part of the Army of North Carolina in the soon to become infamous 34th Regiment – a regiment that fought many bloody battles throughout much of the war. Soon, General Stonewall Jackson took over the command of the 34th and led my great grandfather and the other soldiers in many famous battles. One of the bloodiest was the battle of Fredericksburg where twelve thousand Union soldiers were killed within just thirty minutes. Yet, somehow, my grandfather survived this and all of the other battles he fought during the war – only to be captured, in March of 1865, at Petersburg, Virginia. He spent the remaining two months of the war in a federal prison.

All of these characters had a part to play in the background of my own family and my own genetic make-up – and certainly my own natural tendencies of character and personality. It is very interesting to study family histories and see how genetic and character traits have affected future generations. All of us have many scoundrels in the closet along with a precious few saints scattered here and there. Yet, despite the baggage of our natural inheritance from our family trees, we can all take courage. Consider, for example, the less than ideal family tree of Christ. Isn't it amazing to see that, despite the many colorful and flawed characters in His family tree, He managed to live a perfect life? With over two thousand years of sin added to the genetic pool, it is no wonder that we all struggle with serious character flaws. But, with the help of Jesus, we can have a powerful friend and advocate who will help us polish off these inherited spots from our own characters, becoming more and more like Him.

Watch and Be Ready

Rosa Ann Cora Lee Mooney was my grandmother. She was a vivacious Irish widow who outlived four husbands. She had seven children at the time she joined the little country Adventist church in Luther, Montana. Her second husband, Foster Senecal, was tragically killed when he was crushed between two railroad cars while working on the railway. Yet, he did not leave my grandmother destitute. He happened to be the owner of a large hardware store and hotel saloon in the town of Luther. After all the accounts were settled my grandma inherited a tidy sum of money. She wisely used this money to buy a small farm several miles from town and moved her family there. They had chickens, goats, a couple of milk cows, a mule to help with the plowing and two very spirited horses to pull their buggy to church on Saturdays.

The folks in town thought that she had completely lost her mind when she decided to join the Seventh-day Adventist church. Those "Advents" had some weird ideas. They went to church on the wrong day of the week and didn't eat certain foods like good old pork chops and crayfish. How in the world did she expect her kids to be healthy? They didn't drink, smoke or go to dances. What a boring life they lived! The town folks figured it was all due to the stress over the death of her husband. His death must have messed up Cora's brain and caused her to join this weird sect.

But, as far as the church in Luther was concerned, they were very happy to have Cora Lee and her large family join their small group. The church was still quite small, of course, and had no pastor. A deacon would lead out in a Bible study, lead the singing of hymns and then read a sermon.

Several months after Cora Lee began attending the church a dignified middle-aged gentleman arrived with one young boy in tow. He announced that he would be the pastor of the small church. When the church found out that he also had seven more children they were overjoyed. Not only would they have a pastor but the significant majority of their membership would be active, very active, young people.

Samuel Henderson Kime had been a Methodist preacher who had become an Adventist after reading some pamphlets on the Sabbath which were left in a dry goods store. He took the pamphlets home and studied them and became convicted that he needed to make a change. So, he decided he must leave his Methodist faith and became a pastor in the Seventh-day Adventist church. He helped organize the first Seventh-day Adventist church south of the Mason-Dixon Line in Banner Elk, North Carolina (His son Stewart eventually became the first president of the Carolina Conference of the Seventh-day Adventist Church).

Several years later Samuel moved his family to Washington State where he served as district pastor to several small churches and groups. While there his wife died.

Although Samuel was 23 years older than Cora Lee, his distinguished good looks attracted her interest and, with the encouragement of the small congregation, they decided to marry. So Samuel moved his family, which was composed of eight children, to Cora Lee's farm. Now, there were a total of fifteen children in the merged family. My mother, who was born to Samuel and Cora Lee, added one more to the mix. Then, Sammy, who was born two years later, made the total seventeen. After my grandfather died, my grandmother married her fourth husband, Frank Trainer – who already had children from his wife who had died. The addition of these children gave my mother a total of *twenty-three* brothers and sisters.

Tragically, my mother's full brother Sammy died at the age of two when he ran into the house one day to get a drink of water. He mistakenly picked up a cup of gasoline that was being used to clean clothes. He drank it before anyone could stop him. He aspirated the gasoline and died a few minutes later. His death hung like a dark cloud over the family for years.

Samuel often went away on long trips to preach. He usually went on horseback or took the buggy. Cora Lee was left at home to manage the kids and the farm. It was a big adjustment for a young mother to try to manage so many children all of a sudden – some of which were near her own age! In fact, two of her "daughters" were older than she was but did not live with the family because they were already married.

Cora Lee was a good manager – she had to be! Each child had a job and a responsibility. Beaman, who was five years older than his baby sister, Naomi, was assigned to babysit her. He detested this job because it curtailed his free time to play with his own friends. One day he tried to make a deal to trade her to one of the neighbor's boys in exchange for a very fine looking frog. He even threatened to roll her baby buggy off a cliff but, fortunately, his older brother, Clifford, intervened. Yet, Clifford was no saint.

One day, Beaman and Clifford were given the assignment to watch the two family cows. One cow was dearly loved because she was very tame and followed the family around like a dog. They named her Plunket. At the back of the house, there was a fifty-acre pasture. A railroad track located at the back of the pasture serviced a train that ran stock and goods to Luther. It had an unreliable time schedule but it usually came by in the afternoon twice a week on Mondays and Wednesdays. It was Beaman's and Clifford's job to make sure that on the days the train came through the cows were kept off the track. However, on one side of the pasture there was a very attractive little pond, surrounded by trees and fed by a cold spring. Of course, the boys liked to go swimming in this pond.

One day, when they were supposed to watch the cows, it got so hot that they decided to take a quick dip in the pond to cool off. They were having such a good time that they completely forgot about the cows and the train. They were in the middle of their splashing and yelling when the repeated piercing whistle of the train interrupted their play. They suddenly remembered their responsibility and hurriedly dressed and ran for the tracks - but they were too late. The train had already hit Plunket. There was nothing they could do. She was already dead when they got to her. She had been on the track when the train came around a curve and was not able to stop in time. For punishment Beaman and Clifford had to wash the family dishes for two months. No easy task for such a large family.

When Samuel Kime preached his next sermon, he walked down the aisle of the church thumping his Bible and singing "Watch and be ready!" The boys knew why he was singing that hymn. He seemed to sing it louder as he approached their pew. Their step father's sermon that day was on the nearness of Christ's second coming and the danger of not watching and being ready.

In his sermon he kept repeating the word, "watch, watch, watch!" Each time he looked straight at Beaman and Clifford.

The Model T

Grandma had decided. It was time to invest in one of those newfangled machines called an automobile. Grandpa (Samuel Kime) could travel to churches even faster without having to use a horse and buggy.

After all, the Model T could go up to thirty-five miles an hour on a flat road! So they bought a Model T Ford for two hundred dollars. It was one of the first cars in their area of the country. However, Samuel still preferred the buggy over the Model T. The car was not as reliable as the horse. There were too many flats and you never knew where to find gasoline. Besides, gasoline, at four cents a gallon, was expensive!

On Sundays, Grandma would have one of the older boys drive the car in to town to pick up some of her lady friends for a ride out into the country. Fourteen-year-old Beaman loved to drive and had, surprisingly, proven to be very responsible with the car. However, one Sunday his sanity left him. He saw two lovely young girls walking down the road and decided to show off a bit. "Watch this!" he yelled at them as he stuck his feet through the spokes of the steering wheel. "No hands!" The girls giggled and smiled at him as he drove by. But Grandma, who was also in the car with her lady friends, yelled at him, "Beaman! Behave yourself! Get your feet out of the steering wheel and drive like a normal human being!"

While he was trying to untangle his feet they came to a steep downhill stretch with a sharp curve at the bottom. The Model T began to gain speed and the ladies in the back began to yell wildly. One lady passed out. Beaman frantically tried to remove his feet from between the spokes but found that they were stuck. As the curve appeared he quickly flipped in his seat and righted himself again as the car neatly sailed around the curve and finally glided to a stop. He was then able to untangle his long legs from the steering wheel. Looking at his mother he muttered breathlessly, "We made it!" But, of course, she was not impressed. "Next time," she shot back, "I'm driving!"

Several weeks later my grandpa had to leave home to go on a preaching tour. Grandma decided it was time she learned to drive rather than depending on irresponsible children. "Beaman and Clifford," she announced, "push the Model T out of the barn and bring it around to the front of the house. I need to go to town to get some flour and sugar." And then she added, "By the way, I'll be driving and you boys can teach me how on the way to town. I am sure that driving can't be *that* difficult." Then, she climbed into the car behind the steering wheel and all the children settled around her. Beaman took the seat next to her to advise her on the finer points of motoring. Of course, the problem of managing the throttle, brakes, and shifting, all at the same time, made driving the Model T a challenge for a beginner. Clifford stood at the front of the car and gave the crank a vigorous turn. The Model T sputtered and backfired a couple of times. Cranking the "Tin Lizzy" could be hazardous to your health because, if you were not careful, the crank could jerk with such force that it could break one's arm. Clifford gave the crank another vigorous turn and the Model T purred to life. Tying her scarf around her hat grandma grasped the steering wheel with determination and turning to Beaman smiled, "If you will engage the clutch young man we will head this buggy to town."

It was a wild ride. The car lunged from one side of the road to the other accompanied by the screams of the children being flung from side to side. Beaman and Clifford both frantically grabbed for the steering wheel to bring stability to the lurching car. Grandma wrestled the steering wheel back. She was a little agitated. Her voice rose above the shrieks of the children, "Leave me alone boys! I can do it!" So, they grit their teeth and awaited their fate. After a while, she did start to get a bit better. Over the last few miles of road, she managed to keep the Model T fairly well centered. So, the children gradually settled down to normal chatter.

As the Model T entered town, Beaman pulled the gas lever down to reduce their speed. At that point, the Model T backfired and scared several horses that were tied to a hitching post in front of the blacksmith shop. The horses began to buck and whinny. A couple horses broke loose and began running down the street in front of the car. Grandma tried desperately to stop the car, but executing the proper steps for a novice to stop a Model T require full concentration. Frustrated and confused, grandma reached for the gas lever and pushed down in an effort to slow down. Instead, this action had the opposite effect. The car shot forward and she was thrown back in her seat. Down the block were the rails for the train that went through the middle of town. Several boxcars stood on the track blocking the street. The closer grandma came to the train the more confusion and panic seized her. She began yelling, "Whoa, whoa!" It began to dawn on the children that their mother had lost complete control and they were going to crash. The yelling and screaming of the children added to the confused state of grandma. One by one and two by two the children began bailing out of the car and rolling down the dusty street. By this time the runaway car had attracted an audience. Beaman made one last desperate attempt to wrest control of the car, but his mother's hands were frozen to the wheel. At the last moment, just before impact, he flung himself from the car into the street. The car careened off the side of the boxcar and came to rest on the porch of the dry goods store. The front end of the Model T was smashed. Grandma sat serenely in the driver's seat, her hair a mess and her hat cocked to one side – still with a death grip on the steering wheel.

The children scurried back to lower her down to the ground and assist her as she staggered to the livery stable. On the way home, in a borrowed buggy, she mumbled, "That machine is of the devil.

No more driving for me!" She kept her word until the day she died at the age of 94. She did, however, make a wonderful back seat driver…

At the time of her death she had outlived four husbands and in the process accumulated 23 children, counting his, hers and theirs. Many of those children grew up to be leaders in the community and church. There were preachers, doctors, teachers, administrators, nurses, and missionaries.

Someone remarked about my grandmother, "She was cute and full of spice, but you wouldn't want to marry her if you wanted to live for a long time." Her last marriage, at 81, was her happiest – even though, during their honeymoon, her new 82-year-old husband, Frank, hugged her so tight he broke one of her ribs!

"God," she once told me late in her life, "has been my very best friend. He has blessed me more than I could have ever hoped."

Whose Sister Is She?

Naomi (Kime) Pitman, 1925

The whole family was devastated when they found out that Beaman had run away from home. He was only seventeen. No one heard from him for months. Grandpa and Grandma Kime prayed for him every day at worship. Every now and then tears would well up in Grandma's eyes when anyone mentioned Beaman. About a year and a half after he disappeared, Grandma received a letter from her wayward son.

> "Dear Mom, I am in the navy. I am writing you from Panama to let you know that I am alive and doing well.
>
> As you know I have been trying for years to invent a perpetual motion machine which would make me filthy rich. I threw my last try into the Caribbean Sea. I am also through with my independent life. I realize I can't run away from God and His calling. And, I miss my family.

As soon as I get out of the navy in a few months I plan to go to college at Walla Walla and enroll in the theology course and become a preacher like my father and like my big brother Stewart."

True to his word Beaman joined his brother Clifford and his sister Naomi at Walla Walla College. Clifford was taking pre-med and Naomi was planning to be an elementary school teacher. Both Clifford and Beaman were older than most of the students in the school. They were full of life, single and handsome. Many of the girls were anxious to meet them but these two brothers seemed to be crazy about a freshman student named Naomi. She wasn't what you'd call an outstanding beauty but these two guys were falling all over themselves to walking her to class, meet her in the cafeteria, take her to Saturday night socials and sit with her in church. They held hands and hugged each other good night. Someone reported that they had even seen my mother kiss Beaman on the cheek. This kind of display of public affection was frowned upon by the administration of the conservative college. Beaman, Clifford, and my mother were asked to meet with the dean of students to give reasons why they should be allowed to remain in the school given the reports of such scandalous behavior? My mother, with tears flowing down her cheeks, responded that, "They are both my brothers and we have always been an affectionate family. I love my brothers."

Beaman added, "We are just trying to take care of our little sister!"

The dean of the school looked at them skeptically. "How can you claim to be her brothers when your last names are Senecal and hers is Kime?"

"That's easy!" Clifford said with a grin, "Naomi is our half-sister. We both have the same mother but different fathers."

It was decided to let them stay in school and many ladies rejoiced to know that these two handsome young men were available after all.

Soon after, Beaman met a little red headed girl by the name of Avis Detamore. He was immediately smitten by her. However, things weren't going to be easy for Beaman. Her father was a very strict Seventh-day Adventist minister. And, when Elder Detamore heard that his daughter was dating a former navy man he was very concerned. "Beaman," he gravely explained to his daughter, "is a man of the world. I forbid you to date him!" Poor Avis was crushed, but she secretly continued to see Beaman. Beaman confided to my mother one night, "I love that little red head and I am going to marry her."

At the end of the school year Beaman and Avis mustered the courage to confront Elder Detamore. Beaman cleared his throat, "Elder Detamore, we would like to have your blessing. In fact, we would like for you to do the wedding. But if we don't get your blessing we are planning on running off and getting the justice of the peace to marry us."

Faced with the prospects of having his daughter elope with a wild navy man Elder Detamore decided to cave in and perform the wedding himself - although he was very worried that their marriage would not last. During the wedding service he used the text, "A man that does not provide for his family is worse than an infidel."

However, it did not take very long before Beaman and Elder Detamore became very close. They did everything together from cooking to preaching. He was proud to introduce his son-in-law as the finest young man around to everyone he met.

As far as my mother was concerned, Beaman and Clifford always took care of their little sister. When my mother decided to become a doctor, Beaman and Clifford offered to help. There was very little money, but Beaman, Clifford, and the entire family worked together and scraped up just enough money to help her get through school.

My Dad

My grandfather, Harry Elmer Pitman, came from a wealthy farming family in Madera. He started out life fairly wealthy, but a bit spoiled. Then he chose, contrary to the repeated advice and earnest pleadings of his wife, Hazel, to make a speculative investment in oil. As a result, he lost pretty much his entire fortune. His family was soon struggling to survive in the Santa Cruz area of California.

During this rather difficult time for the family, my father, Harry Theron Pitman, was born in 1912.

As a child, my dad learned to work hard to help his family survive. He helped his father work in the lettuce fields around Santa Cruz and Watsonville. He and his younger brother and sister also helped his mother do laundry for wealthy home owners in Santa Cruz – and then he and his brother Alton and his sister Alvalee would deliver the laundry in an old model T Ford. Later, in his teenage years, he worked long hard hours in the packing sheds in Watsonville.

Though times were hard and money was scarce, he was able to earn enough money to go to Pacific Union College and take pre-med. He was naturally gifted, excelled in mathematics, and had a strong memory. So, even though he worked summers and long hours during school, he was still able to graduate first in his class.

After graduation, he went on to attend medical school at The College of Medical Evangelists in Loma Linda, California. It was a real struggle to make it through medical school because medical school was not quite as easy as college had been. Yet, he still had to work just as hard to pay for his own tuition. There simply was no money available from the family to support him while he was in school. Somehow, though, he was still very successful and did very well in his classes. He was also inventive as far as ways to make money. For example, he started buying cars, fixing them up, and renting them to students (perhaps the first Budget car rental business).

While in medical school, a close friend and classmate, DeVere McGuffin, introduced him to a young woman doctor. The year was 1938. He was immediately attracted to her and her determination to be a doctor. After all, there were hardly any women medical students, much less doctors, in 1938. He decided to try his hand at winning her favor by making sandwiches and bringing them to her during her late night shifts at the hospital. And, what do you know, it worked!

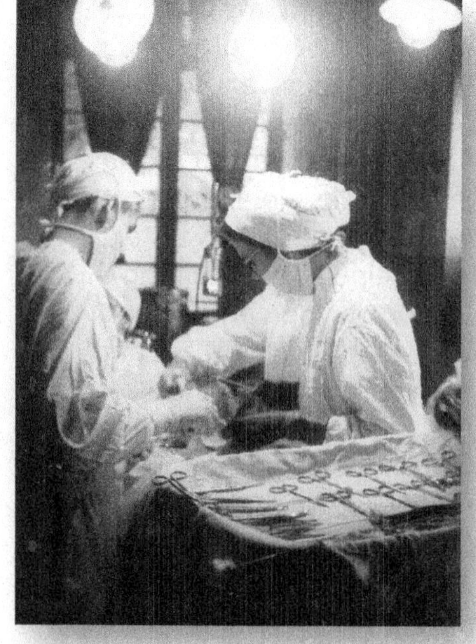

Naomi Esther Kime and my dad were married that same year. After graduating from medical school, he specialized in general surgery at Fresno County Hospital and became the chief resident. My parents went on to have two children, Linda Lee, born the very next year (1939), and me three years later (1942).

Then, in 1943, my dad accepted a call to run a hospital in Chulumani, Bolivia for the Seventh-day Adventist Mission. After some difficulties with the Bolivian Mission president, he decided that he wanted to be independent of the local mission while still maintaining ties with the General Conference. As part of this effort, he signed a lease with the Bolivian government for a hospital in the jungle town of Gaujara-Mirim. He also promised the Bolivian government that he would run the hospital in Chulumani, at the same time, until a replacement could be found.

In order to effectively operate both hospitals he purchased two Vultee BT-13s and had them flown down from San Antonio, Texas. He then hired a Czechoslovakian pilot to help him fly these planes. Everything was on track for a brilliant career as a mission doctor running multiple hospitals and clinics. He had also established a small, but successful, trucking business.

There are times and events that happen in our lives that we cannot understand. I had just turned four years old when, on

My Dad (Theron) and Tony the day of the crash

November 11, 1946, my father was killed at the very young age of 34. He and his pilot, Anthony, were flying along a mountain pass and, evidently, took a wrong turn into a blind-end canyon during some bad weather. There was no room to maneuver nor was the plane able to climb high enough to go over the very high mountains in that region (over 20,000 feet). At the end of the pass, they crashed into Tunari, a mountain located near Cochabamba, Bolivia. They had been flying from Gaujara-Mirim to La Paz to attend a nurse's graduation in Chulumani.

My dad was buried at the Seventh-day Adventist school in Vinto. Later his remains were transferred to La Paz and placed at the Seventh-day Adventist school named in his honor, Instituto Pitman.

I only have a few fuzzy memories of my father. Yet, his early death had a huge life-long impact on me. In this life, we may never know the answers or understand the reasons for why God allows such tragedies to happen – especially to those who seem to be serving Him so well in the prime of their lives. Yet, I have learned to trust God with such things knowing that He loved my father and He has always loved and taken care of my family and me – and has given me the assurance that all will be well; that I will one day see my father again and tell him all the stories that he missed and introduce him to my own sons and grandsons. Such an assurance is truly one of the greatest gifts that God can give each one of us in this life.

My Dad and Me

Theron at 5 years

Theron and his
Mother Hazel

Theron's Funeral at
Cochabamba

Theron's grave in Vinto

My Mom

My mom, Naomi Kime, was born in Luther, Montana in 1908. She was the first child of Samuel and Carrie Kime. However, as already noted, she already had many half brothers and sisters – to include step sisters who were older than her mother. She was a great aunt when she was born!

At the time of her birth, the family lived near Indian country. She can remember Indians come down from the mountains and riding through their farm. Since her father was a preacher and never made much money, the whole family worked on the farm and made spending money by picking and selling strawberries and other produce.

When my mom graduated from medical school, in 1936, women comprised only 5% of American medical students and even a smaller percentage of practicing physicians. She was certainly a go-getter. After medical school, she served in five foreign countries and then went on to practice medicine in California and Tennessee.

From the time she was a young woman, my mom had a strong appetite for learning and educational pursuits. She received her high school education from Walla Walla Academy and then went on to obtain her teacher's training at Andrew's University in Michigan. She taught for two years in Baltimore, Maryland before returning to Walla Walla College for pre-med training. Then, in 1931 she enrolled in the College of Medical Evangelist (CME), now known as Loma Linda University. She attended the CME on the co-op plan. This meant that she took courses for one month and then worked in the hospital the following month to help pay her way.

Being a woman in medicine had its difficulties. She used to tell a story about taking call for another doctor one particular night. In those days, doctors used to actually visit their patients in the patient's own home

(real house calls are somewhat of a novel concept these days). In any case, after being greeted with surprise at the door at the home of a patient, a man asked her to wait while he announced, "Your doctor couldn't come, but there is a sixteen-year-old girl at the door who says she's a doctor! Shall I let her in?"

Following her graduation from CME my mom worked for several years as medical secretary for the Southern California Conference of Seventh-day Adventist. She worked for the Conference by

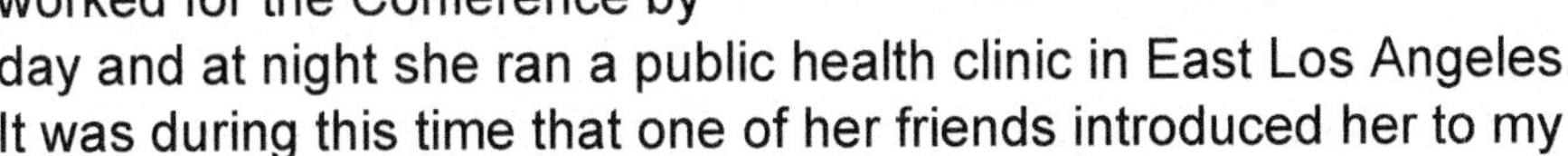

day and at night she ran a public health clinic in East Los Angeles. It was during this time that one of her friends introduced her to my

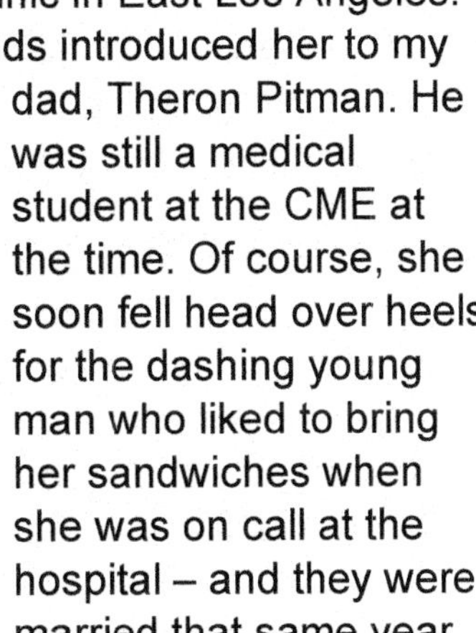

dad, Theron Pitman. He was still a medical student at the CME at the time. Of course, she soon fell head over heels for the dashing young man who liked to bring her sandwiches when she was on call at the hospital – and they were married that same year.

Then, in 1943 my parents went to Bolivia where my mom spent five years in active medical missionary work. She taught at the Adventist nursing school and practiced in Chulumani Hospital for three years and then served as director of the Gaujara-Mirim Hospital in Bolivia for two years. While in Bolivia she met and became friends with three Bolivian presidents, the Bolivian ambassador to the Vatican, and the American ambassador to Bolivia.

After my dad was killed in a flying accident in Bolivia, she was devastated, but remained strong and productive. She never remarried despite numerous offers because, she used to say, "No one could remotely compare to Theron."

She returned to the United States in 1948 with my sister and me and spent three years in a pediatric residency at the White Memorial Hospital in Los Angeles. In 1951 she moved to Tennessee where she served as a pediatrician and school of health director at Madison, Tennessee. She was also on the staff of the Baptist Hospital in Nashville, Tennessee.

It's funny, but even though my mom was a physician, and made a fair amount of money, she didn't like to spend it on herself. It seems to me like my mother was an exceptional role model for Christian stewardship. She was always looking for ways to save money so she could help with some church project or a student in need. She lived in a very small simple house. However, several of the successful community doctors drove fancy cars, Cadillacs in those days. So, as a teenager, I suggested that she buy one. Surprisingly, she humored me and we went to the local Cadillac dealership and looked at various Cadillacs. I then went off to boarding school fully expecting to see my mother driving around in a Cadillac. However, when I came home on leave I found a VW, of all things, parked in the driveway. Surprised, I ran into the house and asked, "Mom, whose VW is sitting in the driveway?!"

"It's my VW," she said and she gave me a wry little smile. She had saved several hundred dollars that she could use to help struggling nursing students in financial need.

My mom also had an absolutely brilliant mind – in some ways. I'd say it was almost photographic. She could quote poetry by the hour and she enjoyed reciting, from memory, long passages from the book "Desire of Ages." She was, at the same time, however, very absent-minded. She was constantly forgetting her purse. On several occasions, she left it sitting on the sidewalk where she set it down to open her car door. She would then get into the car and drive off leaving her handbag all alone. Fortunately, in those days, there were many honest-hearted people who would always bring her purse to her office the next day.

I also remember the many times when she would spend the entire night at the hospital watching over a sick child. One morning after spending the night with a sick patient she wearily made her way to the car, unlocked it, climbed in and drove home. Several hours later the sheriff arrived at our house and asked my mother for the car. She had mistakenly driven the wrong VW home. It was even the wrong color. How her key fit that car I'll never know (perhaps there were a limited number of different kinds of keys issued for certain types of cars in those days?).

In 1959 she returned to Loma Linda where she became a staff member of the department of pediatrics until her retirement in 1974. She became a leader in pediatric healthcare, serving as the senior attending physician and the director of the intensive care unit for the newborn nursery. She was widely published and a well-known lecturer in her field. She performed medical service in Tanzania, Ecuador and in New Guinea and even helped establish a medical school in Afghanistan.

In 1974, at her retirement from Loma Linda School of Medicine, she was named associate professor of pediatrics emeritus. She then became a visiting professor at the University of Guadalajara, Mexico. After two years in Guadalajara, she was called to Montemorelos University in Montemorelos, Mexico. She taught there for eleven years before retiring a second time. She was named professor emeritus at Montemorelos University in 1989. The whole time she stayed at the school she lived in a very small storage room at the back of the school laundry.

It was while she was at Montemorelos that she began having heart problems and found that she slept better sitting up than lying down. She wanted one of those Lazy-Boy recliners, but could not find one in Mexico. So, she drove to McAllen, Texas, to buy one. At the furniture store, she asked if they could deliver the chair to Montemorelos. She was told that they did not deliver furniture to Mexico. "Fine," she responded. "I'll take it there myself."

"Where did you park your truck," they asked?

"It's parked out front," she replied with a smile. They carted the chair out, but couldn't locate the truck. The only thing they saw was a white VW.

"Is that your car," they inquired?

"Yes, it is."

"We can't get this recliner in there!"

"Just strap it to the top of the car."

So, they did - and she drove her little VW with the large chair on top, almost as big as the car it seemed, all the way back to Montemorelos.

On another occasion, she decided the medical school needed some cadavers. So she decided to drive to Loma Linda University, in southern California, to see if they would give the medical school at Montemorelos some cadavers. The school administrators at Montemorelos decided that it would not be a good idea for an eighty-two-year-old woman to be driving all that way all by herself. So, they sent along a young medical student to drive the car for her and "protect her." His skill would soon be called on. As they were driving along, late at night, they suddenly hit a burro that was crossing the road. The accident ruptured the gas tank and pushed the fender into the front tire.

My mom, and this young medical student, were in the middle of nowhere, in Mexico, in the middle of the night. The young man was petrified! "Someone has to go and get some help," my mother gently explained to the young man. But, he just sat there, unable to respond. So, my mom opened the door, got out, and said, "You just stay here and watch the car while I walk back to the town we passed about a half hour ago – Ok?" He still didn't get the hint. So, my eighty-two-year-old mom started walking down the road all by herself.

About two o'clock in the morning an old farmer and his wife drove by in an old beat-up pickup truck. They stopped and took her the rest of the way into town and to the local police station.

Early that morning, before the sun came up, my mom and a tow truck arrived at the scene of the accident. Of course, the brave medical student had disappeared. He'd hitched a ride to the border with a businessman who had stopped to see if he could help.

Her car was towed into town and the local mechanic banged out the fender and repaired the gas tank and in a matter of hours she was on her way.

When she got back to Montemorelos she informed the administration that in the future she would not need any young men to assist her because it was too difficult to babysit them.

After retiring from her work in Montemorelos, she went to live in her cabin in the mountains of Tennessee - taking care of the children there in the Smokey Mountains for seven years. Then, in 1995, she decided to move to Loma Linda, California to be closer to family. She lived for several more years and was able to witness my son Sean graduate from medical school in 1997 – and was able to dedicate him during his graduation ceremonies. The next year she passed away at the age of 89 – having made her corner of the world a bit better because of her love and dedication to serve "the least of these."

I think a little poem my mother wrote summarizes her life well.

"I don't know how to say it,
But sometimes it seems to me
That maybe we are stationed where
God wanted us to be:
That little place I'm filling
Is the reason for my birth,
And just to do the work I do
He sent me down to earth."

The Pilot

In July 1945 my father went to La Paz to check on patients who wanted to come to the hospital in Chulumani for operations. The political situation in that region had been very tense for several months. He also knew that something was going on when he checked on one of his patients who was a high-ranking cabinet minister and heard the man's brother discussing plans for a revolution with several army officers.

The next day my dad was walking down the street when gunfire broke out. He ran as quickly as he could to the home of a friend who was from Czechoslovakia. He pounded on the door. The door opened a crack and my dad shouted at him, "They are shooting real bullets out here." The door suddenly swung open and my dad stumbled in. The house was crowded with people. There were many new faces. So, he sat down next to a dark-haired young man wearing a faded British uniform.

My dad looked over and smiled at the young man. "Hi. My name is Theron Pitman. I am an American surgeon. I run a hospital in Chulumani." He leaned over and extended his hand toward the young man who responded with a smile and a handshake and said, "My name is Tony Kaminek and I am a pilot. I just left England and I have come to Bolivia to teach tactical aeronautics. His voice had a heavy east European accent which made his English difficult to understand. With a big grin he added, "With all that gunfire outside it might mean that I am out of a job!"

They talked and talked as the waited for the gunfire to subside. It didn't take long for them to develop a strong liking for each other. Tony recited a brief history of his life. He had been born in Czechoslovakia. His father was a talented wood carver and carpenter whose talents were much sought after in the restoration of Catholic churches. His father wanted him to follow in his footsteps, but Tony was fascinated by airplanes. These were the early days of aviation. Tony had his first airplane ride at age fourteen, which led to his lifelong love of airplanes. He was very bright and learned how to fly quickly. Soon, he enlisted in the Czech air force. At first, he had a bright future - but then the Nazis invaded Czechoslovakia.

He was impressed into the Luftwaffe as a mechanic for their fighters. It was while working on some fighters one night that Tony and a fellow mechanic decided on a plan of escape. They simply wheeled the ME 109 that they had been working on out onto the runway and pretended to be checking the engine. Tony climbed into the cockpit, gunned the engine and was airborne before anyone caught on to what had happened. He and his friend set the fighter down in Poland and asked for political asylum. In a few weeks he was a member of the Polish air force.

In 1939, when the Germans marched into Poland, he fled to France. When France was taken over by the Nazis he escaped to England and joined an RAF squadron composed entirely of Czech pilots who were stationed in Duxford, England. Originally, all officers, regardless of rank, were commissioned in the lowest rank of the RAF. Tony was given the rank of Warrant Officer, which was the highest non-commissioned rank.

One afternoon, Tony ran into heavy German bombers over the coast of England. His plane was hit by fire from one of the German fighters that was flying cover for the bombers. His Hurricane began to trail oil and smoke and he had to pull out of the fight and headed for home. As his plane was dropping down over the trees to land on the rural airstrip he saw a young woman hanging laundry in her backyard. She was waving at him. He couldn't wave back though or flirt with her. It took all the skill and concentration he could muster to land the plane. Smoke filled his canopy as he yanked the handle and shoved it back. His crew quickly ran up to the plane and put out the fire. It would take a few days to get his plane back into fighting condition. He had a day or two to relax. So, as he sat in his quarters playing cards and drinking coffee, he kept thinking about that girl hanging laundry at the edge of the landing strip.

Finally, curiosity got the better of him. He decided to pay her a visit. He borrowed a bicycle and pedaled over to the house he remembered having flown over. It was a cute little cottage with a picket fence. He leaned the bicycle on the fence and made his way down the cobblestone path to the front door. Working up his courage, he knocked on the door and, in a few minutes, the door slowly opened. There, standing before him, was a courtly old gentleman with a large bristly mustache. Tony's face filled with disappointment. A smile began to spread across the old man's face. "Ah, another one of those flyboys that wants to make the acquaintance of my dear lassie." Then he lowered his voice and, with a wink, he added, "That granddaughter of mine is a real beauty!"

He turned around and went back into the house leaving Tony standing alone on the front porch. He was just getting ready to leave when suddenly there she was - a breathtakingly beautiful young girl. "Did you want to see me?" she said, smiling with her head tilted slightly to the side.

Tony finally caught his breath and found a few fumbling words. "Were you out in the backyard hanging laundry this morning?"

"Oh yes," she answered.

"Well, I was the one that flew over your house this morning."

"Oh really?" she pretended to be surprised. "I must have waved at ten or fifteen. Which one were you?"

"I was the one who had smoke pouring out of the tail of my plane! Your waving almost caused me to lose control. I'm lucky I'm alive - really."

"I am so sorry," she said with a little pout at the edges of her cute little lips.

"That's all right," he grinned. "Your wave put a little sunshine in a pretty desperate situation."

After that evening's introduction, Tony would make a low pass over her house before landing his plane and she would run out of the house and wave. Her grandfather would grumble, "Mary, I guess you'll have to marry the bloke if we're to have peace and quiet around here."

Tony was so timid that Mary was the one who asked him about getting married.

Five months later they married and the following year Mary gave birth to a beautiful baby girl. The war ended, but with so many men looking for jobs it was hard for Tony to find work. Through contacts with friends in Bolivia, he was offered a job with the Bolivian air force. He decided to leave his family in England until he had earned enough money to bring them to Bolivia.

Amazingly he had survived flying for three different countries during the war. He had been shot down several times. On one occasion he bailed out over Holland and was rescued by the Resistance. He stayed in a barn for several days and then dressed as a farmer until he was smuggled back to England.

My father was fascinated by his many stories and adventures. He began to tell Tony about his future plans for his medical work in Bolivia. He had a hospital in Chulumani, had leased another hospital from the government in Gujara-Mirim, and was working on plans to lease another hospital.

My father decided that a plane would help cut his travel time between hospitals. He told Tony that he had recently purchased two Vultee BT-13s from the United States government for $500.00 apiece.

Tony responded with a bit of condescension, "I am acquainted with that plane. The cockpit was designed for the lowest denominator, the most inept pilot, so all controls are oversized and well-marked."

Later that evening as my father was leaving, he turned to Tony and said, "If you lose your job because of the revolution come down to Chulumani and see me. If you want some real excitement in your life, come and teach *me* to fly."

Several weeks later Tony showed up at the hospital in Chulumani and walking into my father's office and announced, "I am ready to teach you to fly." My father jumped up from behind his desk and gave Tony a big hug. "I was thinking of taking a meat plane to the hospital in the Gujara-Mirim. Now you can fly me down there and while we are there you can give me flying lessons.

The following week Tony and my father were at the airfield in La Paz. They packed their luggage and medical supplies into the plane and Tony helped my dad get strapped into his chute and settle down into his seat. Then, Tony pushed the canopy over them, adjusted his straps, and put on his earphones. "Let's get this bird started." He flipped the power switch and yelled out, "Clear!" The prop began to rotate slowly and then picked up speed. It coughed and threw out a puff of smoke and roared into life.

My father pressed the button on the intercom, "Tony, do you mind if we have a little prayer before we take this thing into the air?"

"Sure, go ahead." Tony chuckled. "Are you a priest?"

It was a simple prayer asking God to protect them and watch over their new venture together. Tony pushed the throttle forward and turned the plane into the wind. About three months later, they crashed into the mountains during bad weather and were gone.

Two months after dad died

Teofanes Carreno

Mom and Dad at Carreno's Wedding

There is a popular Bolivian lyric that goes, "They grow well in earth that is good and secluded." This was certainly true of my friend Dr. Teofanes Carreno. He was born in humble surroundings in the small poor village of Cliza, Bolivia (not far from the city of Cochabamba). However, Cliza did have a few attractive features. It is located in a beautiful valley that is full of exotic fruits, beautiful flowers, and all types of natural products. Though poor, its people were very active in business – the business of making chicha that is (otherwise known as corn whiskey).

Yet, his parents wanted something more for little Teofanes. They wanted him to go to a good school and get a good education. So, they scrimped and saved and sacrificed a great deal to send him to school. He also worked hard and earned good grades. And, eventually, he made it all the way through medical school at the University of San Andres in La Paz, Bolivia.

One day, he was getting ready to take his final in his last year of medical school, when a family crisis occurred. His sister, who was living in Cochabamba at the time, became gravely ill. When he heard of his sister's illness, he took the first plane he could find that was going to Cochabamba. When he found his family, they were all very worried. He immediately put his sister into the hospital. After making the necessary arrangements with the doctors for her care, he returned to La Paz to take his term exams and passed the first part with high marks. A few weeks later, when it was time to take the final part of the exam, he found that he was not feeling well. So, he asked the doctor who was on call to examine him. After a few tests and lab work, Teofanes was diagnosed with typhoid fever. To make things worse, it was discovered that he contracted typhoid from his sister – who had been diagnosed with typhoid after he had left her in the hospital. So, he too was admitted to the hospital for treatment. After several weeks he was on the mend and felt well enough to take the second portion of his final exam. However, the directors of the medical school informed him that he would have to wait four more months and take the exam with the students who had failed it.

In the meantime, he asked if he could begin his year of public health service for the government without having first passed his final exam. The government actually agreed to this proposal! However, the best places had been taken. There were only two places left. One was in the town of Trinidad. It was far from home but it was a prosperous jungle town, full of beautiful women who would be very tempting to a young doctor just out of medical school. Yet, Trinidad was known for its immorality. Still, at the time, Teofanes wasn't a Christian and was a bit of a lady's man. Yet, for some reason, perhaps the moving of God in his life, he did not choose to go to Trinidad. Rather, he chose to go the mountain town of Chulumani – a town with far fewer prospects for a young man looking for a wife.

At the entrance to the town of Chulumani was a German hotel that was very popular with the tourists. They had the best food and drinks for miles around and was therefore a favorite meeting place for the town's leading citizens. On the other side of town, on a small hill, was the Adventist hospital. This hospital was directed by two American doctors - my parents. Their only goal was to help as many needy people as possible. They also wanted to prepare missionary nurses to go and serve throughout Bolivia.

In any case, young Teofanes, just twenty-five years old and not yet an official doctor, arrived in Chulumani and was immediately appointed chief of the town's public health department. He was ready to conquer the world. He was like a bird just let free and his first thought was to celebrate a bit. He especially enjoyed going to dances, gambling and drinking. He looked at the Adventist hospital – but that's about all. While he claimed to have respect for what the hospital was doing for Chulumani, he had absolutely no desire to be involved nor did he even visit the hospital.

Still, my parents knew that a young doctor had come to town, and wished to meet him – even if he didn't seem so keen on meeting them. So, one day my father stopped by to visit Dr. Carreno, unannounced, at the public health office. Teofanes was surprised at the friendliness of my father who invited him to participate in the daily activities of the Adventist hospital and requested him to teach in the nursing school. On my father's next visit to Dr. Carreno's office, he was invited for dinner and was told that the Doctora had prepared something special for him. So, he happily accepted the invitation. My mother had set a beautifully-arranged table and the aroma from the kitchen was mouthwatering. She had done a little research and found out that Teofanes' favorite dish was lamb chops. So, that is what she made. He loved it! He really enjoyed himself and thanked my parents again and again for their invitation and for preparing his favorite dish. My mother laughed and explained, "The lamb I fixed you was made out of wheat. It is called gluten. It's not really lamb chops."

Teofanes was shocked. He couldn't believe that the succulent lamb chops he'd just eaten were really made out of wheat!

"Wow! It certainly fooled me," he said as he shook his head.

From that moment on he became very good friends with my parents – and he would even play with my six-year-old sister, Linda, and me on occasion. Linda was easy to play with. She was easy going as a child and had a smile that went from ear to ear. I, on the other hand, was full of mischief, which he seemed to enjoy none-the-less.

After my parents befriended him in this manner, he finally consented to at least tour the hospital. He looked at the departments and met the personnel. He was surprised that the young nurses, who were taking the three-year nursing course, were so mature and well dressed in their uniforms. The hospital had 75 beds, but was full and overflowing with more than 150 patients. Obviously, an extra pair of hands would be a big help. So, it wasn't too surprising when my parents invited him to assist them – though he was a bit surprised when he was asked to help my dad perform surgeries. He was all too happy to help and began working part time in the emergency room and started teaching anatomy in the nursing school.

At night my parents visited him at his public health office and slowly started to share the story of Jesus and His love with Teofanes. Teofanes had, of course, grown up Catholic. In fact, before he decided to go to medical school he had seriously thought about becoming a Catholic priest. But, he wasn't really practicing and didn't really understand Christianity nor had he ever heard or personally read many of the stories about Jesus in the Bible. He had many questions for my parents regarding his own Catholic background. What about purgatory? Why don't you pray to the Virgin Mary? Why do you go to church on Saturday instead of Sunday? My parents tried to answer all of his questions, but he was deeply confused and concerned.

He thought to himself, "Who in the Catholic Church can give me good answers to my questions and explain to me what is wrong with what these Adventists are saying?" Then he smiled to himself as he remembered, "Father Lamberto! My good friend and drinking buddy!. He's got to have the answers!"

That night at the bar he asked him, "Father Lamberto, why do we have so many differences between what we Catholics believe and what the Adventists are teaching about the Bible?"

Without giving it much thought or even putting down his glass of beer, Father Lamberto explained, in a very matter-of-fact, even off-handed manner, "Forget about what the Bible says and go along with what the church teaches. Don't set foot in that Adventist hospital because those people are of the devil. In fact, you already have one foot in Hell by associating with them!"

This response came as a big surprise to Teofanes. By this time he was already friends with my parents and knew them to be good, kind-hearted people devoted to serving the people of Bolivia. Many things began to pour through his mind as he watched my parents and how they lived their daily lives. He saw how they treated people. It did not matter to them if people were rich or poor. They all were given the same tender care. This was completely different from the life he had been accustomed to live. He began to realize that the kind of life they were living brought real happiness. He could not, therefore, reconcile what the priest had told him about Adventists with what he saw in the daily lives and sacrifice of my parents. He could not accept the idea that these people were leading him toward Hell or that they were children of the Devil. So, he began studying, for himself, what my parents were trying to explain to him about the Bible and the love and sacrifice of Jesus.

This did not come without a price for Teofanes. The more he associated with Adventists, the more his former friends distanced themselves from him. Yet, his association with Adventists opened up for him a whole new group of friends – a whole new family. And, this was not without its rewards…

As he worked more and more hours at the Adventist hospital, he noticed that the students were full of life and well trained and very respectful. They also carried out their assignments faithfully and were self-motivated. They did not seek to lessen their own work when no one was watching. He saw the attractiveness of such values and began to apply them to his own life and the manner in which he worked.

Of course, as is only natural for a young single man, there was also one young girl in particular who appealed to him more than any of the others. Her name was Miss Rufina Leon. She was in her last year in the nursing program and was a great help to my parents. She carried some of the heaviest responsibilities at the hospital. And, she was very easy on the eyes. His heart told him she was the one that he would one day marry. It took some time, but Teofanes finally worked up his courage and asked her for a date.

Of course, this "friendship" came to the attention of the Carreno family. They were staunch Catholics and Rufina was a committed Adventist. Soon after they started dating, Teofanes received a visit from his sister, Edna. She explained that she was not at all happy about the path that her brother was taking. She pulled Rufina aside and questioned her, "Why are you converting my brother to your ridiculous religion where everyone is so poor? Why don't you convert to ours? You need to know that my brother has promised that our family will have many beautiful things, a good house, and a lot of liquor so that our friends will be able to have a good time at our parties. We plan to live in high society. You come from a poor family. What has your religion done for you?"

Still, nothing was solved. Teofanes continued to date Rufina and Rufina continued to be a staunch Adventist. Edna and the rest of the Carreno family remained very upset. When Edna returned home she and her mother made a pilgrimage to pray to the Virgin of Copacabana. They pleaded with the Virgin for a miracle. On bended knee and with tears in their eyes they asked her to make sure that their brother did not marry this heretic nurse! When their pleas to the Virgin of Copacabana seemed to fall on deaf ears, Teofanes' cousin, Victor Ortuno, a very prominent man in his hometown, came for a visit. He was very adamant and spoke sharply to Teofanes, "Why are you disgracing the family and our town?! Don't you see we are Catholics?"

Yet, as the days went by, Teofanes' conviction about the Adventist faith began to grow stronger and stronger. Pastor Kepsey came from La Paz and held public meetings. These meetings helped to cement his decision. The opposition from his family and friends drew him closer to God. He believed that God had closed and opened doors and had led him to Chulumani.

On Sabbath morning, December 8, 1945, he was overjoyed to finally be baptized into the Seventh-day Adventist Church. That same evening he married the beautiful Rufina. My parents turned their home into a chapel and decorated it with flowers and stood in the place of their own parents. The principle authorities of the town served as witnesses. My sister Linda was the flower girl and I was the Bible boy. This was a ceremony that Teofanes never forgot and it was the result of the work of my parents simply befriending a young man who was new to their town.

Over sixty years have passed since that wedding. The Carrenos had three children. One became a nurse and two became doctors. In his own family, Toefanes' sister, Edna, who had prayed so earnestly that the Virgin of Copacabana keep her brother from marrying a heretic, ended up becoming a heretic herself. She was also baptized into the Adventist faith. She said, "If my brother made this decision in the face of such opposition, it must be right. I also want to follow Christ." His brother, Abraham, who was a medical student at the time, came to the United States and also married a Seventh-day Adventist woman and was also baptized into the Adventist church. Even Toefanes' parents came to the United States and were baptized beside their children. The grandchildren, other family members, cousins, uncles, and aunts all entered the baptismal waters and then sent their own children to Adventist schools. And, they all married into Adventist Christian families and are all still working today to prepare people for heaven.

In fact, even in his place of birth, Teofanes' entire extended family joined the Adventist Church. There is not one family member who has not followed his example and decided to help others prepare for the soon return of Jesus.

His parents donated their home with its large garden for the construction of a church. It has room for 500 members. They also built a school in honor of Delfin Carreno, the father of the family. There are over 350 students in this school who are preparing for the soon return of Jesus. This school was built with funds given by the family of Abraham Carreno. Now, because of a simple friendship, there are many thousands in the town of Cliza, Bolivia, and in the surrounding towns, who are awaiting the second coming of Christ.

Guajara-Mirim

Guajara-Mirim

The sky is aglow, a crimson red. Above, a hundred clouds reflect the fading rays as the sun as it slowly drops into the forest below. A little village stands in stark contrast to the jungle in the background – a jungle which seems to form an impenetrable wall some fifty feet high and extends over a thousand miles in every direction. Less than a hundred yards away the mighty Mamore River, a quarter mile wide, flows ceaselessly by. It begins its course a month's journey from the interior, passing from distant Cochabamba, the second largest city in Bolivia, before moving on into Trinidad, the jungle capital of the Beni. From there it creeps across endless miles of wilderness before entering Brazil to help form the enormous Amazon River – which eventually flows all the way to the Atlantic coast.

This village is like so many other native villages in this area, most of which have only a few inhabitants. However, at one edge of this particular village there is a newly opened hotel with nice metal beds and white linen (most hotels only offered military-style cots or a hard wooden bench or a mattress on the floor). A small American Catholic Mission Church stands nearby. A little further down the slope, on the waterfront, a dozen or so partly abandoned warehouses are slowly falling into disrepair.

During the Second World War, this was a scene of great activity. From here thousands of natives disappeared into the jungle to search for the precious juice of the rubber tree. Now, all is quiet. A dozen hollow-log canoes lie anchored on the beach. Guajara-Mirim is a town where crooked politicians, criminals, prostitutes, and immoral priests are sent to live in obscurity. It is the Bolivian Siberia.

Just before dark settles on the jungle, a plane descends from the sky and flares out of the grass runway. It rolls to a stop by the shed that serves as the airport waiting room. The trip has been a long and tiring one for Tony and my dad. They slowly climb over the edge of the cockpit and jump down to ground. They walk to the town on tired cramped legs.

Over the next few days my dad, with the assistance of Tony, the pilot, and five local teenage girls, performs over forty operations and delivers three healthy babies.

There were no phones or radios there in those days. However, later that week my dad managed to have a telegram sent to my mother. She was teaching at the nursing school in Chulumani. He asked her to come with a few extra nursing students to help with all the necessary surgeries. The hospital's twenty-bed capacity had doubled and patients were lining the halls and filling the X-ray room. Because of the many tropical diseases in that region, people were always getting sick or injured. Patients were never lacking. Of course, since she couldn't fly, it took several weeks for my mom, together with the nursing students, as well as her two young children, Linda and me, to travel all the way to the Beni.

As soon as my mom arrived at Guajara-Mirim with the student nurses, their work began in earnest. As for my sister and I, we had no responsibilities. It was great! We were given free rein to roam the town like a couple of wild animals. There were so many interesting things to see. I especially liked to play with the local cows. These cows, with their big horns, terrified my sister Linda, but they didn't scare me. I took great delight in pulling their tails and chasing them off the path. It really wasn't much of a challenge because the town's people would yoke the oxen together in pairs so that they couldn't run very fast. This made it much easier for them to be caught and hitched up to their carts. Linda and I also liked to take the path down to one of the streams that ran near the hospital. We'd play in the water there for hours on end.

One day a couple of German ladies flew into town for a visit. They were ornithologists who wanted to go into the deep jungle to study the Macaw parrots which congregated in large flocks there. My mother offered to drive them in the hospital jeep. Late in the afternoon they located the parrots. They shot two parrots to take back to Germany as specimens. Surprisingly, the rest of the parrots responded in a dramatic manner to the loss of their companions. The entire flock flew off high over the jungle canopy crying and screaming. It made a real impression on my sister Linda. She was very concerned and repeatedly asked my mother, "Why did they have to kill those beautiful birds?"

In any case, the ornithologists had obtained what they came to collect and they decided to head for home. However, it was late in the evening and the shadows were beginning to lengthen. The deep jungle is not a place to be after dark. After an hour of traveling, the jeep began to sputter and finally stopped running. They were out of gas in the middle of the jungle – and it was starting to get dark. The ladies quickly decided that it would be better to make a run for it, and starting to walk through the jungle toward town. They did have a flashlight with them, but the batteries were weak and didn't last long. Still, they pressed on. As it got darker and darker, Linda began to hear all the night-time sounds of the jungle and imagined some jungle monsters showing up to carry them off. The ladies tried to assure Linda that all would be well, but it was all very scary, for all of them. Just then, however, they heard the noise of an engine and the darkness was penetrated by a set of headlights. My dad and Tony had come to the rescue! All were very relieved – especially Linda.

After we had been in Guajara-Mirim for a few months my dad decided to build an addition to the hospital. He hired local labor for the construction. The majority of the building crew belonged to the local Communist party. I enjoyed watching these men work. They were friendly and recruited me to run errands for them such as stealing food from the hospital pantry. And, it wasn't long before they decided that they were going to convert me to Communism. They would place me on a high wall and would not let me come down until I shouted, "Companeros, viva el partido Comunista!" (Comrades, long live the Communist party!)

One day they had me high on the wall giving my usual praises of the communist party when, in mid-sentence, my father appeared. He had slipped out of his office to inspect the building. As soon as I saw him I changed my slogan, in mid-sentence, and yelled out, "Companeros, viva...la Iglesia Adventista!" ("Comrades, long live the Adventist church!")

When my father left, the laborers laughed and said to me,

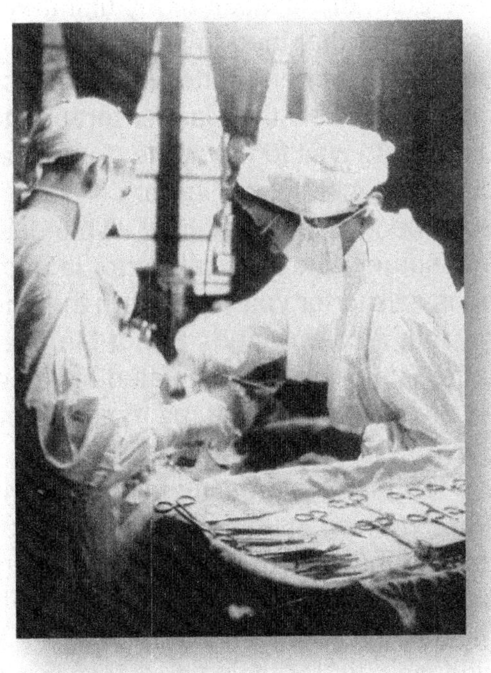

"You're an Adventist Communist."

However, it wasn't long before my association with these men got me in trouble with my father. One day, as I was sneaking out the back door of the hospital kitchen with my arms loaded with assorted food, my father came around the corner and caught me. He took me to the house and gave me a lecture on stealing and then he reinforced his lecture with a belt to my backside. I was very upset about this, of course, and thought about a solution to my problems. So, after my dad had changed his clothes into his scrubs and gone to surgery, I took his belt and went to the back of the house, dug a hole, and buried it. Later I began to worry what my father would do to me, but he never said anything to me about the belt.

While here in Guajara-Mirim, Tony also began to give my father flying lessons. My sister and I would sometimes fly with them. They would practice landings and take-offs on the airstrip at the edge of town.

One afternoon, while Tony and my father were gone to the jungle town of Rio Alta to pick up a patient, a man came to the hospital. He was complaining that he could not urinate. He was in terrible pain. During the examination, my mother was surprised to discover that his penis had been amputated.

"What happened to you," she questioned?

He responded, "I was taken prisoner during the Chaco war. Conditions were terrible. The Paraguayan soldiers beat me and tried to get me to reveal the location of my unit. When I refused to give them the location of my unit they did this to me!"

My mother tried to put a catheter into his bladder to relieve the pressure, but her efforts were unsuccessful. She then decided to operate to drain the bladder through the man's lower abdomen. She decided to wait for my father to get back from his trip so that he could reconstruct the urethra. Finally, my father returned and scrubbed for the operation. When they wheeled Señor Martinez into surgery, he kept calling for la *doctora* Pitman. "I can't believe he is calling for you when I am the one that is fixing his plumbing," my father complained. Señor Martinez was put under and my father successfully completed his reconstruction. However, when he awoke, he thanked my mother, not my father, for the success of the surgery.

So many interesting things like this happened to my parents while working in Guajara-Mirim. On another occasion, my father noticed that one of the kitchen workers was always wearing long sleeved shirts – despite it being very hot and humid. So, one day my dad questioned Rafael, "Why are you always wearing a long sleeved shirt? Roll up your sleeves and let me see what you are hiding."

Rafael stammered, "There is nothing!"

"Then let me see your arms anyway."

Slowly Rafael began to roll up his sleeves. To his dismay, my dad discovered that Rafael was covered with leprosy. He had been working in the hospital kitchen for months. "Why didn't you let me know about this," my father demanded?

"I was afraid I'd lose my job..."

My father put Rafael in a small shed in the back of our house to isolate him. Then, he started Rafael on his treatments in an effort to cure his leprosy. I was upset because Rafael had played and joked with me when I made my way into the hospital kitchen. Now I wanted to have nothing to do with him. My father explained to me that things would be Ok – that I could play and joke with Rafael again when he got better.

Over and over again such unexpected things happened in the Guajara-Mirim hospital. On another occasion, they wheeled a middle-aged man with a thick German accent into surgery. Just as he was going under the effects of the anesthesia he rose up in the gurney, gave a Nazi salute, and yelled, "Heil Hitler!" This was just after the war at a time when many Nazi's had fled Germany trying to escape the allies. Who knows what position this man might have held?

All during this time, my father continued flying lessons with Tony each day and, in return, Tony began studying the Bible with my father and mother in the evenings. Soon, the nuns came to my mother and complained that Tony had told them that he wasn't going to be attending mass anymore and he was thinking about joining the Seventh-day Adventist church. Of course, by that time, how could my mom respond to the nuns except to shrug her shoulders and smile?

My mother and father continued working together at the Guajara-Mirim hospital for several weeks until it was decided that my mother should return to Chulumani to prepare the nursing class for graduation. My father would stay in the Beni for several more weeks before going back to Chulumani to attend the graduation. Those were happy times for my parents, but that was the last time my mom saw my dad. It was also the last time I saw my dad.

One of the last things I remember about my dad was standing behind his seat in the plane and holding on by putting my arms around his neck as we took off for a flight around the town. It was an exciting experience for a four-year-old. He later took my sister Linda up and did stalls and spins with her. Two days later I flew with my mother and sister to La Paz. About a week later, Tony and my dad accidently turned into a blind-end canyon during bad weather and crashed into the mountains near Cochabamba, Bolivia.

The Doctor Will See You Now

As young children, my sister Linda and I had free run of the jungle hospital in Guajara-Mirim, Bolivia. During this wondrous time, we had ample opportunity to watch our parents examining and treating patients. Sometimes, they even allowed us to scrub up and assist them in surgery! – an opportunity which would be absolutely unheard of today. We would actually get to stand on stools and hand them instruments as they needed them.

Of course, these events had a strong influence on us. My sister, in particular, took great delight in playing doctor. Unfortunately, I was always her "patient." I would be the "pregnant lady" and she would be the doctor who delivered the baby. When the delivery room in the hospital was not in use she would place me on the table with her doll and we would go through the whole process of labor and delivery. She would yell. "Empuje Señora, empuje" ("Push lady, push")! I would protest that it did not make any sense for me to be the "pregnant lady"! After all, I wasn't meant to be a mother. I was the boy and she was the girl after all! None of my logic mattered. I was always the "pregnant lady" and my sister the "good doctor."

One day Linda watched my father draw blood from a patient and then smear some of the blood on a glass slide. He then stained the smeared slide and looked the blood through a microscope. That really made an impression on Linda.

So, of course, my dear sister invited me to play doctor with her where I wouldn't have to be the "pregnant lady." "Oh good!" I thought, "What could go wrong?" Soon my seven-year-old sister had "scrubbed" for surgery and then came into the bedroom where I was sitting. She was wearing my mother's white medical coat. The coat was hanging around her ankles and she had a stethoscope wrapped around her shoulders. She was also dragging a pressure cuff in one hand and had a big hat pin in the other.

"Now," she said, "You're going to be the patient and I am going to be the doctor. I would like for you to sit down while I exam you."

I started to protest, but she clasped her hand over my mouth. "Shhhhhh," she whispered. "You have a terrible disease and we have to find out what it is in order to cure it! I'm here to help you!"

She ushered me to a wooden chair and proceeded to wrap the pressure cuff around my four-year-old arm and began pumping.

"Your blood pressure seems to be extremely high," she solemnly declared. "Now, let's check your heart." She plugged the stethoscope to her ears and placed the other end on my chest. "Hum, you don't seem to have a very good heartbeat . . . You must be seriously ill! We are going to have to run a few blood tests to determine the problem."

She reached over and picked up the hat pin. My eyes widened. "You're not really going to poke me with that! Are you?!" I said in a horse, but fairly loud, whisper – still trying to be as quite as possible.

"Oh, this is just a little needle," she said with a knowing assurance in her voice. "Don't be such a baby! I promise, cross my heart, this won't hurt you a bit! Now, give me your finger."

Then, as she gently patted me on the hand she continued in her soft soothing voice, yet with command and authority, "Remember now, I am the doctor and I am going to make you feel better. Now hold up your finger."

As an innocent four-year-old, I naturally believed my sister. So,

I timidly raised my index finger and stretched my hand out to her. She raised the needle and, before I could blink, quickly *plunged* it into my finger!

My eyes bulged and I let out a blood-curdling scream that could be heard by the entire town! I grabbed my throbbing finger and yelled, “You said it wouldn’t hurt! You said it wouldn’t hurt!”

Blood was pouring out the end of my finger and dripping on the floor. My mom rushed into the room. Our doctor-patient relationship was at an end. Linda was highly perturbed. As she was being pulled from the room by my mom she yelled back at me, “Tui, you’re a horrible patient!”

Though her first patient did suffer a bit under her initial efforts at being a physician, my sister eventually turned out to be a wonderful pediatrician. And later, when I became a pastor, this childhood incident furnished me with a great sermon illustration with an important moral to the story – something along the lines of what the devil tries to pass off on us when he suggests that we try this or that “little thing”, some little thing that we know is wrong, and says, “This won’t hurt a bit!”

Pedro Triantafilo

The Triantafilo family was a hard working immigrant family. They originated in Greece, but moved to Bolivia in the early 1930's and settled in the city of Cochabamba. Pouleas, the father of the family, started a bakery business. The entire family worked together to make it a success. And, it wasn't long before the Triantafilos became one of the more prosperous families around.

Of course, their oldest son, Pedro, was groomed from childhood to take over the business. However, he rather enjoyed the easy life and became somewhat of a playboy about town. He would rather go to parties and do a bit of gambling and drinking than manage a business. It wasn't long before he was drinking rather heavily and losing a lot of the family's money playing cards. One night he staggered home dead drunk. His father was very upset and yelled at him, "I've had just about enough of you Pedro! You are a disgrace to the family. I disown you!" The family carried him upstairs, put him in a room, and locked the door. The father needed time to figure out what to do with his wayward son.

Pedro was now a prisoner in his own home. Day after day he had nothing to do but lie in bed, shuffle around his small room, and smoke an endless chain of cigarettes – and think. Once in a while he thought of his sweetheart, the girl his family had arranged for him to marry. But it was all over. Disowned by his father, the future was dark and without apparent hope. He even contemplated the best manner of committing suicide.

Then, one day, he drank another cup of coffee, shook himself from his trance, and looked for another book to read. His supply of books was quite limited. He had read everything except for a couple of religious books, magazines, and a Bible that an American doctor had left at the family bakery. Of course, Pedro was not interested in religion and was not about to read any religious books. He wished he had another bottle of whiskey! Then out of sheer boredom he picked up one of these little books and let it fall open in his hands, but quickly closed it and tossed it aside. He tried to find something else, anything else, to distract his mind.

He could hear the Indian mothers hushing their babies on the street below, and went over to look out the window at them. Pedro's brothers Xavier and Miguel were downstairs making up the "mass" (a large ball of dough) that was then divided before baking the bread. Nine barefooted Indians were hired for doing the work of dividing the "mass" into loaves and putting them into the large adobe oven.

Usually, this time of the day was a happy time when the family would talk, tell stories, and laugh with each other - but no longer. A cloud hung over the place ever since Pedro had been disowned. What was wrong with Pedro? Xavier too was having problems. He had an injured leg and it had become stiff. He could not bend his knee and it hurt him terribly. He had been in the hospital off and on for a year and a half. The family had spent a great deal of money trying to cure Xavier – without any improvement. The combined cost of the family's medical bills and Pedro's reckless lifestyle had sapped much of the family fortune, and set everyone's nerves on edge.

From the window, Pedro could also see his father down below. Papa Triantafilo was very quiet lately. He mindlessly stroked his large mustache that curled up at the ends. He had a distant look in his eyes and the ash from his cigarette grew longer without his notice. Pedro knew that his father was thinking about how to deal with him. Would his father really disown him?

His mother was also down below working very hard as usual. She was stirring up the charcoal stove and placing sheep "entero" in a pan to bake in the oven when the bread was done. She busied herself gathering herbs and flowers that grew in pans and pots around the patio. Pedro really admired his mother. She would work from morning till night to make sure everything was done right. Although she had the option of employing a young Indian servant girl, she wouldn't think of entrusting her work to anyone else. Generally, Mama Triantafilo was an easy going happy woman. She was a bit heavy set and had a very sweet disposition. However, her face now showed deep lines of concern that Pedro hadn't noticed before.

Pedro turned away from the window and sat down once more. Again he picked up the book he had thrown on the floor and looked at it. The book was black and titled, "The Marked Bible." Without really thinking about it or even consciously realizing what he was doing, he opened the book and began to read. Gradually, his mind became more and more engaged in what he was reading. He began to think to himself, "This is good stuff! These stories are actually quite good!" Soon, he became so engrossed in what he was reading that he forgot to smoke or drink his coffee. Then, he started reading the little Bible that was also in his room. Eventually his sister, Angelica, came into the room to bring him his meal. He wanted to tell her about what he was reading, but she didn't want to hear it and slammed the door on her way out.

Down the stairs she went in a huff to the tell rest of her family. "First," she stormed, "he gambles and loses all our money! Then he drinks and smokes himself to death, and now he has gone completely crazy with his new religion!"

However, little by little, Angelica became interested in the stories Pedro would constantly share with her from the Bible. Then she, in turn, would share Pedro's stories with the rests of the family. Soon, the whole family was reading the Bible with Pedro! Papa

Triantafilo eventually "re-owned" Pedro and welcomed him back into the family.

Finally free from his prison, Pedro and Angelica decided to go to La Paz to look for some Adventists (knowing that an Adventist doctor had given their father the religious books and magazines). In order to pass the time on their trip, they took with them the Spanish version of the religious magazine *Signs of the Times*. As they finished the magazine, they turned to a man who happened to be sitting next to them and asked him if he would like to look at their magazine? The man happened to be Pastor Dunn, the educational secretary of the South American Division of the Adventist Church.

Pastor Dunn introduced himself and soon began to tell them about all the Adventist work and missions in Bolivia. Then, Pedro and Angelica told the pastor their story. During their conversation, Pastor Dunn mention that there was an Adventist hospital in Chulumani with an outstanding American surgeon named Dr. Theron Pitman. After visiting the Adventist Mission office in La Paz, Pedro and Angelica decided they would go to Chulumani and talk to the doctor about the problems their brother Xavier was having with his leg. After their visit, they went home and told Xavier about the hospital and the doctor. "I believe God has led us to this doctor," they told him. So, Xavier went to see my father. And, after a few operations, Xavier's leg started to recover – eventually to the point of complete recovery!

Pedro and Angelica went on to become leaders in the Seventh-day Adventist church. They started a Sabbath school class in their own home and soon had as many as fifty people attending on a weekly basis. They also attended the Seventh-day Adventist college in Argentina, learning to become expert teachers and evangelists. Soon, the entire Triantafilo family became baptized and joined the Adventist church.

Who knows how many people have since been led to the light of the good news of the Gospel? all because my dad gave a few religious books and magazines to a man who just wasn't interested - at the time.

Growing Up at Madison

Madison - 7th and 8th Grades

Growing up at Madison

In the summer of 1904 Mrs. Ellen White, along with E. A. Sutherland, Percy Megan, and others, decided to take a steamboat ride down the Cumberland River to visit Nashville, Tennessee. As fate would have it, their boat suddenly broke down about 10 miles north of Nashville at a spot called Neely's Bend. They managed to have the boat towed ashore. And, while they were waiting on repairs, Mrs. White and several of the passengers decided to get off the boat and look around. They found themselves on the 412-acre farm of Mr. Ferguson.

The farm was full of weeds, stones, and gullies. It wasn't much to look at – for all but Mrs. White. When she returned to the boat she said to Sutherland and Megan, "This looks like the place I was shown in vision where God wants us to start a school."

Upon inspecting the farm in more detail, Sutherland and Megan sat down and cried. Everything they saw of the farm looked dilapidated and broken down – very depressing. But they had prior experience with the visions of Mrs. White and believed that God was speaking to her in a very privileged manner. So, they decided to obey the message given. They bought the farm for $12,723.

That same fall the school, Madison College, opened with a class of 11 students. Dr. Sutherland, who had initially sat down and cried when Mrs. White told him of her vision for the school, ended up serving as the school's president - and would continue to do so over the next 50 some years.

Madison College went on to become one of America's most remarkable and innovative schools. It was a school that swung open its doors to any student who desired a good education and was willing to work for his or her expenses. Any qualified student, no matter how poor, was able to receive an education at Madison. Students and faculty worked together on the farm for 5 hours a day before classes. Every building on the school was built by students working together with faculty.

In 1949 my mom was hired to be the pediatrician at Madison College Sanitarium and Hospital and also helped teach in the very well-known and well-respected nursing school. Nurses who graduated from the Madison School of Nursing probably had more practical experience upon graduation than any other graduating class in the nation at that time. So, these nurses were in very high demand and had no problem finding top jobs.

My mom also became very enthusiastic about the work philosophy of Madison. She bought into it hook, line, and sinker. Both my sister and I thought this very unfortunate (at the time at least) because we were quickly drafted into a similar work program by mom. We quickly learned the meaning of real work. However, as I look back on my experience at Madison and all the work that I hated at the time, well, it proved to be a great blessing me – and to my sister Linda. It was a wonderful wide-ranging education. After all, I worked in a laundry, a service station, garden, farm, dairy and in the school's maintenance department. I even had a short stint working at the print shop – until I messed things up so badly at type-setting that they fired me. I never could spell (even this book had to be heavily edited before publication – and I'm sure there are still a number of errors that have yet to be corrected).

We spent sixteen wonderful and exciting years at Madison – my growing up years. Madison shaped my life for the better in many innumerable ways. I had the opportunity to visit and talk with E. A. Sutherland on many occasions and he left no doubt in my mind that God's hand was in that school.

In any case, I hope you enjoy reading just a few of the stories that still stand out so vividly in my mind from those years – years that don't seem so long ago.

Disproving the Big Bang Theory

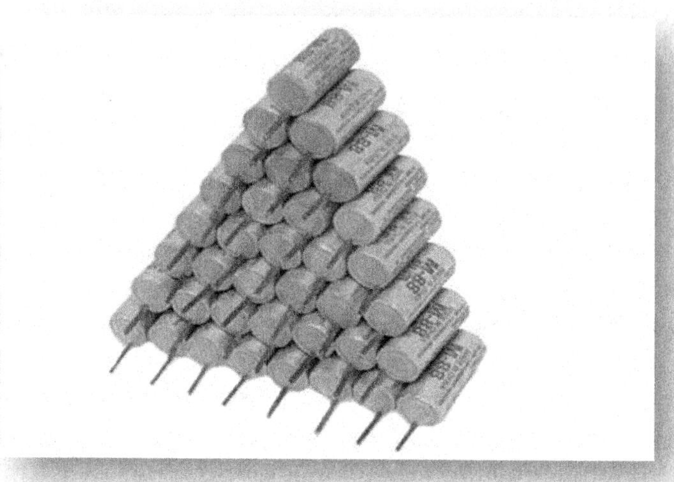

Our teacher was doing math problems with the fourth graders near the front of our one room schoolhouse. She had her back to me so I put down my pencil and took a bit of a break from my homework. It was one of those warm lazy days in early spring. The windows of our school house were thrown wide open and the warm breeze that wafted gently through the open windows soon caused me to drift off into fantasies of swimming and fishing with my friends.

Suddenly, I was jolted back to reality by the clanging of the recess bell. The room erupted into chaos. The teacher began rapping on her desk with her large wooden ruler. I was always fearful of that ruler because when she caught me talking out of turn or sleeping or passing notes she used that ruler on my knuckles. "Children, children!" she called out like a drill sergeant, "Stand still behind your seats and, when I give the order, file quietly out of the room."

We quickly obeyed the order. But of course, the moment we passed the door of the schoolhouse, we ran in all directions like wild Indians yelling and screaming at the tops of our lungs. Soon Miss Matthews made it outside and clapped her hands and called us all together again. "Now children," she said with great enthusiasm, "we are going to play kickball!"

Now this was a bit surprising. We actually liked kickball. My friend Eddie and I started playing defense in the outfield along with a dozen other classmates. But, before the game could start, the school's principal appeared at the door. He called out, "Miss Matthews, could I talk to you a minute." She walked briskly to the school building door. "Continue playing children. I'll be back in a few minutes."

Eddie got excited and, as soon as she disappeared into the school he grabbed me by the arm and said, "I've got to show you something!" Reaching into his pocket he extracted a small silver tube about the size of a roll of dimes and held it out to me.

My eyes grew as wide as saucers. "What is it?"

Don't you know?! "It's an ashcan! This here is one of the most powerful firecrackers you can get. You gotta know how to handle this baby. This ain't for no amateurs."

"Where'd you get it?" I asked, gingerly reaching out one quivering finger to lightly touch it.

"I bought it in the next county over last week when my folks went to visit one of their friends. Ya' know that buying firecrackers is illegal here in Davidson County don'tcha?"

My mother had repeatedly warned me not to play with firecrackers. In order to reinforce her prohibition, she told me a story about how she was called in the middle of the night to assist in a reconstructive surgery on the face of a man who had played with fireworks. It seems the unfortunate victim had been at a New Year's Eve party that night and had had a bit too much to drink. In one pocket of his shirt he had cigarettes and in the other pocket he had a few firecrackers. In a befuddled moment, he reached into the wrong pocket for a cigarette. And, putting the object to his lips, lit up. The explosion that followed nearly ripped off his lips and part of his nose. At the end of this story she added, "I don't want you to break my heart and make me help some surgeon put you back together."

However, a twelve-year-old has a hard time following the counsel of his own mother. Even if she is a doctor, what does she really know? Thinking only of immediate gratification and without really weighing the consequences, I made my decision, "How much do you want for it?

"Well", Eddie responded gravely, "these beauties are hard to find."

"Come on, come on! You have to sell it to me before the teacher comes back."

"Ok, twenty-five cents - and you have to promise never to tell anyone where you got it! – Ok?"

"Oh, I promise!" I said excitedly, nodding my head.

Our school let out at 3:00 p.m. and my mom tried to get home around 5:00 p.m. from the hospital. Sometimes she didn't make it, but most of the time she did. Most days it took me about half an hour to casually walk home. My mother always made a list of chores I needed to do after school. She'd tack the list up on a board in the kitchen before she went to work. I used to think she did it to figure out if I had come straight home from school or not. In any case, I thought there were enough things on that list to keep a grown man busy from dawn to dusk. To make matters worse my sister Linda, who was three years older than me, thought she *was* my mother when mom was away. At that time, she came home from working at the hospital switchboard at 4:00 p.m. It seemed to me that her greatest delight was to inform mom of all my infractions.

In any case, after a few detailed calculations in my head, I figured that if I ran home as fast as I could run, right after school let out, I could have an extra half hour to find something cool to blow up with my ashcan. It did, however, take me a bit little longer to get home than I expected. No matter – no one was there. I figured that if I acted quickly, all would be well.

So, I ran into the house to find some matches. As I came back out of the house, I noticed a small hole in one of the concrete blocks of the pillar that was holding up the four by four post that in turn held up the roof of the porch. The hole was just big enough to slide my ashcan all the way in. I had no idea what awaited me. How was I to know how powerful that little "firecracker" really was?

So, I lit the fuse and stepped back, expecting a nice loud "bang." I shut my eyes and turned my head. All of a sudden, there was a horrifically violent explosion! I heard glass shattering and the sound of hailstones crashing against the side of the house. Hundreds of little pieces of block and mortar peppered my skin like buckshot. Then, in a moment, everything was silent. I opened my eyes to survey the damage. I was in shock! The four by four post hung lazily in mid-air. The cinder block post on which it had rested had vaporized. The corner of the roof that covered the porch gradually tilted downward. The huge front room picture window was shattered and a large piece of concrete, the size of a baseball, lay on the living room floor among jagged pieces of glass. I then noticed a stinging sensation like I had been stung by a hundred bees. I looked at my arms and legs and lifted my shirt. I was bleeding from numerous little puncture wounds all over the parts of my body that had faced the blast. Even so, the very next thought that came into my head was, "Mom is going to *KILL* me! How am I going to explain this to her?!"

I frantically tried to clean up the broken glass and pieces of cinder block. I ran to the phone and called several of my friends asking them if their dads were home and could possibly come over and put in a new picture window and build a new cinder block post before my mother got home at five. My friends all thought it was just hilarious. Some of them couldn't stop laughing!

When mom did finally pull cautiously into the driveway, just a little bit later than usual that evening, she surveyed the damage without a word. She was absolutely speechless! There simply were no words – not even for something like, "What on Earth happened?!"

Eventually, of course, she did find a few words to tell me that my free time was at an end. I soon found myself at work right after school - milking cows in the evenings at the local dairy. It took the rest of the school year and into the summer to pay for all the damage that little silver cylinder had caused.

Now, there are folks who argue that the creation of the universe and our world all started out with a most unusual big bang that created functional order out of chaos. I've never believed that since my own big bang experience. All my big bang brought into existence was calamity and destruction – and a very long school year milking cows every evening. And all from what seemed like a small fairly insignificant 25 cent firecracker. Let me tell you, seemingly small indulgences can end up costing a fortune!

A Visit to the Principal's Office

Patsy Osborn

I think I was about ten years old when I first started to notice girls. Until then, I really didn't give them too much thought – except for my sister when she tried to be mom and boss me around.

Early on, the girls I really liked were tomboys. They could run and play and throw and hit a ball and even fight with the best of us. Virginia and Patsy, in particular, were one of us. Virginia lived just down the street. She was a great baseball player and all us guys wanted to be on her team because she could hit the ball further than most of us. We called her Ginger because she was a hot-tempered spicy little thing.

Like Ginger, Patsy could hang in there with the best of us too – in *anything* we did. She even had a cracked front tooth that she liked to show off. It was broken when she was hit with a bat one day when she was playing catcher a bit too close to the batter...

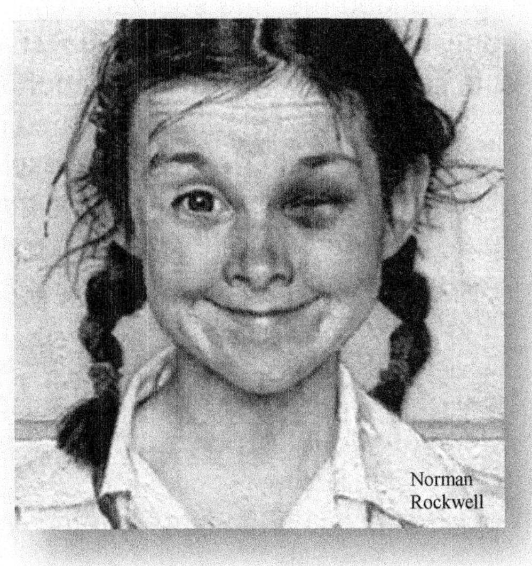

The long and short of it is that Patsy and Ginger were tough and strong and fearless, and none of us guys wanted to get on the bad side of either one of them!

Then, one day, things began to change. Ginger and Patsy started looking different – even smelling different. They weren't as interested in wrestling with us or beating us up. They started wearing dresses on occasion instead of the usual dirty torn-up jeans. They even started combing their hair! There was certainly something different going on – and I noticed some very strange feelings that I had never noticed before. But, I didn't know what they were or how to act around girls anymore. Still, I wanted to be around them and for them to notice me. So, I began playing jokes on them and teasing them to get their attention.

I used to sit behind a particularly cute girl, Suzy. She wore pigtails and liked to swish them back and forth so that they'd hit my face on occasion. I pretended to get all upset, of course, but she continued on as usual. Then, one day during art class, I came up with a brilliant idea. I quietly glued her pigtails together with Elmer's glue. It wasn't until she was called to the blackboard to do a math problem that she realized that her braids were stuck together. Poor Suzy had to cut about two inches off her braids to get them unstuck. This trick delighted my buddies but infuriated Suzy – and our teacher Miss Matthews. She kept me after school to clean the blackboard and sent a note home with me for my mother to read.

Fortunately, my mother was a very intuitive woman. Though she tried to look serious as she read the note, and sternly reprimanded me, she seemed to be hiding a bit of a smile at the edges of her lips. She sat me down and asked me, “Do you like that cute little Suzy girl? I think you do!”

Of course, I vigorously denied it. “No way! Oh Mom, please!”

But mom kept right on. She explained to me that if I wanted to make a real impression with a girl that I wouldn’t get very far by teasing her or gluing her braids together. “You could try carrying her books for her or sharing something she likes from your lunch with her... Just think about it.”

Soon after that, Freddie, Eddie and I got into a brawl right in front of the principal’s office. It had something to do with a note that Eddie found on the playground that morning.

“Dear Patsy,

I think you are very pretty. Do you like me?

Freddie.”

When we threatened to tell the whole school about his sappy love note, Freddie flew into a rage and the fight was on. We were right in the middle of our fist-swinging eye-gouging brawl when the principal walked up pulled us apart. It must have been the last straw in a trying week because he immediately ushered us into the empty classroom next to his office. We all knew what lay in store for us. This was the age when child abuse laws were loosely interpreted. An occasional beating for misbehaving young’uns was viewed as a positive and necessary function of education.

Eddie was the first to be escorted into principal’s office. He was truly heroic. We could hear the thumps and whacks of the heavy paddle board, but not a sound escaped his lips. The beatings stopped. Then, suddenly, the door opened and Eddie walked out with a grimace on his face. He was carefully rubbing his posterior and was walking like a cowboy who had been on a two week round up.

“Next,” growled the principal pointing at me. I got up, a little shaken, and made my way into his office. He shut the door behind me. On his desk lay his large wooden paddle. It looked like a cricket bat with neat dime-sized holes drilled into it (calculated to lessen the wind resistance as it flew through the air). My knees buckled a little when I saw it.

“Now son,” he said gravely, “This isn’t going to pleasant for either one of us, but it has to be done to help you grow up to be a good man someday."

He then proceeded to have a prayer – for his courage or mine I don't know. I don't remember a word of it. I was too busy looking at the paddle trying to figure out how I was going to survive this beating without crying in front of my friends.

After what seemed like an eternity, he finally finished his prayer and said, "Amen". Then, he directed, "Ok son. I want you to put both hands on the desk and bend over."

So, I walked very slowly and very deliberately over to the desk and assumed the position. He picked up the paddle and came around behind me. Out of the corner of my eye I saw him take a full back swing and then start with his downswing. Just before the paddle made contact I jumped to one side. I could feel the breeze as the paddle missed me by centimeters and crashed into the desk. The principal let out a grunt as the paddle fell from his grasp to the floor. As he bent down to pick it up he yelled, "Hold still you little rascal!"

He came after me looking like the mighty Cassie swinging his bat. I jumped again. This time, the corner of the bat caught my leg. I yelled in pain. There was a hit, then a miss, a partial hit, and another miss. I was all over his office. It looked like a bull chasing a matador.

Finally, it was over. He probably felt he had inflicted enough punishment on himself. Or, maybe he was just too exhausted from so much swinging. He opened the office door for me and I limped into the room with where my friends were sitting all bug-eyed.

Freddie had been listening to all the swats, grunts, and yells. By now he was absolutely terrified. He looked like a frightened animal walking into the slaughterhouse. When the door shut behind him, Eddie and I leaned closer to listen to every excruciating detail. We heard the whacks begin. After two or three more whacks Freddie began to cry. Suddenly, we heard a kind of yelp from the principal. "You little devil you!" he shouted! The door flew open and out ran Freddie with tears running down his cheeks. The paddle lay on the floor and the principal was hopping around the room holding his leg. We never did say anything to Freddie about his crying. But we all agreed not to get into any more fights over stupid girls – a resolution that lasted at least a couple of weeks.

As I've grown older, I've thought often of these innocent carefree days. There's always a heart-warming nostalgia for most people when they're asked to think back to the first crushes of their childhood years. I also have very warm feelings for my grade school teachers; even for the principal who said prayers before beating us with his large wooden aerodynamic paddle. These men and women really cared about us and were trying to show us the right way to live. They all made occasional mistakes along the way, as I did when I raised my own two boys. But, the simple knowledge that one knows one is truly loved makes it all Ok.

I like to think about God that way – and know that His love for me and my family will make it all Ok in the end as well…

Chicken Coon

Madison College, in the 1940's and 50's, had the reputation of being a school where a poor person could get an education without going into tremendous debt. If one worked full time during the summer months and part-time during the school year, with no vacations or days off except for Sabbaths, all of one's room, board and tuition would be covered.

The fact is though, even students who were well-off financially and could pay cash up front for their tuition, had to work if they wanted to attend Madison College. Every student at Madison was required to work. Work was part of the curriculum. Students who graduated from Madison may not have had the highest academic skills, but they had abundant practical experience and knew how to work – and everyone knew it. Nurses who graduated from Madison College Hospital were always in great demand.

Of course, as I've already mentioned, my mom was an enthusiastic supporter of the work ethic at Madison. What better way to keep a young man out of trouble than to put him to work?

I got my first job when I was eight years old, pedaling papers at the hospital. When I was twelve, I got my first "real job." There were no child labor laws at that time. The general philosophy was different then. Most people looked upon child labor in a positive manner – as a preparation for life as an adult. Of course, there have always been those willing to abuse child labor; working children under very harsh and unsanitary conditions for extremely long hours – to the point of complete exhaustion and sometimes death. Such forms of child labor are really forms of child abuse and are absolutely evil and those involved are truly criminal in their thinking – devoid of all conscience for what is right and wrong.

For my friends and me, however, our manual labor was a blessing and served to develop good traits of character and numerous important practical skills that we could call upon for the rest of our lives.

At the time, though, picking peaches at 25 cents an hour was not my idea of a picnic or any kind of path toward necessary character development. It was hard, hot, humid work – all day long. We worked on the farm from seven o'clock in the morning until five o'clock in the evening. Mr. Lovett hired three young boys to help the older boys in his orchard and garden. When we were not picking peaches we would pick okra from a one-acre patch. Because the okra had little hairs that would stick into your skin, it was necessary to wear long sleeves and gloves to pick it. The sweat would just pour down our faces and down our backs. Then, if I forgot for just a moment about what I was doing, and tried to wipe the sweat off my face with the back of my glove as I was picking the okra, those little spines from the okra would get stuck in the skin of my neck and face. That was like pouring salt into a wound since it would make me itch and scratch the rest of the day like a dog with fleas – which would only make things worse and worse.

Another one of the bosses I worked for growing up answered to the name of Chicken Coon. I'm not really sure how he came by that name, or nickname, but perhaps it was because he ran the poultry department at Madison? Chicken Coon had originally come from a distinguished family of preachers and had once been a preacher himself. But, he had been defrocked when he was discovered having an affair. In any case, since he had once been a preacher, he maintained the use of biblical terms and phrases to flavor his communications. When he became angry with someone, he would often yell out, "You Uncircumcised Pharisee!" (which, I suppose, is even more of an insult than calling someone an "Uncircumcised Philistine"). So, it was always very interesting working for Chicken Coon.

I first met Chicken Coon when, at the end of one particular harvest season, he requested that the school's farm send him a couple of boys to help with the school's poultry business. So, there was a call for volunteers. The problem is that working with chickens isn't much better than picking okra. So, no one exactly jumped at the opportunity. As fate would have it, however, Gerald and I drew the short straws and were chosen, along with two other boys who had been working at the laundry, to help Chicken Coon that season.

One of the dirtiest jobs at the chicken farm was cleaning out the hen houses. It was terrible. We would attach the manure spreader to two large Belgian work horses that the farm owned and pull the spreader next to the open windows of the hen houses. We would cover our faces, except for our eyes, with handkerchiefs - and then start shoveling chicken manure and shavings out the window into the spreader. Then, when the spreader was full, we had the horses pull the load to an open field where we spread out the chicken manure as fertilizer for the next growing season. Of course, as we shoveled the stuff, the dust from the dried chicken droppings would float over the wagon and cover us from head to foot. It's a wonder that we didn't come down with every disease known to man.

Another of one of our jobs on the chicken farm was picking up eggs and taking them to the washing and packing house that was located in the middle of the poultry yard. Three large hen houses were on either side of the washing and packing house. As we went through the hen houses we would gather the eggs into large metal baskets and carry them to the central washing and packing house. Since Gerald was the biggest, he assigned Eddie and me to pick up the eggs and lug them to the house where he and Lynn would clean and sort them according to size and then pack them. The washing area consisted of a large sink that was situated in front of an even larger window that stayed open during the hot days of summer.

One hot afternoon, Gerald was issuing his commands to us as usual. And, as usual, he ordered Eddie and me to go and pick up the eggs. We meekly obeyed, picked up our baskets, headed for the hen house at the end of the poultry yard, and began picking up the eggs. There was one hen in that house that laid exceptionally large eggs. We called her Matilda the Hun. When we got to her nest we found one of the largest eggs that I had ever encountered in my brief poultry career. This egg was about the size of a baseball. As I picked up the egg and cradled it in my hand, I was overwhelmed with an evil desire. After Eddie and I finished filling our baskets we lugged them outside and set them down before we began our journey back to the wash house. "Eddie," I grinned, "How far do you think I can throw this egg?"

Eddie smiled from ear to ear and said, "Maybe you can hit the wash house?!"

So, I reached down and carefully picked up Matilda the Hun's giant egg and softly ran my fingers over it as I calculated the proper trajectory. "Well, here goes!" I drew my hand back and let it fly. It flew gracefully over the first hen house, then the second, and, finally, it cleared the third one as well. We stood there in silence. There was no sound. All was still. Then, suddenly, we heard a tremendous yell. A few moments later, eggs started flying *our* way! Around the corner of the chicken house came Gerald, running toward us at top speed caring his own basket full of eggs. From his face, we could tell that Matilda's egg had sailed successfully through the window of the washroom and made a direct hit. It couldn't have been any more beautiful. From his forehead downward, Gerald was covered with egg. As he charged at us, Eddie and I each grabbed several eggs and began to defend our position. Eggs were flying everywhere like we were in the middle of a hail storm.

Then, in the heat of the battle, Chicken Coon drove up. It took him but a moment to take it all in. "Stop! Stop!" he yelled over and over again before escalating into, "You Uncircumcised Pharisees!" When we didn't stop he got really mad and started yelling at us, "You children of perdition! You're all fired! Fired I tell you! I will *not* have any of you *unfaithful stewards* working for me!"

Of course, none of us were all that broken hearted about not having to work at the poultry farm anymore. But, my mom was absolutely horrified that I had been fired from my job. I don't know if it was the influence of my mother or the fact that it was hard for Chicken Coon to find anyone else willing to do the job. But, whatever his motivation, several days later he drove by our house and offered us our old jobs back. “After all,” he said. “Jesus did forgive sinners. I suppose I could do no less.”

The Tomato War

When I turned thirteen, I went down to the college farm and asked the farm manager, Mr. Cantrell, for a job. He took a step back and sized me up. “You’re a little puny don’t ya think? Are you sure you are up to it?”

“Oh yes sir!” I said, with as much bravado as I could muster.

“Well, show up tomorrow and I’ll try you out. You’ll have to put in a little extra effort to keep up with the other fellas.”

I was overjoyed to get the job because the farm was where the real macho guys worked. I wanted so much to be all “grown up” like them. And, it was certainly true that anyone working on the farm in those days had to be tough and act responsibly.

Like me, Gerald was fourteen going on twenty. I greatly admired him because he was tough, big and strong – much bigger and stronger than I was at the time. He also knew and used a lot of cuss words that would make a sailor blush. At first, I thought he set the moon. Unfortunately, however, my own feelings of admiration were not reciprocated. In fact, as time went on, I became his personal punching bag. I felt sure that his greatest pleasure in life was finding new and creative ways to torment me. Fortunately, Gerald’s older brother would often step in to preserve my life.

Most of the time, however, we all were too busy working to be playing around or fighting with each other. My days at the farm began at four o'clock in the morning. Altogether, we had to milk a herd of about fifty cows each day. We began by setting up the milking parlor. First, we would run the glass tubes from the parlor to the cooling room where milk was collected into large metal cans to be picked up and sent to the processing plant.

As we worked with all those cows every day, day in and day out, we got to know them pretty well. Each cow had her own individual personality. In fact, one of our Jersey cows was actually our pet. She had been hand raised since she was born and had a strong affinity for people. We called her Lovey Dovey. When I would go out to get the cows in the morning from the pasture and bring them in for milking I would climb onto her back and ride her in to the milking barn. When it came time to milk her, she would patiently stand there and eat her food while we washed her bag and milked her. Many cows would swat their tails in your face and kick at their milking cups and urinate and defecate on the floor. Every once and a while a cow would kick her milking cup off the suction hoses and all the muck on the floor would get sucked up into the milk lines. Then, we would have to stop everything to clean out the lines. Of course, this was never a concern when milking Lovey Dovey. She seemed to like it and would patiently stand there chewing her cud. When I finished milking her, I would always slip her a little extra feed. Then, she would hang around the barn waiting for us to play with her a little after work.

There were also several other interesting animals on the farm. For example, Gerald, of all people, developed special feelings for a cat he named "Little David." This cat was missing about half of one side of its face. When Little David was just a kitten he had crawled onto the motor of the milk truck to keep warm in the winter. Then, when someone started up the truck that morning, the blade from the fan clipped off part of one side of his face. This little kitten fell out from under the truck and Mr. Cantrell picked him up, took one look at the poor little thing, and said, "There is not a lot we can do for this little fella. We need to put him out of his misery."

To my amazement, Gerald interceded for that kitten and pleaded, “Mr. Cantrell, how about letting me have him?” So, Mr. Cantrell handed the little quivering bundle over to Gerald.

Somehow, Gerald nursed that little kitten back to health and, during the process, developed a deep attachment for him. At first, Gerald brought a box into the milking parlor and laid the little kitten on the top of a pile of rags that were placed inside the box. Every morning he gave the little kitten fresh milk from an eye dropper and every afternoon he would repeat the process. For a while, it didn't look like the little guy was going to make it. But, after several days, he began to improve. And, after several months, he turned into a sleek beautiful cat. His only flaw was his terribly disfigured face – a face which was so ugly it was kinda cute in a way.

Even as a kitten, Little David was something else. He had great courage. He would attack and kill rats that were as big, and sometimes bigger, than he was. He was a little “giant killer” - Hence his name, “Little David.”

Gerald and Little David established a bond that lasted until the day Little David died. When Gerald was in the barn milking, that cat would walk over and sit down beside him. If Gerald did not make it to work Little David wouldn't show up either. Gerald told me that Little David would often bring him dead birds and small animals as gifts and signs of his love for Gerald. I didn't believe him until one day when I was doing the milking and saw Little David dragging a very large rat through the doorway. He dragged it over to where Gerald was standing and set it at his feet. Gerald bent down and patted the cat's head and scratched his ears. He told Little David what a good and brave cat he was for bringing in such a huge rat. I even began thinking that, perhaps, Gerald wasn't so bad after all. He actually had a tender spot. Then Gerald caught me staring at him.

“Pitman,” he shouted, “get rid of this rat!”

Fearful for my life, I cautiously picked up the rat by the tail and made my way out the door and flung that rat as far as I could into the feed lot.

I thought to myself that perhaps Gerald only had a soft spot for animals while he hated humans – me in particular. I spent hours thinking how I could revenge myself on him for all the injustices he had inflicted upon me.

Several weeks later Mr. Cantrell came into the milking barn with our assignments for the day. Gerald and his brother were assigned to go and cut hay with two other boys at the river bottom. My assignment was to hoe weeds in the tomato patch with several other boys. It was a hot day and the work was hard. As the day progressed, a plan of revenge began to form in my brain. I noticed that every hour the wagon from the hay field would drive by piled high with bales of hay. I also noticed that Gerald was driving each time. He took great delight in hurling insults at us as he drove by – especially at me.

Finally, I could take it no longer. My very honor was at stake and demanded satisfaction. But, I needed some help to carry out my plan. So, I held a hasty conference with my co-workers and explained my plan. They all liked it and were fully on board. We all worked very hard and by late afternoon we had stockpiled a mountain of rotten tomatoes at the edge of the field that lay nearest the road. In the distance we could hear the tractor coming along with the last load of the day. As it drew closer and closer we casually made our way to the end of the rows of tomatoes and pretended to be busy hoeing. As the tractor came within range, we noticed that we weren't the only ones who had come up with a diabolical plan. The boys from the hay field had piled mountains of dirt clods on top of their bales of hay. Soon, they began to launch their attack and we immediately retaliated with a barrage of rotten tomatoes.

Of course, our main target was Gerald who, by virtue of driving the tractor, had forfeited the protection of the hay bales. He had no way of finding cover and, to my utter joy, our tomatoes repeatedly found their mark. Soon, he was covered with rotten tomatoes. He had tomato juice and seeds dripping off his nose and down the sides of his face. What was even more glorious was that the tomatoes stunk to high heavens. The occasional dirt clod hits we suffered were more than worth it!

Revenge was sweet indeed, but short-lived. Several days later Gerald and I were sent to a field to pick up some irrigation pipes. We had to pick up these long aluminum pipes and transfer them to another field. Some pieces of pipe were longer than others. So, we picked up the smaller ones first. I use the term "we" loosely here, you understand, because, since Gerald was older and bigger, he commanded me to pick up the pipe and stack it all by myself while he drove the tractor. This is how it went until Gerald saw a skunk run into one of the longer pipes up ahead. So, he got off the tractor and called out to me, "Hey Pitman! Come help me stack this long piece of pipe."

"Wow," I thought to myself. "He may have some small piece of humanity left in him after all. He's actually helping me out here!"

Of course, Gerald failed to inform me that a skunk was inside the pipe. Just as I bent down to pick up my end of the pipe, Gerald picked up his end rather quickly and gave the side of the pipe a firm whack with his hand. The skunk tumbled out of the pipe all primed and ready for bear. I was just as surprised as the skunk! We both stood there transfixed for a moment, but only a moment before the skunk went into action. He unloaded everything he had on me. I was covered with skunk spray from head to toe and reeked to high heaven.

Gerald thought it was the funniest thing he had ever seen and fell on the ground in convulsive laughter.

For days no one could stand to be around me - not even my mother! I had to burn my clothes and take an unusual number of baths – to include a bath in tomato juice. I tried all kinds of soaps and solutions in an effort to remove that awful smell. Nothing really seemed to work. Even the friendliest of the cows would run away from me whenever I came near.

Those were the days. I remember them fondly. Gerald and I eventually became friends. He obviously did have a good heart. Someone who is that kind to helpless animals has to have a good heart. And, eventually, I learned the wisdom of the Biblical advice, "Do not repay evil for evil. On the contrary: If your enemy is hungry, feed him; if he is thirsty, give him something to drink. In doing this, you will heap burning coals on his head."

The Streakers

There's nothing quite like summertime for a child. Growing up in Madison, I always looked forward to my summers – especially summer Sundays. Once school let out for summer break, I did have to work. However, most of the time, my friends and I didn't have to work on Sundays.

Perhaps our favorite place to hang out on summer Sundays was Schuler's pond. This scenic pond was secluded and surrounded by large trees. During the especially hot days of summer my friends and I would go there to swim, fish, play, build forts, and fantasize about all the great things we would do when we grew up. Sometimes, we would ride our horses right into the pond and swim them around as we rode or swam beside them. Sometimes, we camped in the nearby woods and built forts. Once we rolled several fifty-gallon drums down to the pond and built some rafts and pretended they were pirate raiding ships on the ocean. We'd attack each other's ships with our eye patches and stick swords, and try to see who could throw all the guys from the other "ship" into the water first. Once, we even made plans to build a submarine. Fortunately, this particular plan never materialized because my mother found out about this project and put a stop to it. Most likely, we would have all drown on our maiden voyage - much like the Confederate sub, the Hunxley, which spent most of the Civil War drowning Confederate sailors rather than fighting off the enemy.

Of course, we all enjoyed fishing as well. We stocked Schuler's pond with the fish we caught in the Cumberland River. We knew just the right place to catch hundreds of fish. Just below the college garbage dump was the outlet for the sewer. Tons of raw sewage would flow into the river from this spot and thousands of fish would gather to gorge themselves on it. Catching fish here was as easy as falling off a log. And, since we didn't actually eat the fish, we were not too concerned what about went into them. We just liked the excitement of catching them.

Then, when we got tired of fishing, we would grab our .22 rifles and go up to the dump to shoot rats. The rats at the dump were about as plentiful as the fish at the sewer outlet – and very large. The rats were certainly much larger, on average, than the fish we caught. One day, however, our friend Lynn hooked a thirty-eight-pound carp! It was the biggest fish any of us had ever seen. We were so impressed that we actually gave this particular fish a name. We called him Mortimer.

At first, we didn't know what to do with Mortimer, but soon decided to take him to Schuler's pond. Our friend Richard volunteered his dad's car. So, we hooked a trailer to the car and put a large washtub on the trailer. Then, we loaded Mortimer into the tub and drove cautiously to Schuler's pond. By the time we got there, most of the water had spilled out, but Mortimer was still alive.

Eddie and I gently carried him to the pond and lowered him into the water. He lay on his side for what seemed like an eternity. Then, all of a sudden, he flipped over and knifed his way into deep water. Occasionally we would see the water rippling and knew it was old Mortimer chasing another meal. He lived for several months eating smaller fish until the hot days of summer began to lick up the water and the pond began to shrink. One day we arrived at the pond and found Mortimer floating dead on the surface, probably due to the very warm water and lack of oxygen. We pulled him out and held a solemn funeral service for him before burying him a short distance from the pond.

Sometime later Eddie called me on the phone and wanted to know if I wanted to go fishing with him and Lynn?

"Sure, when are you going?"

"As soon as Lynn and I can find some bait."

"Oh, bait isn't any problem at all. We can dig for worms behind my house where Lou (my horse at the time) usually does her thing. There's always a pile of worms there."

Sure enough, it didn't take us long to dig up a large can of worms.

We did well fishing that morning, but, after a while, we grew bored. It was getting hot and, since the site was secluded, we decided to strip and go swimming. We just peeled off everything and piled our clothes on the bank and plunged in. The pond was not your crystal clear lake, you understand. The water was tepid and home to every germ in the universe. If you believe in evolution, that pond is the place where life first started. In many places it was covered with a greenish-yellow scum. My mother could always tell when I'd been swimming in Schuler's pond by the musty smell that would still be wafting off my body when I came home. She used to warn me swimming in such a dirty pond was dangerous. I might end up contracting some flesh-eating bacteria and lose fingers and toes – or worse! I just shrugged my shoulders before running off to do it again and again. And, perhaps I did better at fighting off sickness and disease when I went to Bolivia as a missionary later on because of the resistance I developed swimming in Schuler's cow pond?

In any case, there we all were that day, swimming without a stitch on, as happy as could be. Lynn had hung a rope from one of the limbs of a large oak tree that grew close to the water's edge. We would run to the top of an earthen dam with the rope in one hand and swing out over the pond to see who could land the farthest from shore. We also gave points for the biggest splashes.

We were so immersed in our play that we didn't notice the arrival of Patsy and Ginger. Ginger let out a very loud wolf whistle and both of them started laughing hysterically at us. We were completely blindsided. We just stood there for a moment in shocked disbelief. Our friend Lynn was, however, in midflight on the rope swing, but decided the better part of valor at that moment was to bail out early. He landed with a splash right in front of us in two feet of water. Of course, we were obviously glad that the water was so muddy, but were trapped as helpless as fish in a barrel as the girls stood there laughing at us from the bank. Then, to add insult to injury, they picked up all of our clothes and took off with them. They yelled back over their shoulders, "We're just going to wash these for you. You'll have them back in no time!" We could hear them laughing and giggling as they disappeared from view. We yelled at them, "You'll be sorry! We'll get you for this! Bring um back!" We called down the wrath of the unknown gods and everyone else we could think of on those girls, to no avail. They just kept on walking. In a few minutes we couldn't hear them anymore.

We held a little council meeting, still standing waist-deep in the pond, trying to decide what to do. Finally, we decided that we would have to make a run for it. Since my house was the nearest, it was most logical to head there. So, we quickly jumped out of the water and raced from one large bush or tree to another. When we got to the edge of the woods we stopped to check out the traffic on the road in front of my house. We all noticed that there were several parked cars on either side of the road.

I suggested, "It would probably be best to enter at the back of my house through the basement door. You guys can wait in the basement while I sneak up the stairs through the kitchen to my bedroom and get some clothes."

So, we all ran, dodging from car to car, before finally making it into my basement safe and sound – without anyone seeing us (that we know of). We all let off a sigh of relief!

"Phew! That was a close one!" Freddie gasped.

"Sure was!" I panted.

Then, I ran up the stairs to the door of the kitchen. Quickly, I grabbed the door handle, flung it open, and raced into the kitchen toward the hallway that led to my room. About halfway through the kitchen, I noticed that my way was blocked. I was absolutely horrified to discover that our kitchen was filled with a sizable group of my mom's lady friends who were preparing goodies for an afternoon baby shower. I stood there, naked as a jaybird, frozen for a moment like a deer caught in the headlights. Time just stopped. No one moved or said a word. Then, in a stroke of genius, I said, "Have a nice day!" and quickly dashed around a couple startled ladies and down the hallway to my room. After a brief pause, I heard raucous laughter coming from the kitchen.

My mom assisted in discretely passing clothes to my friends in the basement. However, I remained in my room until late that evening when all the ladies finally left the house. Of course, I never wanted to see those ladies again! Even my own mother could barely control laughing out loud whenever she saw me. For the next few days, every time my mom saw me, she would turn her face to the side and cover her mouth with her hand.

But no, we never did tell on Patsy and Ginger…

Pedro the Squirrel

Dr. Schuler was a general surgeon who lived in a large stone house down the street from us. He owned about five acres and since he had grown up on the farm he still felt the urge to grow things. So, he went into organic gardening on a big scale. He had his basement garage crowded with boxes full of compost and manure. He called it his worm nursery. The worms, he said, would aerate the soil of his garden. In the spring of the year, he would plow up several acres in his back yard, raid the college hen houses and the dairy feedlot and pile truck load after truck load of this aromatic material onto his garden. Of course, as one might imagine, things started to smell pretty bad behind Dr. Schuler's house about this time every year.

Now, Dr. Schuler also liked to raise other things besides the plants in his garden. It seemed to me that his wife, Ruth Schuler, was always pregnant. They ended up having eight children together. Two of their daughters were near my own age. Joan was a bit older, but Ginger almost exactly my same age. We used to have great fun playing around together as kids.

You would think that with all of his own kids and all of his background on the farm that Dr. Schuler would also be an animal lover. You certainly wouldn't have thought that he would be afraid of animals – certainly not a little squirrel in any case.

You see, I liked squirrels, still do, and had hand-raised several of them when I was a young boy and would let them go into my backyard when they were old enough. Most of them stuck around and were pretty tame, even as adults. They lived in the backyard in several big oak trees. Of course, when they were still little, too young to survive outside on their own, these squirrels had the free run of the house. My mom wasn't entirely enthusiastic with this arrangement because the squirrels left their little droppings everywhere and chewed on anything they could get their little teeth on. Yet, she was also an animal lover and did allow the baby squirrels to stay inside till they reached adulthood. But, once they were old enough, she insisted that they must be "outside pets."

Of course, even as outside pets, they would often come and visit me for a handout as I sat on our back porch. And, if the door was left open they would make a beeline to get inside. They liked being in the house. I felt sorry for the outside squirrels. So, I made a small hole in the sheetrock behind the refrigerator into the kitchen. They would come through the open garage door in the basement, up the stairs, and through the hole behind the refrigerator into the kitchen. Obviously, my mom was never made aware of this particular arrangement. She thought that big rats were running around the house at night and tried numerous times to "get rid of the rats." I was constantly picking up the poison boxes and traps she set out. I was in mortal fear that I would miss one and one of my little friends would get wiped out.

Then, one night, my mom came home late from the hospital. She had been up most of the night with a critically ill patient. She was very tired and came into the kitchen to fix herself a little snack before she went to bed. She was fumbling around for the light switch when suddenly something jumped on her. She immediately thought about the rats and started screaming. I sat up abruptly from a dead sleep, jumped out of bed, and headed for the kitchen. It turned out to be one of my squirrels that had been rummaging around the kitchen looking for food. When my mom came through the door the squirrel decided to do what he usually did with me when I came home – give her a friendly greeting by jumping on her shoulder. Needless to say, it didn't take long before my mom forced me to confess where the secret passage was located. It was very sad, but the next day the hole behind the refrigerator was patched.

Some time later, I went to the back yard to play with my squirrels. Pedro was the youngest and tamest of the group. My mom wasn't home, so I decided to take him into the house to feed him some nuts. I set him down on the kitchen floor to run around a bit while I went to my room to change clothes. As I was passing through the living room, I noticed the new *National Geographic* my mom had left on the coffee table. I stopped, picked it up, and then sat down in the rocking chair to quickly flip through the pictures. All of a sudden, I heard a little squeal. To my horror, I instantly realized that I had rocked the chair onto Pedro. One of his back legs was really hurt. He tried to run, but he could only drag that one leg. As I stooped down to pick him up he started to squeal and suddenly chomped down on my index finger. His sharp little teeth cut like a razor. I quickly set Pedro down and grabbed my finger. His teeth had cut to the bone. Blood began to flow and drip onto the carpet. I ran to the bathroom where my mom kept the bandages. As soon as I bandaged my finger I grabbed a towel and went looking for Pedro. I found him under the dining room table. I reached out to him and gently picked him up with the towel.

I got on my bike and pedaled as fast as I could for the hospital. I figured if anyone could fix up Pedro it was Dr. Schuler. When I arrived at the hospital I dropped the bicycle on the front lawn and rushed down the hall to Dr. Schuler's office. His waiting room was full, but I rushed up to the receptionist and told her it was an emergency and that I needed to see Dr. Schuler immediately. Very quickly Dr. Schuler's nurse appeared and escorted me into Dr. Schuler's office. He sat behind a large imposing desk. As he quickly looked me over, he didn't seem very concerned. He leaned back in his chair, put his hands behind his head, and smiled at me, "Now Tui, what's the emergency?"

"It's Pedro! He's hurt bad. Could you help him?" I placed the towel on his desk and carefully unfolded it.

The moment he saw the squirrel he leaped to his feet and started yelling, "Get that thing out of here! That's nothing but an overgrown rat! They bite and carry rabies!"

He stood back quivering against the wall as if I had unleashed an attack dog. I was shocked! The nerve of him! Had he just called my dear Pedro an over-grown rat?!

I quickly gathered up the towel and Pedro and made a hasty retreat. The patients in the waiting room looked at me with startled expressions as I charged out of his office as fast as I could go.

I stood in the hall trying to decide what to do with Pedro. There was Dr. Gant, the psychiatrist, or Dr. Horseley, the ear, nose and throat doc. Oh, and there was Dr. Slate, the OB doctor. But, after a minute or so of thinking, I finally decided to take Pedro to see my mom. She specialized in babies and since Pedro was little, maybe she could do something for him. Although she had screamed that night when the squirrel had jumped on her in the kitchen, I had also seen her gently pet and feed some of my squirrels. So I ran down the hall to my mom's office.

When I told her about Pedro, his hurt leg, and what Dr. Schuler said about him, she laughed and laughed. But, when she regained her composure, she tenderly unwrapped Pedro from the towel and placed a tiny little splint on his tiny little leg. Then, as I reached to pick Pedro up, she noticed the bandage I had around my own finger.

"What happened to you?" she inquired.

"Pedro bit me when I first rocked the chair on his leg and tried to pick him up."

As she cleaned and re-bandaged my finger she said, "You'll be fine. Dr. Schuler is wrong on this one. Squirrels rarely get rabies and have never been known to transmit rabies in the United States." She patted me on the head and then looking down at Pedro she said, "I don't know how much good this little splint will do, but keep Pedro in the house for a while and see how he does." I was in shock. Was she really telling me that Pedro could actually stay in the house?

We pampered Pedro for quite some time. He loved every minute of it. And, his leg did gradually improve, but not fully. It always slowed him down a bit. He did Ok with his handicap for a while. But, one day, when he was outside, a cat saw him and took off after him. Normally, this wouldn't have been a problem for Pedro. But, being unable to be quite as quick as usual, the cat got him. I saw it happen and ran as fast as I could to rescue Pedro, but it was too late.

I emptied one of my mother's shoe boxes and buried Pedro under his oak tree in our backyard. I cried a little. I asked my mom if she thought God would resurrect Pedro when He came to take all of us home to Heaven with Him someday? She thought for a minute and said, "I can't say for certain, but I know God is willing to do whatever it takes to make Heaven the happiest place possible for each one of us. So, perhaps He will bring Pedro back just for you." Then, she bent down and looked me in my eyes. She had a little tear starting down her own cheek. She gave me a hug and told me how sorry she was that I had lost my little friend.

Pioneering Heart Transplants

Several years before Dr. Christiaan Neethling Barnard performed the world's first human-to-human heart transplant on December 3, 1967, my buddy Freddie and I endeavored to perform the first rabbit-to-rabbit heart transplant.

I was about twelve years old at the time. My mom was, of course, a firm believer that, "idle hands are the devil's workshop." She therefore endeavored to keep me occupied doing "useful work." In addition to my working long hours at a dairy farm during the summer months, my mom decided that I also needed to do a few more things around the house, like mow our yard. So, early one Sunday morning I dragged out our powered lawn mower. While it's true that we did have a powered lawn mower (not entirely common at that time), I'm not all that convinced that the one we had was any better than the non-powered mowers of the day. Ours was very hard to crank for one thing and, once I did finally get it started, it blew out clouds of smoke that were so thick that it was sometimes hard to see where I was going.

In any case, I finally got the thing started and had begun carefully mowing close to a rock wall that ran along the side of our house when, all of a sudden, the mower coughed and belched out a wad of dead grass along with a shower of light brown hair. I quickly realized that I had run over something. So, I turned off the mower and pulled it back from what I'd just run over. Reaching down, I pushing the grass aside and I found a partially-intact rabbit's nest. As I looked more closely at the nest, I saw a tiny baby rabbit nestled inside. So, I picked him up and cupped him in my hand. His eyes were wide open, but he lay perfectly still in my hand. The only thing moving on him was his tiny little nose. And, I could feel his little heart thumping away very fast inside his delicate little body.

If it's possible for a twelve-year-old boy to have maternal instincts, that was me at that moment. I experienced an immediate bond with that frightened little thing and felt very protective of him. I did look for his mother for some time, but she never turned up. So, I decided to keep him and named him Scampi.

Of course, I was told by local authorities that it's essentially impossible to raise wild rabbits. They always die no matter how much love, food, and tender care they're given. But, with the help of my mother's baby formula and a small doll bottle, Scampi survived the first several days and began to thrive. It wasn't long before he was eating lettuce and carrots all on his own. Soon after this, he began to forage around our yard for his own food. Any time he sensed danger he would scamper back to me and I would pick him up and put him back in his cage where he felt secure. He also felt secure if my dog was close by in the yard. They had really hit it off and had developed a strong affinity for each other. They actually liked to run around and play with each other.

Scampi did very well for about a year. Then I started noticing that he was having some trouble running around the yard. He'd quickly get all tired out. I took Scampi to see my mom in her office at the local hospital. She looked him over and examined him carefully. Then, she put down her stethoscope and explained to me that Scampi was suffering from a form of heart failure. "I don't believe your rabbit is going to live much longer," she said. "I'm surprised he lived this long. The poor thing is suffering you know. We probably need to take him to the vet and have him put to sleep.

I'm really sorry Tui. I know you love this rabbit. You let me know when you're ready."

I was shocked at the poor prognosis. Surely there was something else that could be done?! I didn't know what to do or say. Quietly, I left my mom's office and walked home with my head down, gently petting Scampi and rubbing his him behind his ears as I walked down the dusty road. I went to my room and sat down at the edge of my bed just thinking and petting Scampi. All of a sudden an idea struck me like a bolt of lightning. "Why not find an injured rabbit with a healthy heart and give the healthy heart to Scampi?!"

Freddie's father was a well-known surgeon at the Madison Hospital – the same hospital where my mom worked. So, Freddie and I would often meet at the hospital in the evenings while we were waiting for our parents to finish their rounds. These waiting sessions would give us opportunities to plan our next excursions and escapades. So, during our next "session" I told Freddie about Scampi and about my idea for a heart transplant. Freddie thought for a moment, trying to visualize the whole thing. As his imagination became more and more vivid, his face contorted a bit and the bridge of his nose started to wrinkle.

"Yeah, I don't think it's such a good idea," Freddie began. "Where could we possibly perform such an operation? We can't get into the surgery suites at the hospital. We don't have the proper instruments. We don't have any experience with this sort of thing. It has never been done before. And, what if we get caught?"

"Everything you say is true," I nodded. "But just think how famous we'd be if it worked!" After about an hour or so of discussion and arm twisting, I finally got Freddie to agree to at least assist me with the surgery that would make us rich and famous.

"Well, how are we going to do it?"

"Late at night the surgery shuts down except for an occasional emergency. I figure we can smuggle Scampi up there and exchange his heart and no one would be the wiser. We can scrub up just like your dad and Dr. Schuler. We've watched our parents scrub and operate a million times. How hard could it be? We'll use one of those sterile instrument packs and I know where they keep the sutures. The surgery table is big enough to put Scampi and the donor rabbit side-by-side so we can each stand and operate on opposite sides of the table. We'll put them both to sleep with Sodium Pentothal. Then, we'll shave them and use Betadine to sterilize their skin over the sites of operation. You'll operate on the donor rabbit while I'll operate on Scampi. We'll have to be quick and exchange the hearts before they die on us you know."

Freddie frowned, "You sure this will work?"

"No, but what choice do we have? Scampi isn't going to make it unless we try. This is his only shot!"

Freddie broke out in a wide grin. "Ok, let's do it!"

So, a few days later I happened to find what I thought was a mortally-wounded rabbit on the side of the road. I called Freddie up on the phone and said, "We're on for tonight. Meet me at the hospital at ten o'clock."

One of the operations lasted a bit longer than usual, so we waited for them to finish up. Then, when everything was clear and the OR had shut down for the night, we headed in for our ground-breaking surgery at about 11:00 p.m.

Everything was proceeding as planned. We scrubbed in and obtained all the necessary equipment. Both Freddie and I gloved up, put on large surgery gowns and surgery masks. We heavily sedated both rabbits with Sodium Pentothal before shaving the operation sites and sterilizing the skin with Betadine. We then used sterile drapes to cover up the rest and create a "sterile field." Finally, both of us stood ready with our scalpels in hand. I looked over my mask at Freddie.

"Ready?" I asked?

Freddie nodded.

"Ok, let's get to it."

We'd just started to cut into both rabbits and had clamped off a few bleeders with mosquito hemostats when the surgery doors flew open and Mrs. Wear, the no-nonsense head nurse of the surgery unit, strode in. She was a large rather heavy set woman and was very intimidating. She took one look at us and boomed out, "What's going on in here?"

We panicked. Freddie dropped everything, let out a few expletives, and flew out past Mrs. Wear, past the double doors, and down the hall. Everything seemed to be happening at once. Our donor rabbit suddenly came out of his anesthetic and hopped off the operating table, dragging a couple hemostats with him. When Mrs. Wear saw that a rabbit, of all things, jump off the operating table and hop toward her, she let out a blood-curdling scream. Now was my chance to escape, so I followed Freddie's lead.

I'm not sure how Mrs. Wear found out who the "surgeons" were since we were all gowned and masked and everything. Perhaps our short stature and the fact that I left Scampi on the table were a couple clues. In any case, a few days later my mom sat me down and talked to me in very stern terms about our personal use of the hospital surgical unit. I think I did catch her once, however, trying to stifle a twinge of a smile before she quickly regained composure.

A week or two later Scampi and the donor rabbit appeared at our house in a cage. Both were doing well. Someone had done a very nice job of suturing them back up. And, somehow, the donor rabbit had also survived his original injuries. Unfortunately, Scampi did end up passing away, about a month later, from his continuing heart failure.

So ended our dreams of contributing to the advancement of medicine - and of the Nobel Prize that would surely have been ours had we not be derailed in the midst of our historic moment.

Just One of the Gang

Every school has its clicks and bullies and the grade school at Madison was no exception. When I was in sixth grade there were several boys in the seventh and eighth grade who not only excluded us smaller and younger boys from their activities, which would have been just fine with us, but they also seemed to really enjoy tormenting us. Larry was one of the main ringleaders. He was a seventh grader and was exceptionally big for his age. Often he would bully me into giving him the best part of my lunch. “You'd better not tell anyone or I'll knock your lights out!” he would snarl as he held his very large fist an inch or so from my nose.

Soon I found out that I wasn't the only one who was being milked for food and money. At one point my friend Freddie saw what was happening to me. Afterward, he pulled me aside and confided, “That bum fleeced me out of my allowance money three times this last week. I am getting tired of him demanding ‘protection money' from me. He told me that if I didn't pay up he'd sic some of his buddies on me!"

Soon after this Larry actually beat up Eddie pretty good after school when he refused to "trade" his new bike for Larry's old one. Fortunately, someone walked by and broke up the fight before Eddie was hurt too badly. Larry yelled back as he was leaving, "I'll finish you off really good later! This isn't over by a long shot!" The next day, Eddie arrived at school wearing a rather large "shiner" over one eye. He explained to Freddie and me what had happened to him and of Larry's threat. So, we decided to join forces and blindside Larry with a surprise attack of our own. After school, Freddie and I rode our bikes as fast as we could to a stand of woods near the entrance to the Madison campus. We knew that Larry would ride by there on his way home. We hid ourselves behind some bushes and, within a few minutes, Larry rode up. He leaned his bike up against a tree and stood there looking down the road toward the school. He had his feet spread about shoulder width and his arms were folded across his chest in a menacing pose. He was just waiting for Eddie to come that way to "finish him off."

Everything was going according to plan. Soon, Eddie came down the road on his bike. He stopped a few yards in front of Larry, laid his bike on the ground, and walked nonchalantly up to Larry and grinned up at him – still wearing his black eye. "Well, if you aren't the brave little one," Larry laughed as he looked down at him.

"I guess you weren't satisfied with just one black eye! Get ready for your medicine little boy!"

Then, Larry reached down and grabbed Eddie by the neck with his left hand. And, with his right hand he reached as far back as he could reach before he started his downswing. Eddie closed his eyes tight and his lips drew into a grimace. Of course, during this time, Larry was so intent on Eddie that he failed to notice Freddie and me hurling ourselves at him from behind the bushes. Before he could even get is right fist all the way back to punch Eddie, we were instantly on him swinging our fists and screaming at the top of our lungs like wild Indians, "Ahhhhhhhhhh!"

Eddie quickly opened his eyes and joined in the attack. Larry went down much easier than I thought he would. He fell like a sack of potatoes. Eddie and Freddie held him down while I tied him up with the rope we had with us. Then, we just left him there crying by the side of the road.

The next day at school, Larry showed up with a very swollen lip and two black eyes. He told everyone that he had had an accident with his bicycle. None of us said a word about what really happened, but everybody knew. I think some of the girls had seen what had happened and the news had already spread. In any case, Larry never did bother any of us again.

After our success with fending off Larry, my friends and I decided that we needed to form our own gang for self-protection. Our founding members included Eddie, Freddie, Lynn, Richard and me. Of course, if you have a gang you need a secret hideout to make plans and meet for special celebrations. Between the school and the farm was an area that was heavily wooded. It was an ideal spot to build a hideout. Of course, as with all great hideouts, our hideout had to be so well hidden so that no one else could ever find it.

So, for several hours every Sunday for months on end, we would go and work on our hideout. It was an underground hideout. So, we spent most of our time digging a huge hole in the small clearing we'd chosen. Finally, our hideout was as deep and wide as a good-sized room in a house – approximately 20 by 15 feet square and about 10 feet deep. As a covering, we cut down thin trees and laid these thin logs across the top of our hide-out in parallel. Then, we piled dirt on top of the logs and smoothed it out.

As a final layer of camouflage, we put leaves and grass on top of the dirt to make it blend in with the rest of the area. After finishing the roof, we fashioned a hinged trap door out of a discarded piece of plywood and then covered it with leaves and grass.

Some of the older boys at school got wind of our hideout and tried to find it, but our camouflage was so natural looking that they never did discover it.

One day at school, we decided to have a special meeting at the hideout. In order to avoid being followed, each of us headed in the direction of our own homes so that no one would think to follow us. Then, about halfway home, we changed course and headed for the hideout. We crawled down into the darkness of our underground room, lit our candles for light, and sat around our small table making our plans with the smug feeling that we were pretty much invincible and were, of course, the coolest guys around with such a great hideout.

As we were basking in our coolness, our whole world suddenly came crashing down. In an instant, the entire roof of our dugout disintegrated as an entire cow came crashing down through the roof, tail first, and landed right in the middle of our table. Luckily, no one was killed as we fell all backwards toward the four corners of the room.

We quickly climbed out of our hole and stood on the edge observing the damage. The cow, though invisible under all the wreckage, was still alive. She was thrashing about a bit and moaning. We looked at ourselves. Although no one was seriously hurt, we did have cuts and bruises all over our bodies. Lynn had a little blood trickling down his cheek from a cut on his head. But mostly, we were in shock! In an anguished tone Eddie sputtered, “How we gonna to get that cow out of there?!”

“I don’t rightly know,” Lynn said, with a dazed look in his eyes, shaking his head. “I think she’s hurt pretty bad.”

Of course, it had to be Lovey Dovey, everyone's favorite milk cow. Of all the cows on the farm, why did it have to be her? She had been raised by hand from the time she was a calf and always hung around the barn after milking to get petted and be given special treats. I really liked her. As already mentioned, I used to actually ride her back to the milking barn when I went out to bring in the cows for milking. I couldn't believe that *she* was the cow that had fallen into our hideout!

"What is this cow doing out in the woods?" Richard said as he held his hands outstretched toward the hole.

"She must have broken through the fence and followed us," I answered. "She is like a dog. She likes to be with people... and she knows me."

After trying to get Lovey Dovey out of the hole for over an hour, we finally decided to go to the farm and ask for help. We arrived at the dairy office covered with dirt and sweat from head to toe. But, by that point, having dealt with boys like us for many years, nothing much ruffled Mr. Cantrell. He briefly glanced up from his paperwork, "What can I do for you boys?" None of us really wanted to be the one to tell him, but, after what seemed like a very long pause, Eddie finally spoke up, "Tui has something to tell you," he blurted out.

My eyes bugged out as my mind raced and I thought to myself, "Why did you have to volunteer me you knucklehead?!" Mr. Cantrell was looking at me now. "Yes Tui, go on." What's on your mind son?

I was scared and my voice was trembling as I blurted out, "There's been an accident in the woods at the northern end of the pasture. One of your cows fell into a hole and we can't get her out! You've got to come quick and help her. I think she may be hurt."

At this, Mr. Cantrell jumped to his feet and raced out the door with us trailing behind him. When Mr. Cantrell saw Lovey Dovey, he went down in the hole and examined her. He soon discovered that she had broken her leg. He shook his head. “We’re gonna have to shoot her I’m afraid. It’s the only humane thing we can do for her now,” he said as he looked up at us.

She was buried right there where she was. Needless to say, Mr. Cantrell was very upset at us. Lovey Dovey was also his favorite cow.

That summer our little gang worked long hours at the dairy cutting and grinding corn for cow feed until we had accumulated enough money to pay for a new Jersey milk cow – but no cow, no matter how fine of a milker, could replace Lovey Dovey.

My Contribution to the Space Race

On October 4, 1957, the Russians initiated the space race by launching a tiny little satellite named Sputnik. That same year President John F. Kennedy announced that America would be the first nation to put a man on the moon. All of America, especially all of the young people, caught the space fever. And, during those days, there were no regulations regarding the construction of homemade rockets.

One Friday, Lynn stopped by the filling station where I was working and announced excitedly, “Did you hear about the big rocket launch that some of the guys are going to have on Sunday by the Cumberland River?”

“No! What time ya’ll gonna to launch it?”

“Sometime in the early afternoon. Ya gonna go?”

“You betcha! I mean, if can get my boss to let me off a bit early. I usually have to work on Sundays.”

Fortunately, my boss let me off early that Sunday afternoon. So, I eagerly ran off to join my friends at a large pasture that bordered the Cumberland River to see them shoot off their rockets.

These were all homemade jobs, of course. So, they came in all sizes and shapes. Some were very imaginative. One was made out of a hollowed-out broomstick, a few were made out of steel pipe, and one was made out of the cardboard cylinder from a roll of toilet paper.

As with most experimental efforts, the majority of the rockets never made it off the ground. Some never even ignited. A few made a lot of smoke but not much else. A couple blew up the moment they were ignited and shrapnel flew everywhere. Then, there were those that made it a few feet off the ground before tipping over and crashing back into the ground. A few of these didn't topple all the way over, but would fly sideways at a high rate of speed – sometimes in our general direction and we'd have to run at top speed for the protection of trees and gullies. One of these particular rockets impaled itself halfway into a tree. Then, there were those two or three rockets that rose majestically into the sky for several hundred feet before deploying their parachutes and sailing gracefully back to Earth.

It was an exciting afternoon and I went home determined to build a rocket of my own! Not just any rocket, of course. I wanted to build one that would eventually put man on the moon!

I was a freshman in high school at that time. Every afternoon after school I pumped gas and did odd jobs at the local service station. This was the age when you really got true service at the "service stations" around the country. For each customer, I would run out and pump their gas, check the oil, tire air pressure and water levels in the batteries, add water to the radiator, and even wash their windshields! - all for just 31 cents a gallon.

My boss usually went home early and left me to close up the filling station at the end of the work day. So, many evenings I stayed late to use the garage at the back of the station to work on my rocket. It was nine feet tall and made out of aluminum conduit. I built it in three sections. The bottom stage was two inches in diameter, the middle stage one and a half inches, and the third stage one inch in diameter. For my propellant, I decided to use a mix of gunpowder, sulfur and zinc dust – all mixed in with a little bit of car oil. The oil, I calculated, would slow down the rate of burn and keep the mixture from exploding. When it was finally done and all put together, I painted it red with white stripes and named it, "The Shark."

It was a very emotional moment when I finally bolted the last stabilizer into place. That evening, Freddie came by to check on my progress. I led him to the back of the station where my rocket was sitting on top of my work table. We took a few steps back in order to properly admire my creation. It was magnificent. Freddie thought so too. "Tui, you've outdone yourself! She's a beaut!"

Then, Freddie, who fancied himself a mathematical genius, pulled up a chair and sat down at a nearby desk to scribble out some calculations. After a few minutes, he set down his pencil and declared, "I calculated that this here rocket will reach an altitude of over three miles!"

I tried to sound nonchalant as I said, "Oh, that's nothing. If this one is successful, it will be the prototype for a much larger one I'm planning to sell to the government for moon travel and space exploration . . ."

"Hey," laughed Freddie, "I bet Eddie could be our astronaut! He always wants to be the first try anything."

"True, but this is more dangerous than the submarine idea he came up with. Maybe though, after the first four or five successful launches, we could build a prototype big enough to send him up for a test flight?"

"Yeah, It's probably wise to test it a few times first before sending Eddie up in it," Freddie agreed.

Soon, the big day arrived for our first launch. Eddie, Freddie, Lynn, Richard and I loaded the rocket and all of the necessary equipment into my old '39 Plymouth and drove down to the river. The rocket was so long that part of it remained sticking out through the back window of my car. As we pulled up to the launch site, our excitement was almost unbearable. We set up the rocket on its wooden launching platform and then ran contact wires from the platform to a tree we'd chosen to serve as our block house.

As we all huddled behind that tree, Eddie began the countdown: 10, 9, 8, 7, 6, 5, 4, 3, 2, 1, Blast Off! - at which point I touched the ends of the ignition wires to the battery. Nothing happened. Everything was still. Then, after what seemed like an eternity, I saw a small flame flicker at the bottom of my rocket. A second later, the entire rocket was engulfed in a huge cloud of smoke. As we stood there motionless, with our mouths wide open, the tip of "The Shark" slowly became visible above the cloud of smoke and gradually began to climb skyward. Faster and faster it flew, higher and higher. We all stood there, transfixed by the sight. The flies that were buzzing around could have flown in and out of my mouth without notice. Soon, it reached the first set of low-lying clouds and was gaining speed as the first stage completed its burn. Then, in an instant, my trance was broken by a tremendous explosion. There was a huge fireball and my rocket was blown into a million pieces that began to rain back down on us.

My friends all shouted, "That was amazing! You've got to do it again Tui! You've got to do it again!"

So, far from being discouraged about my initial failure, I determined to start work on a larger and more sophisticated rocket. This time, of course, Freddie wanted to be in on the action. It was decided then. I would build the body of the rocket and Freddie, who also fancied himself an electronics expert, would build the rocket's "brains." (Of course, years later when we'd all grown up, Freddie almost electrocuted himself trying to fix his wife's kitchen toaster).

We were soon busy at work planning the design for our new rocket when, as fate would have it, some of the other boys in our neighborhood succeeded in sending their rocket through the next door neighbor's roof and into his living room before it embedded itself into his living room wall!

A few more events like these caused the government to step in and make laws that effectively curtailed my contributions to the space race. I still think though that Freddie and I could have given Wernher von Braun a run for his money.

Of course, one of these days we're all going to blast off from this old planet for a fantastic space journey. I am so looking forward to the day when Jesus takes everyone who loves Him on a wondrous trip through the vastness of space to our real heavenly home. They'll be no need for rockets or space shuttles. We'll be able to travel at will throughout the vastness of the universe. That's going to be something more wonderful and spectacular than even Freddie and I, in our wildest dreams, could ever have imagined.

The Prodigals

It wasn't that we were mad at the world or at our parents. It was more that we wanted to prove our independence. I was fifteen and wanted some excitement. I guess watching all those old black and white westerns and growing up with horses inspired us to seek adventure on some ranch in Texas. I don't recall who came up with the idea first, but after some discussion, it was decided. We would become Texas cowboys and come home the next school year loaded with money. None of us were old enough to drive except for Richard. He was sixteen and had just gotten his driver's license. We decided it probably wouldn't be such a good idea to tell our parents because they would try to stop us.

For the remainder of the school year, we began saving the things we would need for our trip. We acquired several old guns and stored up a large cache of can food in the shed behind Richard's house. Richard's parents had given him an old 1948 Plymouth that we were going to use as our getaway car. We would make our escape on a Sunday morning during Christmas break, telling our folks that we were heading off to camp out by the local Cumberland River and fish. That way we would have a good head start before anyone missed us.

Sometime about midnight my friend Lynn threw a few pebbles against the screen of my attic window to let me know that everyone was ready to go. I slid the screen up and threw out my duffle bag. It was filled with extra clothes, boots and various odds and ends, and was very heavy! Lynn was standing right under my window and was completely flattened when my duffle bag landed on him. Fortunately, it didn't do him any real damage. He half hollered up at me, "You knothead! Why didn't you let me know you were going to try to kill me?!"

"Quiet!" I said. "You want to wake up the whole world?"

Lynn was rubbing his head and picking himself up off the ground when I finally got over to the window and looked down at him. "Sorry," I said in a loud whisper. "I forgot you were right under the window. I'll be down in a minute."

I silently made my way out of the house and ran to the waiting car. We were full of adrenalin and never slept the rest of the night. We talked excitedly about what we were going to do with all the money we would make as cowboys. However, the further and further we got from home the less and less enthusiastic we became.

On the second day of our trip, we realized we were running out of gas. We had stored several five-gallon containers of gasoline in the trunk of the car, but had just emptied our last of them into the gas tank. It was lunch time so we pulled over to have a bite at a rest stop and think over our situation. As we sat around our picnic table silently eating cold beans from tin cans, we were a pretty quiet and somber bunch. But, no one wanted to be the first to let on that we were worried or chicken or anything like that. Finally, Richard stood up and broke the silence.

"We've got problems," He began. "This old car uses more gas than I thought! And, we've just poured in our *last* five gallons. Not only that, but this old car is burnin oil like there is no tomorrow. We've only two cans of oil left."

Then, he sat down without offering any solution to our problems. We sat on the bench staring at each other for some time, waiting for someone to come up with a plan.

After a few minutes of this, Eddie cleared his throat, "How much money do we have amongst us?" We dropped our spoons and lay aside our cans of beans. One by one we reached into our pockets and pulled out our change and dollars bills and put it all into a pile in the middle of the table. It was a very small pile. Lynn let out a low whistle, "You mean this here is all we got?" Eddie began to count the change and bills. It came up to all of $12.34...

"Oh man," Richard said as he gloomily shook his head. "There is no way we are going to make it to Texas on $12.34!" After pausing a second or two he continued, "I thought each of us was planned on bringing at least twenty dollars! – right? Now, here we are in Arkansas and there is no way we're going to make it all the way to Texas. There's just no way! I need some time to think about this..."

So, we all sat quietly as Richard thought... and thought. Lynn finally broke the silence.

"How come Richard gets to make all the decisions? He's only a year older than me!"

Eddie snapped, "Who's car we riding in?"

"This is a very hard decision for me," Richard shot back, trying to defend himself. "You're all welcome to come up with a plan of your own you know! You guys don't seem to understand that we have real problems here!"

"Like what?" Lynn asked.

I finally chimed in, "Richard is right. We do have problems: no gas, no money, and no plan."

"And a car with steering so loose that if you slow down under forty it wanders all over the road like a drunken sailor!" Eddie added.

"That's right!" Richard said with a bit more authority. Then, he hung his head, kicked the dirt, and said, "There's one other thing I haven't told ya fellas about."

"What's that?" We all chorused.

"My mom. You see, she has heart problems. I just found out about it as we was leaving. I didn't want to tell you guys bout it cuz I thought you might chicken out if I didn't come along with ya'll. But, I've been uh thinking that the stress of us leaving might be too much for my mom. Her heart might not be able to take it."

At this we all perked up a bit. Lynn was the first to respond to the obvious implications of Richard's story.

"I for one don't want to be the cause of your mom dying!"

"Uh, Me neither!" Lynn and Eddie chimed in together.

I nodded my head in solemn agreement. "So, what do we do now?"

Richard looked around the table, squinted his eyes a bit, and held out his hands toward us, "Let's head for home! If we make good time our folks will think we was just extended our fishin trip. We have just enough gas to get us to Memphis. After that, I don't rightly know what we'll do about gas. We'll just have to play it by ear."

We all nodded our heads in agreement and comforted each other with the thought that we had to sacrifice our dreams to become Texas cowboys, and the fabulous wealth that was sure to follow, in order to save the life of Mrs. Mitzelfelt.

We arrived in Memphis late that evening. The gas tank needle pointed to empty. As we drove slowly down the street a shiny new Ford pulled over to the curb and parked. A couple got out giggling and staggered down the street toward a brightly-lit bar. It was New Year's Eve and they were celebrating. As we passed them, Eddie yelled out, "Mind if we borrow some gas?" Either they misunderstood or they thought it was a joke. In any case, the man slurred back, "Sssure, hep yur self."

"You heard him," Richard said as he maneuvered our car to the curb.

"I'll get the gas can and the hose," Lynn volunteered as he climbed out of the back seat of the car and headed for the trunk.

"Have you ever siphoned gas before?" Eddie asked.

"No, but it can't be all that complicated. Ya just stick the hose in the gas tank, suck on the other end a bit, and then stick your end of the hose in the gas can till you fill it up. Then, ya put your finger on the end of the hose to stop the gas from comin when you're done."

This sounded simple enough. So, we all made our way to the shiny new Ford parked behind us. Lynn unscrewed the gas cap and slowly inserted the hose into the gas tank. Eddie held the gas can and waited impatiently. Lynn lowered his head and sucked on the end of hose. Nothing happened. He wiped the end of the hose with his hand and bent down again. "You're not suckin hard enough," Eddie urged.

"I'll get it this time," he shot back as he began to suck on the hose with a bit more vigor. Then, all of a sudden Lynn jerked back his head and spewed out a mouthful of gasoline! He started coughing and sputtering uncontrollably. Eddie paid no attention to this. "Quick," he said, "put the hose into the can!" After several trips between cars, we finally had enough gas – though the Ford had almost none left by this point. We left a hastily scribbled thank-you note and headed off again.

It was almost 1:00 a.m. when we entered the outskirts the small town of Jackson, Tennessee. The place was deserted. Unfortunately, however, the sheriff was still awake. His car was parked at the end of the road at the entrance to the town, right under a speed limit sign. So, Richard was forced to slow down as he passed by the sheriff. This was a real problem. Richard's car had bad ball joints and would begin to wander from side to side if the car went too slow. Suddenly, the sheriff turned on his flashing lights and pulled out after us, following close behind as we weaved back and forth across the road.

We had a short discussion among us as to whether we ought to flee or stop. Richard yelled back at us, "Don't you know this car can't do over fifty-five?!" So, he slowly pulled the weaving car over to the curb.

The sheriff stuck his head into our window and directed the beam of his flashlight, in turn, onto each one of our faces. "Well well now! What have we here?" he said with a grin. He was large and heavy. His smile revealed a large gap between his front teeth. "Ya tag says you'all from Davidson County. Ya boys seem to be a fur piece from home. What cha been doin? Fishin?" He chuckled. "Not talkin boys? That's jus fine. Ya boys is goin a spen the night in jail with me tils I finds out what's a goin on."

The sheriff put Eddie, Lynn and me into his beat-up patrol car. While the sheriff was talking to Richard, Eddie whispered, "I believe we could have given the sheriff's old car here a run for his money."

The town jail was just as dilapidated as the patrol car. It had two cells. One was occupied by the town drunk and the other was empty. "Now ya boys will be privileged to occupy the best cell of our humble establishment," he said, swinging open the creaky door and ushering us in. "Ya fellas make yourselves comfy now, ya hear?!" Then, he shut the door and turned to leave and then stopped. "Any of ya fellas gots a phone number so as I can communicates with ya ma or pa?"

We looked at each other, each hoping the other would pony up. But, of course, none of us wanted our own parents to know what we'd done.

The sheriff continued, "Ifans I don't gets a phone number ya fellas can stay here and rot as fur as I care!"

At this, I suddenly blurted out my phone number.

"Ahhhh, that's more like it," he responded with a smile. "Ya boys behave now! See that thar man over in the next cell? He jus kilt his wife and cut her into a million little pieces and stuffed her into a garbage bag. Ifan ya boys don't behave, I'll put ya'all in thar with him!"

He chuckled as he ambled out of the room and into his office. There was a bunk in the cell bolted on the bars next to the other cell, but we all sat on the floor on the opposite side of the cell. We could hear muffled sounds coming from the sheriff's office as he talked on the phone. The man in the cell next to us just lay there motionless on his bunk, snoring loudly. But, we all stayed as far away from the bars of his cell as possible, just in case.

Early the next morning my mom and our next door neighbor, Mr. Wiggins, walked into the jail. They had driven most of the night to get there. I had mixed emotions. I was so happy, but at the same time, I felt very ashamed to see her standing there in front of our cell. I saw tears trickling down her cheeks. I expected to get an ear full, but instead she blurted out, "I am so glad that you're safe! We thought that you had drowned in the river! We've been looking all over for you boys."

I've always dearly loved my mom, but I can't think of a time I loved her more than that moment. I knew then how the prodigal son Jesus talked about must have felt when his father gave him that big hug and welcomed him home after he ran away.

As we walked out of the jailhouse, the sheriff smiled cheerily and waved at us as he said, "Now ya'll come back and see me some time, ya hear?"

The 88

The 1955 “Eighty-Eight” Oldsmobile Holiday coupe (aka “Rocket 88”) was a beautiful car. It was two-toned with small fender skirts and flipper hubcaps. It was one of the fastest stock cars produced that year. I have no idea why my mom chose to purchase that particular car that year, but I wasn’t asking any questions. I was simply ecstatic.

I was just 13-years-old in 1955. I was still too young to have a driver’s license, even in those days, but my mom did occasionally let me drive the 88 - with her in the car. My sister Linda, who was three years older, was able to drive it all on her own. She would ride with mom to the hospital and, while mom was seeing patients, Linda would get to go to town with some of her girlfriends.

One day, while coming back from town, she had a flat several miles out. And, since the area was mostly farmland, there wasn’t anyone within site or ready walking distance that might help a bunch of stranded girls. So, they decided to try to change the tire on their own. After all, how hard could it be? They opened the trunk, pulled out the jack, placed it under the fender skirt and proceeded to jack up the car. Of course, the more they cranked on the jack, the more the fender of the car warped - until there was a huge bulge in the fender. Just about that time some boys from the school came driving by that way and recognized them. They pulled over and offered to help, but it was too late. The damage was already done. I was very upset at my sister, but mom was very calm when she found out. I don't think she said anything to Linda other than, "Oh, that's Ok. I'm sure it can be fixed." I was sure at the time that if the shoe had been on the other foot, my foot to be precise, that much more would have been said – and done! You see, there was still a bit of sibling rivalry between Linda and me.

Linda and I sometimes had trouble getting along during our childhood years. She thought that since she was older, and bigger at first, that she had the right to boss me around. Of course, early on I had reached the conclusion that I didn't need her advice or direction. We were both very hard headed and determined to have our own way. So, one can imagine that our arguments got very heated at times - so much so that one day a neighbor called mom at the hospital and told that her she needed to come home and separate the two of us before we killed each other.

Of course, over the years, we did grow closer and closer to each other, until, eventually, we ended up actually liking each other.

I believe the beginnings of a turning point in our relationship came on one particular day. I must have been about eleven years old at the time. Linda was just beginning her early teenage years and was definitely interested in boys by then. In any case, on this particular day, she was sitting by the window about mid-morning when she saw her boyfriend walk by our house. She ran outside and he stopped to talk to her for a minute. Although she wasn't supposed to do this, she invited him into our house. Mom wasn't home and it was against the rules for Linda to be alone in our house with her boyfriend. But, who would ever know? As they headed for the house down the sidewalk, I was able to hide myself behind the curtains in the living room with a squirt gun. They sat down on the couch in the living room and began talking. After a minute or so of chit chat, he put his arm around her shoulders and leaned in for a kiss. At that moment, I parted the curtains and yelled, "Gotcha!" as I shot them point blank with my squirt gun.

Linda was livid and yelled at me, "Tui! I'm going to kill you!" Meanwhile, her boyfriend headed for the door calling back, "I'd better go. I didn't know your little brother would be hanging around spying on us." At this, Linda huffed off to her room and slammed the door.

I should have known to let good enough alone, but I just had to rub it in one more time. Later that morning when she was in the bathroom brushing her hair I came up behind her and whispered in her ear, "I am going to tell mom all about you, kissy lips!"

I saw her eyes in the mirror start to narrow and, before I could even flinch, she twirled around and hit me on the head with her hairbrush after a full 180-degree swing.

I staggered a few feet and slumped to the floor like a sack of potatoes. I was out like a light. Eventually, I started to regain fuzzy consciousness. As my eyes began to focus once more and put together shapes and forms I started to recognize the face of my sister. She was bent over me sobbing uncontrollably, "Speak to me! Speak to me! Oh Tui, what have I done?!"

I never did tell mom about Linda and her boyfriend and Linda became more friendly and compassionate with me. We still got into the occasional altercation, but not so frequently or heatedly as before. Even my anger over Linda jacking up the fender of the 88 was short-lived. It was soon fixed and looking as good as new until one day, about three years later, when mom was called out of town for several days. She felt that since Linda was almost nineteen and I was now almost sixteen we could be trusted to handle things at home on our own until she got back.

On the day mom left on her trip, Linda had to work late and so mom asked me to go with her to the airport. She said, "I really shouldn't be doing this, but you're just a few months shy of being old enough to get your own driver's license. So, I'll let you drive the car back to the house after you drop me off - if you promise to take the back roads all the way home."

"Sure thing mom. Not to worry," I said in as reassuring and manly a voice as I could muster. But, of course, I was very excited to finally have the chance to drive the 88 all by myself.

"Make sure," she added, "that you leave the car parked until I get back. Linda can drive it if there is an emergency, but I don't want you driving it while I'm gone."

At school the next day Richard and Eddie told me about Tom, a young war vet who had just come back from Korea and had started up at our school. Since the G.I. Bill was paying for his education he decided to use the money to buy a new Chevy Impala. Tom thought he was something else driving that new car around campus. He was going around telling everyone that his Impala could beat any car in a two-mile run.

"Oh man, my mom's 88 can beat him any day," I bragged when Freddie told me about Tom's new car. Freddie smiled at me, but then shook his head, "You can't prove it because your mom will never let you race the 88."

Without thinking, I blurted out, "She doesn't need to know about it – right?"

"How's that?!"

"Well my mom is gone on a trip right now and she left the car at home. And . . . I've got the keys."

At this Freddie got all excited and ran off to set the whole thing up. Soon, everything was set. The race was arranged for the next afternoon. My sister was working, so I was able to get the car without a hitch. I stopped by the school to pick up Freddie and Eddie. They hopped in the car with me and we drove down to the ironically named Neely's Bend Road where there was a long stretch of straight road. When we arrived, there was Tom and his friends sitting there waiting for us. They had measured off the two-mile run and attached a red bandana to a mailbox at the finish line. A black line had been painted across the road for the starting point. I let Eddie out at the finish line and then drove back to the starting point and let Richard out so that he could witness the start of the race. "I hear you've got a pretty hot car," Tom smirked. "You really think you and your 88 can actually take me and my Impala? You ever raced it before? You ever raced anyone before boy?"

I tried to look and act the part, but I was feeling a little intimidated. After all, this guy was five or six years older than I was and was a veteran of the Korean war! But, I pulled the comb out of my back pocket and slowly slicked back the sides of my hair.

"Yea, no problem. This here 88 is the hottest thing around these parts. Your little Impala ain't nothin."

It was quite an act because the entire time my heart was pounding so fast and so loud that I was sure those next to me could hear it. My palms were all sweaty and I could hardly keep my knees from banging together. After all, I'd barely driven anything at all, much less raced a car at top speed before.

After our a few more seconds of our face-to-face stare down, we got in our cars and lined up at the starting point, both gunning our engines as Richard lifted the white handkerchief. Then, he swung his hand downward and yelled "Go!"

Our wheels spun furiously and let off a great deal of smoke as we took off. I took the early lead as my 88 leaped out of the starting gate. I was running close to fifty when the Tom and his Impala began to gain on me. As we passed the one-mile mark, I was a bit ahead, but soon we were running neck and neck, both clocking about 70 mph. Then, he slowly began to inch ahead. I don't know how fast we were going when we passed the finish line, but he crossed first, at least a car length ahead of me.

As soon as we made it through the finish line, at full speed, I tried to slow down quickly because, just beyond the finish line, there was a gradual curve. Tom made it around Ok, but, because of my inexperience driving, I overcompensated and began to slide. Then I overcorrected the other direction, lost control of the car, went off the road, and drove through someone's yard, clipping their mailbox. After leaving deep ruts all over the place in their lawn, I did, however, manage to get the car back on the road. When I finally got the car stopped, I jumped out to examine the damage. Fortunately, it was pretty minimal. I was very relieved. There was just a little scratch in the bumper, and that's about it.

I didn't really feel too bad about losing because, although Tom was ahead at the finish line, I had beaten him most of way, had been first to reach 60 mph, and had taken the one-mile mark – and had survived my first race. Over longer distances, of course, the overdrive in the Chevrolet at that time was just too much for the 88 to overcome.

Later that evening I told Linda that she needed to get gas in the car because mom would be coming home the next day and she need to go to the airport to pick her up. The gas tank was near empty. Since the filling station was close to the house and on a private road she said, "Why don't you go? I am tired." Happy to obey my sister for once in my life, I grabbed the keys off the kitchen deck and yelled back, "I won't be gone long!"

It didn't take me long to go to the service station and fuel up, but during that time it started to rain a little. It was just a light drizzle. On my way home, I saw Eddie, Ronnie and Freddie walking on the side of the road. So, of course, pulled up to them.

"Where you guys headed?"

"We're going to Richard's house to see if someone there can give Freddie a ride home."

"Hop in," I grinned. "I'll take you there. It's only three or four miles."

They opened the door and all piled in. "We want to come along too," Eddie said as he slammed the door shut behind him. A few minutes later we were pulling into Freddie's driveway. On the way back, Ronnie got into the front seat with Eddie and me.

"I heard this baby is a hot machine!" Eddie said as he slapped me on the back. "There is a little stretch up the road from here. Why don't you show us what she'll do?"

A bit more confident after my race with Tom, I pushed my foot down on the accelerator and the car spun out as she shot forward. The speedometer needle quickly began to climb. We were doing at least 70 mph when we came to the first slow curve. Without a second thought, I slowly applied pressure to the brake pedal. However, the road was slick from the drizzling rain and the car began to fishtail a bit. I suddenly started to get a bit anxious and tightly gripped the steering wheel till my knuckles turned white. I couldn't slow down fast enough to stop the fishtailing from increasing in intensity. The next thing I knew, the car started to slide sideways down the road. I tried desperately to correct, but without any response from the car. It was completely out of control by this point and started to spin around and around. All I could think to do was yell, "Lord, save us!" I remember a flash of bright light and then nothing. I lost consciousness.

When I gradually came to and realized where I was, I started to look around me. The windshield had shattered into a million little pieces and the steering wheel was bent almost in half. Blood was pouring profusely down my face. The back seat of the car was pushed up over the top of the front seat at a crazy angle. The radio was still blaring. I saw flashing red lights. The first thought that came into my mind was, "I've got to get out of here!" For some reason, I tried to start the car, but nothing happened. From somewhere under the dash I heard Ronnie screaming, "You've killed Eddie!" I looked around desperately. Eddie was nowhere to be seen. Outside it was dark and raining. There was no light except for the flashing lights coming from the sheriff's car that had just pulled up behind us. I crawled out and went around to the passenger side of the car. The passenger door was wide open. I pushed and shoved and finally moved the seat back enough so that Ronnie could squeeze out from under the dashboard. Miraculously, aside from superficial cuts and bruises, neither Ronnie nor I were significantly hurt, but we still couldn't find Eddie. I turned around and walked out into the darkness and rain and called for him. "Eddie! Eddie! Where are you?!"

This was a nightmare. What was I going to tell my mom? I turned around and looked at the car. I had hit a telephone pole going backwards at around seventy miles an hour. The bottom portion of the pole was embedded in the rear end of my car all the way to the back of the front seat. It was a true miracle that Ronnie and I were still alive. But what about Eddie?

Then, about 20 yards off to our right, in some bushes near the highway, we heard someone moaning. It was Eddie. He had broken through several smaller bushes and was pulling himself out of a giant bush a little farther along. He was repeating, over and over again in kind of a daze, "Oh my thumb! Oh my thumb!" He was holding his hand and his thumb was twisted at a crazy angle. As we watched, he pulled on his thumb and it popped back into place. After looking again at the car, I simply couldn't believe that all three of us had survived the crash.

By this time, there were people all around. The wrecked car was blocking the road and preventing people from passing in both directions. People began milling around looking at the wreck. This was dangerous because the power pole had broken in half and the live high power lines were lying all around on the wet ground. Fortunately though, no one was electrocuted.

I'm not really sure what took the sheriff so long to get out of his car. Perhaps he was trying to radio in to get an ambulance. Or, perhaps he thought that it was such a horrible wreck that there would be no survivors. Or, perhaps it was only my warped sense of time at that moment that made what was probably only a few minutes seem like an eternity. Suddenly though, there he was, standing right next to the three of us and shooting out questions without too much concern in his voice.

"Anyone know who the driver of the car was?" he asked.

"Me," I said as meekly as possible. He stood there for a minute staring at me. Rivulets of water were running down his face.

"Are you Ok, son?"

"I, I, I think so."

"How old are you?"

"Fifteen," I mumbled as I looked down at my shoes.

"I suppose you don't have a driver's license."

"No sir."

"What's your name son?"

"Tui Pitman."

"You any kin to Dr. Naomi Pitman?"

"Yes sir. She's my mom."

"Well boy, besides still being alive, this is your lucky day. I happen to owe you mother a big favor." (I later found out that my mom had taken care of the sheriff's daughter).

The next day the sheriff went to the airport to pick up my mom and explain to her what had happened. Again, she was far more worried about me than the car. She made sure that I was patched up properly and in no time at all my cuts and bruises were all healed up.

A few days after the accident the insurance agent came by to talk to my mom about the wrecked 88 and perform an appraisal. She explained to him, "My boy used the car without my permission." At this, the agent smiled at her and said, "I am sure that when you were young you did one or two things that you wish you could do over . . ." Then, he took out his checkbook and proceeded to write my mom a check for the full value of the car, out of which my mom paid $50 to the electric company to install a new telephone pole. The installation actually cost quite a bit more than this, but once the rep for the electric company found out that it was my mom, he insisted that the price was "just $50 Ma'am." The sheriff never did write us a ticket nor did he ever file an accident report.

To this day I have a small knot on my head from that accident that continually reminds me of God's power and grace. With God, we don't get what we deserve. Of course, I still don't know why God decides to save some people while others, who are far more deserving, are killed every day in such accidents? Perhaps we will never know the answers to such questions in this life, but it seems to me that God has given us evidence to know that He is in charge, that He dearly loves each one of us, and that He's got a plan to make it all better in the end.

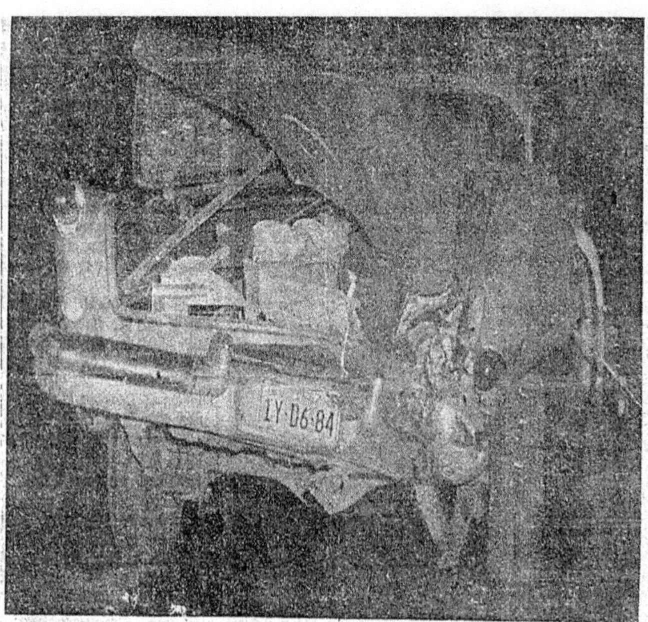

TUI PITMAN, 15, of Madison, driver of the 1955 Olds pictured here, lost control of the car and slid into a telephone pole last Wednesday at 6:45 p.m., according to Chief J. L. Boatwright of the Madison Police. Passengers in the car, which was going east on Neely's Bend Road to Madison, were Eddie Thorton, 15, and Ronnie Bush, 16, of Madison College. Chief Boatright said all three boys were taken to Madison Sanitarium, where they were treated and released.

My Hillbilly Friends

My mom was a very frugal woman, but that doesn't mean she was miserly with her money. She just had to have a good reason before she spent it.

One summer Professor Tucker, who had recently retired from teaching at Madison College, invited us to spend a weekend at his mountain cabin in Grundy County, Tennessee. His cabin was located on twelve acres of wooded land and sat right on the edge of a mountain bluff that overlooked a beautiful valley. Mom fell in love with the place. So, when she found out that the Professor Tucker was thinking about selling, she made Professor Tucker an offer on the place and he accepted.

She was very excited to finally have a place in the mountains. We visited the place several times a year, traveling the winding mountain roads all the way from Madison to stay in our cabin for a week or more. Many of these trips were sort of working vacations for my mom since she did quite a bit of gratis medical work for the underprivileged in the local community.

I loved going there because I was free to roam miles of untouched wilderness filled with beautiful woods and crystal streams and waterfalls. During this time, I developed a close relationship with the Eubanks family who lived about a half mile from our cabin. The Eubanks had ten children. The two oldest boys, Preacher (Raymond Jr.) and Andrew, became my very close friends. They knew the mountain like the backs of their hands. They'd grown up in those woods and knew where all the best swimming and fishing holes were located. They knew the best places to hunt for squirrels and rabbits and how to turn them into "mouth-waterin stew," – at least it was mouthwatering to them. They were definitely about as country as it's possible to be, I suppose, and proud of it – as were pretty much everyone around those parts in those days. In fact, during some of our explorations through the woods, we ran into several stills and sometimes were chased away by shotgun-toting red necks in overalls – just like you'd see on TV.

One of these times, we walked up on an old man sitting with his back against a large oak tree. He cradled an antique 12-gauge shotgun in his arms. We'd seen the smoke of his still off the bluff from my mom's cabin.

"Wat ya boys doin pokin round this part of the woods so nears ma still?"

"Oh, we're just huntin squirrels."

"Thar ain't no squirrels arounds here. I feared yu'alls a goin in the wrong direction if yu'alls knows what I mean!"

He looked up at us and gave us kind of a squinty-eyed wink and patted his shotgun before continuing on with his advice.

"Ifin ya fellas wants some of them thar squirrels I recon ya aughta look fur em in the utter direction," he said as he pointed back the way we'd just came.

On another occasion, we were following an old logging road that led to the "Stone Door" where there were steep granite cliffs that plunged hundreds of feet into the valley below. The view from the top was absolutely fantastic! There was an Indian trail that ran down through large crevices between the cliff faces into to the valley and then through the woods toward the Tennessee River. As we started down the logging road, we were laughing and telling jokes, minding our own business, when suddenly a middle-aged man jumped out of nowhere, right in front of us, and began yelling and waving his arms at us, "Turn around! Go back! Turn around! Go back!" If that weren't startling enough, we were doubly surprised because he was stark naked, except for his boots.

Since we all had guns and were rather curious we ignored his commands and kept on walking. When the naked crazy man realized our intentions, he whirled around and dashed off back the way he'd come. So, naturally, we began to jog after him. We soon understood why he had been so anxious for us to turn back. There, in a small meadow, was a picnic lunch spread out on a blanket. Next to the blanket, hiding behind a small bush, was a young girl about half the man's age – also stark naked. The man grabbed the picnic blanket and, throwing the contents to the wind, headed for the girl. He threw the blanket over her head and said, "Let's get out of here!" Then, he hustled her into a pickup truck that was parked nearby and took off like a singed rabbit. He was in some kind of hurry and certainly didn't want the girl to be recognized.

So, we all laughed and then decided we were a bit hungry. There was plenty of food around from the picnic party we'd interrupted. So, we all sat down and enjoyed the tomato sandwiches and potato chips that were left behind, and washed them down with the cold soda pop that they'd abandoned in a cooler filled with ice. They even left their clothes! - all piled neatly nearby.

Andrew went over to take a look at the piles of clothes and soon came back laughing out loud.

"You know fellas, it's too bad none of us gots a good peep at that there girl. But, I sur enough knows who the fella wus," he said as he held up a wallet in his hand. "You ain't gonna believe this, but accordins to this here driver's license he's a preacher man! And, he's a livin in McMinnville. Won't the 'Reveren' be surprised when I brings him his wallet?! I recon I'll be gettin a pretty good reeward nots to mention it to the Good Reveren's wife!"

There's no telling what one might find in those woods on a

"day's outin". It was always an adventure hanging out with the Eubanks boys.

They lived a simple life, as did most folk up there in the mountains. They ate most of the small game on the mountain, like squirrel, possum, coon and rabbit. They were all crack shots too. They kind of had to be. The whole Eubanks family knew how to handle guns. They say that one of the boys in particular, the one they called Preacher, could light match sticks with his .22 rifle – legend has it anyway. Raymond Sr. loved fishing. He would bring home a long string of fish every weekend for his wife to clean. They also had several large hogs in a crudely built pen out back in the yard behind their house. One of their pigs was a pet they called Arthur. He was very friendly and loved to greet visitors with grunts and squeals and would run back and forth begging to be petted. Their home was simply furnished with Salvation Army throwaway. They papered their walls with magazines and newspaper. The doors were always wide open. The chickens, dogs and cats had to be chased out of the house on occasion, but mostly no one bothered. The dishes were left scattered and unwashed around the kitchen. Food, plants, and clothes were stacked all over the place. When Mrs. Eubanks invited you to eat, she'd tell you, "Sit down fer a spell." She would sweep the assorted remains of the last cooked meal off the table. Then, she'd baptize one of the dirty dishes in old sudsy water and wipe off the excess with a dirty towel and pick out some corn bread from a frying pan on the stove and pour on some black eyed peas from a kettle and hand you the plate. The food always tasted good, but I always had this hidden fear that I would probably die very shortly from some unknown disease. Many times I had no idea at all what I was eating. But, I learned it was best not to ask too many questions.

Despite all of this, or perhaps because of it, the Eubanks were pretty healthy people for the most part. Mrs. Eubanks knew every plant that grew on the mountain. She knew which plants were good for medicine and which ones would make you sick. Much of her spending money came from the plants that she'd harvest and sell for medicinal purposes.

You see, the Eubanks lived, what they would call, the good life - and they would have it no other way. Except, perhaps, for the chain smoking of the father of the family, Raymond Eubanks. When

Mr. Eubanks came home from working for the county repairing worn out roads at the end of the day, his favorite thing to do was to set himself by the kitchen door and smoke cigarettes. He never used a chair. He just squatted down and smoked one cigarette after another. He would pull out a thin sheet of paper and then a bag of tobacco that he always carried in his shirt pocket and deftly sprinkling a small pile of tobacco into the paper. With his teeth he would synch up the bag and put it back into his pocket. Then, he'd lick the edges of the paper with his tongue and, with one hand, he would roll his cigarette. As soon as he had finished smoking one he would light up another. Sadly, he ended up developing severe emphysema and had real difficulty breathing for quite a number of years, but still continued to smoke just as heavily as ever until finally dying of throat cancer.

It was sad to lose Mr. Eubanks in this way. He was the nicest man and would give you the shirt off his back – if you really wanted it. It's a shame that the tobacco habit is so difficult for many people to kick once they're hooked on it. It's a terribly vicious addiction that leaves so many wonderful lives completely wrecked in its wake.

As I got a bit older, I had to go away to college in Chattanooga. However, Chattanooga isn't very far from Grundy County. So, for most of my free weekends, I'd head up to the cabin and take along some of my college friends.

One weekend I decided that it would be fun to explore a cave we'd found at the foot of the mountain. There were neat formations and miles of passageways. My friends Preacher and Raymond had found the cave and shown it to me a few years before. This cave had been used during the Civil War to mine saltpeter – a key ingredient for gunpowder. The miners would use small hollowed out logs to transport the liquid saltpeter to the entrance of the cave for further processing. Many of these hollowed out transport logs still remained there in that cave today. There were huge piles of bat guano in the cave as a result of millions of brown bats that lived in the cave.

In any case, I was excited about exploring it with my college buddies and also invited Preacher and Andrew to go with us. So, early in the morning we loaded Dale's jeep with our gear and drove down the mountain highway until we found the old logging road that led us close to the cave entrance. We spent a wonderful day exploring the cave. Everyone had a great time. Then, late in the afternoon as the sun was beginning to set, we headed back up the mountain. As we were nearing the cabin a car with about six guys in it pulled up beside us. They were all quite drunk and began cursing and yelling insults at us. Before we realized what was happening they had sideswiped us and forced our jeep off the road and into a ditch. No one was hurt, but my college friends were outraged.

"What on Earth just happened? Who are those guys?" my friend Dale shouted!

Preacher, never one to get too excited about anything, cleared his throat and slowly explained, "Them fellas is from Utah Flats and theys after me."

"Why are they after you?!" I asked in surprise.

"Sems like I got into a fight with one of um this past Fraday nat at the furin legion dance - cus they was a messing with one uh my sistas. One of them fellas was bigger than me. So, I decides to run right home real fast like and fetched my pa's brass knocs. Then, when I a comes back to the dance, I kinda worked him and a nutter fella over a tad. Theys left the dance a heap put out. I recon ya fellas come along rat in the middle of it."

We pulled the jeep back onto the road and drove back to the cabin. We didn't sleep well the rest of the night. Dale slept with his .38 under his pillow and I had a shotgun by my bed as well. Several others took turns as watchmen. When we all got up later the next morning, it didn't take us long to pack up our stuff and head back to college.

The main problem was, of course, that the Eubanks daughters were very good looking girls. The mountain boys just swarmed around them like flies to honey. Understandably, Mrs. Eubanks was very protective of her girls. It was a tough world up there and Mrs. Eubanks had to be tough as well.

For example, shortly after my wife Faye and I got married I took her up to the Tennessee mountains to spend a few days at my mom's cabin. The cabin was musty and needed a good cleaning since no one had been there for some time. I was working on repairing the screen door when Faye called out from the back bedroom, "You need to come see this!" I wandered slowly back to the bedroom. Faye pointed to the floor and then to the mattress. There was a huge blood stain on the mattress and a large blood stain on the floor.

"What in the world happened here?! Are you sure this place is safe?"

"I have no idea," I replied, but don't get all upset. I'm sure there's a perfectly good explanation.

She was doubtful. I could tell that she was still pretty concerned.

That afternoon I took her to meet the Eubanks. She really liked them right away. During our conversation, we told Mr. and Mrs. Eubanks about what we'd found in the cabin – all the blood stains on the mattress and floor.

"It musta ben them fellas from Utah Flats." Mrs. Eubanks laughed.

"I'll tell ya'll abouts all the particulars. Ya see, they come a sneekin round my place, tryin to molest my girls, not too long after my boy Preacher had a fight wit um. I let um knows that they ain't a welcome arounds my house. But, late one afternoon I seen em sneakin thru the woods a comin towards my house after my girls. I says to myself that they is up to no good. Sos I quick grabbed my gun, twas loaded with bird-shot. I yelled at em and told em I'd given em fair warnin. I believes they was skeert plum to death when they seen me comin at em wit ma gun. They commenced a runnin and I knowed it wer no use for me to aim at um. Sos, I jus pointed the gun in thar direction and pulled the trigger. Then I heered one of them holler, 'She got me' as they stumbled off thru them thar woods. I ner seen em fellas again. I reckon they climbed into yur cabin sos they could recuperates from all the birdshot I put in em."

In a strange sort of way, Faye was much relieved to hear this story. She was most interested in the life and many amazing stories Mrs. Eubanks had to share with us.

My mom also had numerous interesting encounters in those mountains as well. She loved the people in those mountains and wished to continue to help them, especially their children, even after she retired. So, she ended up moving there and living in her cabin for about six months out of every year. Once, after returning from one of her absences, she found that someone had robbed her house of some of the antique furniture and silverware she'd left there. She had no idea who did it or where it all went. One day, however, while driving down the road, she noticed that the garage door of the sheriff's house was partially open. As she glanced over at it on her way by, she happened to glimpse part of a couch inside the garage. It looked very familiar. So, she stopped the car and walked over to the garage to take a closer look. Sure enough, there were her things all stacked in the sheriff's garage! – of all places. Now, this was a quandary. She decided to drive home and think for a while about how she might approach the sheriff. After asking around, she discovered that the daughter of the sheriff and her boyfriend were supporting their drug habit by breaking into people's houses and robbing them.

Still, she didn't quite know how to handle this type of situation, so she decided to pay a visit to the county judge. When she entered his office he was sitting behind a large desk with his feet propped up on top of it. He was leaning back in his chair with his eyes closed and his fingers interlocked across his portly stomach. She walked a little closer and gently cleared her throat, "Uhmmm." A bit startled, he opened his eyes and, seeing my mom, swung his feet off his desk and stood up. Still a bit dazed he held out his hand and asked, "What can I do for you ma'am?"

She told him of the situation with the sheriff and his daughter and all. The judge gave her a knowing half smile as he began to explain, "People live by a different code around these parts. Don't go accusing the sheriff's daughter directly or bringing charges. If you did so, it would not be a great surprise if, in the middle of the night, your cabin were to catch fire – you know? You see, it would be better to figure out another way to get your property back than confronting the situation directly."

So, mom thought about this advice long and hard, for about two seconds, before deciding to go and visit the Eubanks. If anyone knew how the mountain community worked, it was the Eubanks. She told them what had happened and asked Preacher and Andrew to go with her to the sheriff's house to reclaim her furniture. They were pretty stout boys by that time and had a reputation for not messing around. They took mom over to the sheriff's house in their beat up truck. A billow of black smoke followed them as they pulled up into the sheriff's driveway. The three of them walked up to the kitchen door and mom knocked on the door a couple times. The sheriff's wife opened the door.

"Yes, how can I help you folks?"

Mom smiled sweetly as she took her hand, "I've come after my things that you have in storage in your garage. I really appreciate your daughter's willingness to take care my furniture while I was away. That was so thoughtful of her. You must thank her for me – won't you? These two fine boys have volunteered to assist me in taking my things back home."

"Oh," the lady responded, "I had no idea all those things were yours! My daughter and her boyfriend brought them over here several weeks ago and asked us to keep an eye on them. I am glad they could help you. Go right ahead and take them home. Would you like to come in first for some coffee or something?"

Mom never had another problem getting anything stolen from her cabin again. I guess the word went out to leave her place alone.

I have kept in touch with the Eubanks through the years. The kids have grown and married. I often stop by and visit with Andrew. We're still good friends. He's still a great fisherman and I go fishing with him on occasion. Of course, he smokes like his dad did. I keep telling him to at least think about trying to quit. He always says,

"Someday I will."

I really miss Preacher though. They called him Preacher because he never did smoke or drink and never swore. He was kind and gentle unless he saw someone getting abused or hurt who was defenseless. When he saw such things, the fire would come into his eyes - and that was pretty much the end of whomever was responsible.

Preacher was drafted into the army during the Vietnam War. Just before he was due to come home from Vietnam he volunteered to go on a mission for a buddy who was sick. As he was jumping off the helicopter into a jungle clearing he was shot and killed by a sniper. They brought him home in a pine box. I still miss him.

When I visit the cabin I often take the short walk down the highway to a little white Methodist church. I unhook a metal gate that surrounds the little cemetery behind the church and walk in. There around me lie scattered tombstones. Preacher's tombstone is in the very back. There's a faded picture of him in uniform still on his tombstone embedded in plastic. On the stone is written his date of birth, the date of his death, and then these words, "Sergeant Raymond Eubanks Jr. 'Greater love has no man than this, that he lay down his life for a friend'."

I've often thought that this world would be a much better place if we had more preachers like Preacher; with fewer words and greater love for those in need of comfort and protection.

Traveling

Traveling

My mom loved to travel. She traveled all over the word for the United States Department of Health in order to study the nutritional needs of children. In the process, she also helped to set up several medical schools in developing countries. I could never name all the countries she visited, but I do know that they included China, India, New Guinea, Thailand, Egypt, Pakistan, Jordan, Philippines, Sumatra, Syria, Lebanon and several countries in Africa.

Occasionally, I was able to go with her on her adventures around the world during my teen years. She considered it a key part of my educational experience. When she found out about an interesting trip, she would make arrangements for me to come along and would pull me out of school at random points in the school year. This was good, and bad. It certainly was a great educational experience for me, but it was somewhat difficult for me as well because, when we returned from our trip, I would have to try and pick up my studies with the rest of the class wherever they happened to be in their coursework. All this traveling and moving around also meant that I ended up attending four different academies in four years. Overall though, I loved it.

One particular trip we took to Tanzania, in East Africa, lasted three months. At the end of our stay at Heri Mission Hospital there, near Lake Tanganyika, I told my mom that I'd like to do some traveling on my own. I was nineteen-years-old at the time. To my surprise, she agreed. She actually thought it was a great idea. So, I spent the next six weeks traveling all over Europe all on my own. I slept on park benches, in barns and on trains. It was an exhilarating experience; one that I'll never forget.

Even after finishing my academy years and starting college I continued to travel with my mom, but did much more traveling on my own as well. I remember taking one trip to Mexico with three of my college buddies, Alberto, Roger, and Richard. My friend Richard (aka "Gordo") had just joined us at Southern College (now Southern Adventist University) straight out of the marines. He was still just a tad rough around the edges – especially for an Adventist college.

Once we made it across the border into Mexico, we drove for an hour or so before stopping at a little town. We were headed for an Adventist school in Montemorelos, but were getting a bit hungry. So, we stopped for a bite to eat at a little café. Of course, my buddy Gordo was a bit on the stout side (hence his nickname). He ordered just about everything on the menu . . . along with a tall glass of Tequila to wash it all down. Then, he ordered another, and another. I leaned over and warned him, "You do recall that we're going to be staying at the home of the principal of the *Adventist* school? – right? It would be kind of embarrassing if we were to show up at his house with you drunk out of your mind."

"No problem! I could drink all day and never get drunk!" he grinned as he dismissed my concerns with a backward wave of his hand and ordered yet another tall glass of Tequila.

After downing a quart of the stuff, he managed to walk in a semi-straight line to the car. Then, about fifteen minutes later, everything hit the fan. Before we knew it or could do anything about it, Gordo suddenly sat bolt upright, leaned over slightly, and, in a projectile manner, threw up all over the backseat of the car. The stench was quite impressive. I remember it vividly to this day. Yet, Gordo was still stone drunk, as drunk as I've ever seen anyone get. It was quite scary actually. He was constantly trying to open the back door of the car. It was all we could do to keep him from trying to get out and "stretch his legs" at 60 mph.

"Hey guys," I announced as I turned my head toward the backseat, "We really need to sober Gordo up before we reach the school."

The sun was going down rather quickly and it was getting colder and colder by the minute. So, when we spied a cow pond near the road, we drug Gordo, limp and passed out by then, to the edge of the freezing water, and, taking him by his hands and feet, swung him back and forth a few times and threw him in.

The response was instant. Gordo was suddenly very much alive. He came running and screaming out of that pond like he'd been lit on fire and ran around the pond about three or four times at top speed. After catching his breath, someone handed him a towel and a change of clothes. We also got him a rather large cup of coffee to try and get him sobered up as quickly as possible.

Finally, Gordo did start to sober up a bit. However, even though he was halfway sober when we finally arrived at the principal's house a few hours later, and had new clothes on and all, and had drunk a large cup of coffee, he still smelled strongly of Tequila. It was impossible to get rid of that smell. So, of course, no one was deceived when we walked through the door. The principal was, however, a most kind and generous man. He never said a word about any of it, but treated us all, even Gordo, as if we were the finest and most clean-cut of all the Christian youth he'd ever seen. This really made a lasting impression on me. I've never forgotten that man's Christian courteousness and tact.

After staying at the school there in Montemorelos for a few days, we travel to Mexico City and rented mountain climbing equipment. We had plans to climb Mount Popo, located just a few miles from the city. We were told that Cortez had, long ago, sent his soldiers to climb to the top of this mountain, which included traversing the mountain's dangerous glaciers, before going down into its extinct volcanic crater to gather sulfur for making gun powder.

After hearing this story we said to ourselves, "How hard could it be?" We figured that if they could do it with their primitive equipment, we could easily do it as well.

We spent the first night at a wooden lodge built on the mountain side for climbers. The cabin was placed high enough so that climbers would have some time to acclimatize themselves to the altitude. We figured that we didn't really need very much time for acclimatization. So, just as the sun was coming up the next morning, we head out up the mountain.

We made great time at first without incident. After all, we were all strong healthy young men in the prime of life. Then, as we were climbing a narrow path that led to the first ice field, Gordo suddenly passed clean out and, before anyone had a chance to react or do anything about it, he fell off the path and rolled a long way down the hillside. Luckily, it wasn't a very steep hillside at that point and he seemed to be Ok by the time we got to him. He'd only suffered a couple minor scrapes, but he felt sick to his stomach and could not continue. We managed to pull him back up to the path and stayed with him a few minutes until he was able to walk by himself. By then, Alberto wasn't feeling exactly on top of the world himself. So, he volunteered to go back to the cabin with Gordo and take care of him.

Only Roger and I were left, but we were feeling fine and decided we'd go ahead and finish the climb and be back down in a few hours. Of course, it ended up being a much more difficult climb than we'd ever anticipated. First off, the distance to the first ice field was far longer than we realized. We couldn't reach it that day. We had to spend another freezing night on the side of the mountain before reaching it the next day. Still, we were determined to conquer this mountain. So, we put on our crampons to give us some extra traction on the ice, pulled out our ice picks, and headed off. We were about half way up the ice field when one of my crampons came loose and I began to slide down the mountain. I had about a quarter mile worth of ice below me on which to slide before I'd reach a sheer cliff that dropped off hundreds of feet onto the jagged rocks below. I desperately hacked at the ice with my pick, but it wasn't holding and I was gaining speed. I started to get desperate and said a little prayer, "God save me." At that moment, after having slid about thirty feet, my pick held and I stopped. I was so relieved and grateful! "Thank you God!" I said out loud as I rolled over on my back, still hanging onto my pick for dear life. I yelled to Roger, "I need your help with this crampon!"

"I'll be there as soon as I can," he yelled down at me! "This ice is tricky!"

After what seemed like an eternity, he managed to work his way down to me and, with tremendous effort, we were able to reattach my crampon and continue our climb. It never entered our minds that perhaps, just perhaps, we'd bitten off a bit more than we could chew. Yet, somehow, a miracle to be sure, we actually made it the rest of the way to the top of Mount Popo, and back down again, without further incident.

A few days later, after having survived Mount Popo, we drove to Acapulco, Alberto's hometown. Before coming to Southern, he'd worked in Acapulco as a tourist agent, but decided he needed to learn more English to help him advance in the tourism trade. Since Alberto had grown up in Acapulco and had worked for a few years as a tourist agent, he seemed to know everyone there. One of his friends worked taking scuba divers to dive in the bay, and he offered to take all of us out, free of charge. He took us to dive at a very interesting place where a German U-boat had sunk a freighter. Coral had started to grow on it and the fish there were spectacular. It was also interesting examining a sunken freighter up close. We could even see inside it in places where there some large holes and rusted out spots.

On our second day in Acapulco, we went shopping. We drove up a narrow oneway street to some shops that were selling blankets and parked our car in front of one of the shops. While we were inside a shop buying blankets, a policeman rode up on his motorcycle and parked behind us, without our knowledge. When we finally finished our shopping, we all climbed back into our car without noticing the motorcycle. Roger was driving. He started up the car and put it into reverse to back out from in front of the shop. Suddenly, we heard a crash and kind of a crunching sound and felt the car bounce a couple times. Then, we saw the motorcycle out of our front window. We'd knocked it over and driven over its front tire, twice. It was smashed and the rim of the front tire was badly warped. It was beyond repair and completely undrivable.

Roger stopped the car and started to open his door, but Alberto yelled at him, "We need to get out of here in a hurry. Don't stop! They will throw us in jail and we will never get out!"

At that, Roger quickly slammed his door and restarted the car. Just then the policeman came out of the store and saw his motorcycle lying there all smashed in the middle of the road. He began swearing and ran out beside our car yelling at us to stop as he jogged beside us gesturing frantically. Roger's eyes bugged out a bit and he pushed the gas pedal to the floor. We took off down a one-way road – the wrong way. Somehow, we managed to avoid the other cars and found our motel. Not taking any chances, we grabbed all our stuff and threw it into the car and left town within minutes. We headed for the border and were back in the good ol' US of A by the next morning.

While I had many close shaves on these traveling adventures with my mom and my college friends, I did learn a great deal about the world and about people in general – people from many different cultures and walks of life. I learned that while cultures and customs may be a bit different in different places and countries around the world, people are basically the same. They all have similar needs and desires and cares and burdens. And, they're all looking to find fulfillment and meaning – something to make their lives worthwhile. They all try to achieve this in many different ways. Some ways are better than others, but those people who seem to be the happiest are those who, like my own mother and her innumerable humanitarian missions around the world, have given their lives to serve others out of a true concern for the welfare of those in need. This is true despite the religious background or social status of a person. Those who find their own meaning in serving the needs of those in need are the most fulfilled. And, I'm sure that one day such will hear the words of the King, "I tell you the truth, whatever you did for one of the least of these brothers of mine, you did for me." – Matthew 25:40.

Horse versus Mule

When I turned eighteen I received an invitation from Bill Jameson to spend my summer with him in Peru. I had met Bill on a trip to Bolivia with my mom the year before and immediately bonded with him. He reminded me of a defensive end for the Chicago Bears. He was six foot three and 230 pounds of muscle. Bill was so full of life that it was hard for me to imagine, at the time, that someone with his personality would ever choose to be a preacher. So, one day I built up my courage and asked him why he had chosen to become a preacher? He stopped what he was doing and looked over at me without saying anything for a minute or so. Then, he quietly started to tell me his story.

"You see, I was a medic during the Second World War. My company was part of the final drive into Germany at the end of the war. As we were heading into Germany we came across one particular German town where we encountered strong resistance and our advance stalled. We had to fight from street to street and house to house to clear the town. On the corner of one particular street, the Germans had a machine gun nest set up on the second floor of a schoolhouse. From this vantage point, they stopped our lightly armed unit. They had us pinned down and had killed and wounded quite a number of guys in my unit already.

I remember squatting behind a pile of rubble, waiting for the arrival of one of our tanks to help us take out the machine gun nest. Then, I heard one of our guys yell out, 'Medic! Medic!' When I looked over my shoulder I saw one of my own buddies, Strig, lying there wounded on the opposite side of the street. His real name was Tony Strigliano, but we all called him Strig. He was hit bad and his blood was pooling on the ground around him. I knew that I would almost certainly be killed if I tried to cross the street right in front of that machine gun nest. Yet, I felt that I had to at least try to help Strig. So, although I'd never been much of a praying man before, I decided that now might be a good time to start praying.

I said 'Lord, if you get me through this alive, I'll serve you for the rest of my life.'

Then, I grabbed my medical bag, jumped up and ran across the street as fast as I could go. However, I only made it about half way when, all of a sudden, here came this German jeep around the corner with several German soldiers in it headed right at me. They looked determined to run me down and, before I could even flinch, they did just that. In an instant the jeep hit me and I yelled out loud, 'Lord save me!'

I felt the front and back wheels of the jeep run right over me and then the jeep was gone. I just lay there for a few moments trying to figure out exactly what happened. At first, I was just surprised that I was still alive. Then, I was surprised that I didn't feel any pain. I remember thinking that perhaps I had been paralyzed and just couldn't feel anything. But, when I tried to move my arms and legs, I could! And, I still didn't feel any pain. I felt and looked myself over and everything seemed to be in order. My clothes were torn here and there and I was bleeding a bit from a couple minor cuts and I had a few bruises, but everything seemed to be Ok.

Then, I heard Strig again. He was calling out to me, 'Help me Bill! Help me!', and I snapped back into the moment. I rolled over, grabbed my medical bag which I'd tossed several feet away when I got hit by the jeep and scrambled over to Strig. The machine gun in the school house lit up and peppered the road behind me, but too late. By the time the bullets got close to me I'd already grabbed Strig and pulled him into a doorway. I bandage him up and he stopped bleeding. Perhaps, though, he stopped bleeding because he just didn't have any blood left? I held him in my arms and prayed, but, in just a few minutes, he took a deep breath and was gone."

Bill's voice started to break at this point and he took a long pause. He stared off into space for a minute. His face grew very serious. This startled me since Bill was always so cheerful and gregarious. I'd never seen him like this before. After a minute or so of silence, he said,

"From that moment on I knew that God was real and that He had performed a miracle in my life. I don't know why He saved me and not my buddy Strig. He was barely nineteen years old. Yet, I do know that God did save me for some reason in a miraculous way that I cannot deny. That is why I am a minister today."

I guess it was because of that traumatic yet miraculous experience in his life that Bill did not seem to fear anything. He had a sense of Divine protection that seemed to give him a feeling of invincibility. I think this is one of the reasons I liked him so much. There was something very special about him.

Bill was also a lot of fun and was very entertaining. Even his Spanish was entertaining – much to the chagrin of my mom. My mom had agreed to let me spend some time with Pastor Jameson. Since my dad had been killed she wanted a positive manly influence in my life and she thought that Bill, about twice my age at the time, was just the ticket. Still, she didn't want it all to be fun and games. She wanted me to improve my Spanish as well. So, my mom arranged for a Spanish professor from Walla Walla to tutor me. She was a very strict and proper professor who felt that I should spend eight hours a day, six days a week, studying Castilian Spanish verb conjugations and general sentence structure. Of course, I had other ideas. I wanted to spend more time with Pastor Jameson traveling around the country visiting with the common ordinary people of Peru. My professor was very unhappy about this. She wrote my mom letting her know, in no uncertain terms, that Bill Jamison would have a terrible influence on me because he "butchered" the Spanish language. I think I spent two days with her before I abandoned my official Spanish studies altogether and headed off for full-time adventure with Bill. And, much to her credit, my mom never did object.

The first of many trips I took with Bill was into the Peruvian jungle. We flew in an old twin engine Cessna and landed on an airstrip that had been carved out of the jungle next to a river. The plane was rented. It was owned by two Frenchmen who lived there right by the airstrip in thatched huts with their Indian wives. After we landed the plane, we pulled up next to their huts and talked to them a bit as we loaded our supplies into canoes. Then, we paddled off several miles downstream to a mission station called Navati.

The Indians in this area of the jungle would hunt one another in retaliation for some presumed wrong and then shrink the heads of their victims. This practice had actually decreased over the years as the result of missionary influences. It's amazing what just the simple story of Jesus and the gospel message of hope and love for one's neighbor can achieve for what may seem like complete savages. It changes lives.

The Indians who actually lived at the mission station had become Seventh-day Adventists Christians. Although these Indians had given up revenge killing entirely, they did like to show off a bit. They liked to show me the special poisoned arrows that they had once used in years passed to kill each other and the games that they used to play to develop their skills at dodging the arrows that were shot their way.

Of course, they did still go hunting for wild game. In fact, I went on several hunting trips with them. I helped them hunt and prepare wild turkeys. Of course, I really wasn't much good with a bow and arrow. However, they were just amazing to watch. For them, shooting wild turkeys high up in the topmost branches of the forest trees was like shooting fish in a barrel. And, speaking of fish, they were also very good fishermen. At first, I wondered how they could catch so many fish so quickly. Then, I went with them on a fishing trip and saw them use a most interesting fishing technique. They would dam up streams and then they would mash a poison root called Barbasco and wash the fluid from the root into the water. Then, after a few minutes, the fish in that area would float to the surface and the fishermen would simply wade out into the water and pick up the fish. Not very sporting, of course, but certainly very effective.

At first, I would go swimming with them as well, but quickly realized the danger of swimming in the local rivers when I saw several of the Indian men with large scars on their legs.

"How did you all hurt yourselves like that?" I asked.

"Piranha," I was told.

When piranha fish get isolated in packs where there is little food, they will work together as a team to kill and pick clean anything that walks or falls into the water in that area. They can reduce an entire cow to skeletal remains in minutes. Of course, most of the time one has only to worry about an occasional chunk being taken out of one's legs here and there . . . which was cold comfort to me.

The Indians laughed and said, "Oh, the piranhas aren't your real problem. Whatever you do, don't pee while you're in the water because the needle fish will swim up the source of the urine and attach itself inside of you. Then, you'll be in real trouble."

The jungle certainly isn't a place for a novice. I wouldn't have lasted more than a day or so there by myself. There were so many dangers and pitfalls all around – to include very large crocodiles sunbathing along the banks of the river right close by. I quickly decided that swimming was perhaps not the best idea unless absolutely necessary. I also quickly learned to keep my shoes on. At first, I wanted to do everything like the natives.

So, I went barefoot until a big red ant bit my toe and paralyzed my whole leg for several hours. After that, I decided that I didn't have to be a native after all.

Still, I did have my shining moments with the natives. One night, as I lay sleeping peacefully in my hammock, I suddenly awoke to some kind of commotion in the chicken coop. So, I slipped on my pants, grabbed my pistol, and carefully made my way to the hen house. As quietly and delicately as possible, I unlatched the door and cracked it open just a bit. My flashlight was off as I carefully slid it inside the cracked door and turned it on. The beam shown onto a startled Ocelot (a medium-sized wildcat) with a chicken in his mouth - and several other dead chickens below. He quickly darted out an open window with the chicken still in his mouth and started climbing over the fence that surrounded the chicken house. I drew my pistol and fired a single shot just as he cleared the fence. Amazingly, the bullet went right through his heart.

The village chief was very impressed when he saw the Ocelot. "Señor Pitman, you're a great hunter!" When we left that area this chief gave me, as a sign of friendship and to remind me of my stay there, his own bow and arrows!

Bill and I went on many more similar trips to villages all around Peru. I soaked it all in. It was quite a heady experience for an eighteen-year-old - and I loved it!

Our last trip together, was, however, particularly memorable. On this trip, we traveled to the highlands of northern Peru. At first, we traveled in Bill's van as far as the road went and then we had to load our supplies onto mules and horses. Our trip was supposed to last two weeks. During this time we held evangelistic meetings and medical clinics and pulled teeth. It is always very important and helpful to minister to people's physical needs as well as their spiritual needs – as Jesus did in His ministry.

Of course, in traveling from town to town I began to understand how folks who lived in the ninetieth century must have felt since we went everywhere on horses or donkeys. Eventually though, I got used to it and my saddle sores went away. On one of these trips between towns, as we were plodding along, Bill thought of something to spice things up a bit. He rode up beside me and grinned.

"Hey Tui, I've got a great idea. Why don't we have a race to the next town? It's only about ten or twelve miles away."

I looked up and shook my head, "Of course you want to race. You've got Samson, that big old white mule. All I've got to ride is Mickey here, this little runt of a horse. How fair is that?"

Bill thought for a moment before grinning at me once again.

"I tell you what I'll do to make it a little more even. I'll give you a twenty-minute head start! Fair enough?!"

"Fair enough," I said, smiling back at him.

"You had better start right now!" he laughed.

I tried in every way possible to get that little horse to actually run, but the fastest gear I could get out of him was a moderately fast but tooth-jarring trot - and that only with the vigorous use of a little switch I cut off a tree. After about 50 yards of this, I looked back at Bill. He was just sitting there on his mule looking intently at his watch. Mickey's trot was killing me but I had no other alternative if I wanted to win the race. About thirty minutes into my trot I heard a loud commotion behind me. It was Bill and Samson. Samson was running like an out-of-control locomotive and Bill's arms and legs were flapping in all directions – along with all of his equipment. In an instant they flew past me in a cloud of dust with Bill yelling at the top of his lungs, "I'll see you in town Tui!"

"Well," I muttered to myself, "So much for winning the race. But, I'm not a sore loser. I'll plug along the best that I can."

Then, a little miracle happened. When I looked up again to watch Bill and Samson disappearing in a little cloud of dust, I was surprised to see Samson start to buck like crazy and sling Bill around like a rag doll. Turns out, they'd bumped into a tree full of bees and both Samson and Bill were being stung all over. It didn't take long before Bill was launched like a rocket into the bushes alongside the trail. I avoided the bees and yelled, as I trotted by, "I'll see you in town Bill!"

I turned in my saddle to look back as Bill slowly untangled himself from the bushes and began to collect his equipment that was scattered all over the place "from Dan to Beersheba" – as Bill used to say. I knew it would take him quite a while to collect everything and catch that angry mule. So, I began to take heart.

"I'm actually going to win this thing after all!" I chuckled to myself.

However, after about forty minutes, I heard that familiar sound behind me. I looked and there was Samson, ears pushed back, nostrils flaring, traveling at top speed with Bill on his back – arms and legs flailing. Again, they flew by me like a hurricane as Bill called out, "See ya in town Tui my boy!"

However, just over the hill in front of me, they ran into a flock of goats that were being herded home from pasture. The goats scattered, setting off a chorus of clanging bells that hung around their necks. This startled Samson and again he began to buck. This time Bill was launched onto a pile of rocks and thorn bushes that lined the path at that spot. As I trotted past, Bill was moaning and mumbling to himself he lay there amongst the rocks and thorns.

"Do you need some help? Bill my man?" I said as I grinned down at him from my slow but trusty steed.

I figured he'd quit at that point and concede the race.

"No," he grimaced. "I'll die first before I quit! I'll get you yet."

Over and over again the same thing happened. I'd get way ahead before Bill and Sampson would fly by, yet again, only to run into more trouble. Bill was thrown off Sampson five more times during that race (seven times total). The only problem for me and my winning was that he never gave up. It didn't turn out for me like the story about the tortoise and the hare. When Bill was thrown, he got back up . . . again and again and again. The last time he was thrown, he was so close to town he could see it. He had about a ten minute lead on me. But, he was so sore and beat up that he couldn't get back up on Sampson. So, he limped along dragging Samson behind him by the reigns into town.

One of our local church members was working in his field close to town and when he saw Bill limping along past him. He called out to Bill and helped him climb back onto Sampson - and then led them both into town. I arrived two minutes later.

After our race, we both decided that for the next few days walking was far less painful than riding. Bill was covered with bee stings, small puncture wounds (from the thorns), and bruises from head to toe and I had two big symmetrical blisters on my backside that could have been put in the Guinness Book of World Records.

On our way back to Lima, we finally traded in our horse and mule for a car. We also took a young man with us who had never been out of his little village in the highlands of Peru. It was his first automobile ride.

The road back to Lima ran along cliffs that bordered the Pacific Ocean. At one point there was a sandy desert on the other side. It was late at night when we reached this desert area. We were making good time, traveling at about forty miles an hour, when we came around a curve and ran right up onto a sand dune that had blown across the road. I was driving at the time and had tried to slam on the brakes, but the road was slick with sand and we skidded right up onto the dune.

At that moment Bill, who had been asleep, woke up and, grabbing the steering wheel with all his might, yelled,

"Jesus save us!"

The van turned and slid down the sand dune toward the ocean below. Fortunately for us, a large amount of sand had already gone over the road, down the cliff, and into the ocean. So, it cushioned our ride as we slid down fairly slowly before stopping right at the water's edge. We sat there in silence for a few minutes. Finally, Bill spoke.

"God is good. Let's thank Him for sparing our lives tonight."

So, the three of us bowed our heads and thanked God for another miracle.

Early the next morning a couple men in a big truck came along and saw us. They ran a wench cable to our van and slowly pulled us up onto the road again. When we looked at the van for damages, there was only one little dent in the fender where the cable rubbed it a bit. When we got back up on the road, we got out of the car and walked along the road a bit to look at the sand dune. We discovered that the only place where we could have ridden safely down a slope of sand was right where we did it. If we had gone down at any other place, we would have tumbled down a sharp cliff face and into the ocean.

I never forgot Pastor Bill Jameson. He was like a father to me during an important time in my life when I didn't have a father of my own. And, he left an important lesson with me. The Christian life isn't about being worried about failure. We are all weak erring human beings - and God knows it. We are constantly tripping, stumbling and falling. The secret to succeeding in the Christian walk is to keep getting up and keep coming back to God, putting our hand in His, and saying, "Let's try that again."

Kamikaze and the Baboon

Dr. Berkenstock pushed his chair back a few inches, scooped up a spoonful of custard and announced, "This stuff is cracking good! This here pudding will warm the cockles of your heart." Then, he slowly put the spoonful of custard in his mouth, closed his eyes, and rolled it around with his tongue, savoring the moment. "Mmmmm-um, this is outstanding!" he said as he flashed a smile over at Mrs. Berkenstock.

It certainly was delicious custard. The Berkenstocks had asked my mom and me over for dinner and it seemed to me like I hadn't eaten food so good in a very long time. Evidently, Mom thought so too because she asked, "Where did you get the eggs? Aren't they usually hard to come by around here in Tanganyika?"

"Oh, you're absolutely right!" Dr. Berkenstock gestured with both hands before starting into his chicken story.

> Several years ago I was having the hardest time finding eggs that weren't old or contaminated. You never know what you're buying in the native markets. So I decided to get some chickens of my own. I checked out several farm journals and

finally decided to order some young pullets from the United States. I was told it would take several weeks to get them here. So, I had time to build a chicken coop behind my house with a high chicken wire fence and a cover to keep em safe from predators. I thought I'd start out with twenty young chicks. I figured that if I got at least a dozen good hens out of the batch and a few good roosters that I would be able to provide good wholesome eggs for our family and for the hospital as well.

Then, about a month later, Albert, my delivery boy and purchaser, drove into my yard and cheerfully announced, "Your little chicks are here!"

We carried them to the back of the house and I excitedly let them out of their cage and into their new home. In a few weeks I discovered that out of the twenty chicks, only one of them was a rooster. And, he wasn't much to look at. He was a scrawny little thing, but thought he ran the place. He was irritable and arrogant and was always harassing and terrorizing the poor hens. I'm sure he thought of himself as a giant. He was absolutely fearless and would attack anything or anyone who came into his domain. I called him Kamikaze. He even attacked me! The one who fed him every day! Imagine!

Fortunately though, the rest of my chicks grew into beautiful plump hens. I was looking forward to having fresh eggs shortly, but with all the harassment from Kamikaze I wasn't quite sure if my hens would ever have a quiet moment to lay any eggs. But, after a little while, things settled down just enough for them to start laying a few fine eggs.

Things were going along good for Kamikaze and his kingdom there for a while. Then, about four months later, a family of baboons moved in next door to my chicken yard. They lived in that huge mango tree right over there in my backyard next to my chicken yard.

I didn't know what to do about the baboons. They can be quite a nuisance of course. In our area of the country they destroy thousands of dollars' worth of crops every year. Also, they're not strictly vegetarians and are known for occasionally eating small animals like dogs and cats . . . and chickens of course.

What's interesting about baboons is that they are very intelligent animals. I've heard they can count up to four. They can keep track of at least four hunters who are out looking for them and hide until all four have left the area. However, if there are more than four hunters in the group, they lose count and come out of hiding before all of the hunters have gone away.

As another example of their intelligence, I once heard a story of a signalman for a railway company in South Africa who had a pet baboon named Jack. The signalman was crippled and had a wooden leg. So, he trained Jack to perform several jobs for him. Jack actually learned to operate the signal levers at the proper times for the trains to go on the proper railways. The old baboon even stayed at his job switching the signals after his master died! People brought him food and kept him going for a long time. But, one day, Jack just disappeared for some unknown reason.

In any case, I kind of respect baboons because of their intelligence. So, I didn't exactly want to kill them or anything. I didn't rightly know what to do, so I just let them be for the time being.

Every day I would open the gate to the chicken pen and throw in a handful of corn, Kamikaze would charge me, wings a flapping and neck outstretched. I would give him a shove with my foot back into the pen, feathers all aflutter, and shut the gate. The hens would come running and peck the corn while Kamikaze stood watch with a commanding pose. The hens would leave corn along the edge of the fence because the baboons would descend from their tree and stick their fingers through the fence and pick up the cornels of corn to eat. Of course, the chickens were scared of the baboons. When the baboons would arrive at the fence the chickens would all head for the safety of hen house. That is, all the chickens but Kamikaze. He would strut around and rush the fence, over and over again, flapping his wings and crowing loudly. He would actually try to attack the entire family of baboons single handed!

I could tell that one big baboon had a real fascination for Kamikaze. Each day he would come down and sit by the fence and stare intently at him. Although Kamikaze was a bit on the scrawny side, the old baboon seemed to drool a little as he sat there staring at Kamikaze.

I didn't notice it till later, but this baboon was, day-by-day, quietly pulling the fence strands apart at the bottom. And, day-by-day Kamikaze became more and more accustomed to the presence of that big baboon. After a while, Kamikaze felt so confident that he would walk right up to the edge of the fence where that old baboon was sitting and peck at the corn that lay right and the very edge of the fence in front of the baboon. And, he would occasionally lunge at the baboon and peck at him in an effort to keep him away from his corn.

Soon, however, the hole that the old baboon had formed in the fence was just large enough for his entire hand to fit through. He left a little bait for Kamikaze too. Several kernels of corn were scattered close to the hole in the fence. When Kamikaze saw them, he strutted right over and started pecking away, getting closer and closer to the hole in the fence. Then, quicker than you can blink, BAM! That old baboon had Kamikaze by his scrawny legs.

Kamikaze was absolutely shocked at the indignity and started pecking at the baboon's hand and flapping and beating his wings at the baboon. Then he started cackling desperately and crying at the top of his lungs as the baboon slowly and deliberately pulled him through the hole in the fence. Then, before I could do anything, the old baboon tucked Kamikaze under one arm and raced up the tree to one of its topmost branches and sat down on a limb. He put Kamikaze between his knees and began to pull out his feathers by the handful. With each pull, Kamikaze would let out a loud cackle. Then, the old baboon would lean out over the limb and watched the feathers float to the ground. He continued to pull out feathers until the Kamikaze was plucked clean. Of course, after that, he wasn't much more than a quick snack for the old baboon.

I had to wait several months more to acquire another rooster to take Kamikaze's place. Of course, the new rooster turned out to be much more calm and cautious. Unfortunately though, the baboons were emboldened by the success of the old baboon. The entire family now descended around my chicken fence every day and started making holes in it. So, I finally decided that if I wanted chickens, I'd have to get rid of the baboons. I pulled out my shotgun and pelted a few of them - and they finally moved on. And, that is why we had such good custard today for dessert."

I have often thought of Dr. Berkenstock's chicken story over the years. I've even used it now and then as a sermon illustration or a children's story. Everyone jumps when I tell the part about the old baboon sitting there and the suddenly GRABBING the rooster - and the kids love it. At the end of the story, I explain to them that most of us are like Kamikaze at some point in our lives. God has built a wall of protection around us by providing us with ten rules to make our lives happier in this world. Sometimes we are tempted look at these rules as unnecessary restrictions and God's way of preventing us from having any fun and getting what we want out of life. So, we live our lives as close to the edge as possible, failing to realize that the seemingly harmless old baboon on the other side is just waiting for the prime moment to have us for lunch.

As I've gotten older and a bit wiser compared to my early years, especially after having children and grandchildren of my own, I've learned to love and respect God and appreciate the fences that he has put in place for me - and my family.

The Driving Instructor

The morning rays came stabbing into my head as I turned over in bed. It was going to be another very hot day. As I rubbed the sleep out of my eyes I thought to myself, "This is the day I'm going to teach Jason how to drive."

The smell of breakfast cooking drifted over me from the kitchen. The house boy yelled above the clatter of the pans and dishes, "Bwana, your breakfast is ready!" I hurriedly stumbled to the wash basin and splashed cold water on my face. Driblets of water ran down and landed with little explosions on the dry dusty dirt floor.

I had arrived at the Heri hospital during the hot season. The country was a kaleidoscope of color and excitement. There was also danger because Tanganyika (now Tanzania) had recently been liberated from colonial rule. The popular word of the day was

"Ururo", which meant "Freedom." Of course, freedom was often chaotic. It meant that the rules that used to be in place were gone. For example, freedom from the British government meant that it didn't matter on which side of the road one chose to drive. All were free to drive as they saw fit – and they did!

Of course, there was also a lot of freedom in medicine back in those days. For instance, the director and surgeon of the Heri hospital was a white South African man. He was a very interesting and creative surgeon who used his fishing line for sutures if regular sutures weren't available and rigged the suction hose that he used for surgery so that it would water his garden at the same time. His vegetables always received plenty of protein. Also, because of the extreme heat, he wore shorts and operated without a shirt – bare-chested. Of course, he did wear an apron that protected him somewhat from the spray of the occasional punctured artery. He always used a spinal tap when performing surgeries (for anesthesia) which seemed to have a tendency to cause the patient's blood pressure drop precipitously on occasion. Whenever this happened, and someone brought this to his attention, he'd look up cheerily and say, "Don't worry. They'll make it! Hardy buggers, they are!"

This particular surgeon was also fond of tomato juice. When he first arrived at the Heri Hospital he used to go on rounds to visit his patients with a glass of tomato juice in his hand. As he talked to them and examined them, he'd sip away at his tomato juice. Word soon got out that the good doctor was drinking the blood of those who didn't make it.

To add to his reputation, his houseboy started telling everyone that the doctor was a cannibal. He said that the doctor ground people up into powder and put them into boxes and then ate them for breakfast. It was perfectly logical after all. The house boy explained that he had actually seen the doctor open up a can with a picture of fruit on it and out came the very same fruit that was pictured on the can. He also saw the doctor open a can with a picture of corn on it and corn poured out. Of course, it only stood to reason that the doctor kept pictures of the things that he was planning on eating on the cans and boxes in his kitchen. It is no wonder then that the boy's eyes would widen as he explained that on many mornings he had actually seen the doctor open a box with a picture of a black woman on it and pour out the white powder from the box and mix it with some milk. Then, the doctor would put the mixture into a skillet and fry it. When it became nice and brown he would put butter and syrup on the cakes made out of the powered remains of the black woman and eat it!

Of course, after a few stories like this people stopped coming to see the doctor. Finally, when someone told him why no patients would see him, he stopped drinking tomato juice in public and explained to his house boy that it was really wheat flour (pancake mix) in the box with the black lady on it.

While patients did eventually start to cautiously come back to see the doctor, occasional misunderstandings still came up every now and then. For example, one day the doctor's gardener almost killed himself when he drank a mixture of DDT and bean soup. He'd watched the doctor kill worms that were on his plants by dusting them with some DDT powder. So, when the doctor commented about the gardener's large abdomen and told him that he had tapeworms, the gardener put two and two together. Rather than use the prescription the doctor had given him to purchase medicine from the pharmacy, he decided to use DDT instead. He noticed that the doctor kept the DDT in a shed with the door unlocked. So, one day after work, the gardener slipped into the shed to get a little DDT power to treat his tapeworm problem. He thought that he would only use just a little bit of it so the doctor would never miss it. By the next day, he was, however, very very ill. He continued to get worse and worse and almost died. He did survive, however, and mostly recovered, but not quite. Unfortunately, from that point on he always seemed to be just a few bricks short of a full load.

I stepped into all of this as a young volunteer. I thought it would be a good experience for me. I had no idea what I was getting into, but it did end up being a good experience for me. I learned a lot about many things.

When I first arrived at Heri Hospital I was given the job of purchaser. This job required me to take a road trip to Kigoma about twice a week to purchase supplies. Jason, a nurse assistant, was assigned to help me on my trips to town. I always drove and he always rode shotgun, but he really wanted to learn to drive himself.

He harassed me for weeks on end about it. Of course, he'd never even seen an automobile before he saw the hospital's jeep, Mabel.

I'm not sure why I named her Mabel, but the name just seemed to fit for some reason. Originally, Mabel had arrived with the contractors who built Heri Mission Hospital. After the hospital's construction was completed, they had abandoned her. After some time, she'd been rescued from the junk yard and was kind of patched together and hand painted a rather sickly shade of green. And, she was getting old. Several generations of missionaries had struggled to keep the old jeep in running condition before I got there. Not surprisingly then, it was very difficult to get her started in the morning... or at any time for that matter. So we'd always end up having to push-start her. We'd get her rolling for a few yards and then pop the clutch . . . and eventually she'd start. That's why I always left her on a hill when I parked somewhere. Otherwise, I'd have to find a few people willing to help me push-start her again. Her brakes were also in terrible shape. It always helped to start pumping them vigorously a few minutes before you expected to stop. And, there was so much play in the steering wheel that it took several frantic rotations to make it around a corner. Driving her anywhere proved to be a wild adventure all by itself. Miraculously, however, no catastrophic accidents had ever occurred - yet.

On occasion, when we'd made good time on a trip, we'd have some time to do a bit of exploring. So, one day Jason asked me if I would like to visit his home.

"Sure, why not," I said, "I'd love to see where you grew up."

When we arrived I found eight or nine huts surrounded by a wall of sticks. In the middle of the courtyard stood a weathered tree. Jason told me that this tree was his family's god. Then, we walked over to his house and he introduced me to his father. His father had six wives. The youngest was fourteen years old, thirteen years younger than Jason, her stepson. The oldest wife, Jason's mother, was fifty-four, but looked more like eighty-four.

After greeting them all, I asked Jason, "Why does your father have so many wives?"

"Oh, the wives demanded it," He said as he shook his head from side to side. "When there's too much work, they go to my father and tell him to marry another woman. My father is a very kind man and gives into their wishes even though he can't afford a new wife. A young healthy woman is expensive. At least two cows!"

In his tribe, women did all the heavy work while the men sat around, drank beer and talked politics – and reproduced. Jason had twenty-one brothers and sisters in all.

Tui and Jeep at the burial place of David Livingston's heart

Several days later we were driving by a village and saw a group of men sitting under large mango trees. They were gathered around a large pot. Jason explained that this was the local pub. I stopped the jeep and watched as a long straw was passed around the circle. Each man, in turn, would take a long drag on the straw before passing it off. Even from my distance, the smell was overpowering. "Where do they get that stuff?" I asked as I waved my hand in front of my nose.

"It's made out of bananas," he explained. "The women take bananas and chew them into a mushy paste and then spit the paste into a large pot. Then, they dig a hole and put the pot into it and cover it with banana leaves and then with dirt. After that, they leave the buried pot for a few weeks. Then, after several weeks of fermentation they dig it up and you have a brew that will knock your eyeballs out!"

Oh man, I've gotta take some pictures of this!" I said to myself as I pulled out my camera. When they saw me with my camera, several members of the group staggered to their feet and came toward me. They were upset that I was taking their picture. I discovered later that they believed the camera would capture their souls, and they were not fond of that idea. Fortunately, however, they were all dead drunk and couldn't move very fast, but Jason was very worried, especially when the men started trying to climb up on the jeep. As he tried to push them off, he shouted at me, "Let's go, let's go! These men want to kill us."

Some of them actually had their spears with them and were taking blurry-eyed aim at us. So, I slammed the accelerator to the floor and Mabel roared to life, throwing a barrage of gravel and dirt at our pursuers as we sped away in a cloud of dust.

Only then did Jason decide to tell me that several weeks before a European doctor and his friends had been attacked at a market while taking pictures. Several of the doctor's party had been hacked to death and it was only the miraculous arrival of the army that saved the doctor's life.

After that, Jason argued that he definitely needed to learn how to drive. After all, what if I were to get injured and couldn't drive. It would be best if he knew how to drive so that he could drive me to safety. The logic was rock solid, and Jason was so eager to learn.

So, the promised day had finally arrived. After I finished washing my face and hands I went to get some breakfast in the kitchen. I'd barely finished eating when there was a knock on the door. I cracked open the front door and there stood Jason with a huge grin spread across his face.

"I am here to learn how to drive Mabel!" he said and he bounced up and down like a little kid at Christmas time.

We spent the first part of the morning discussing the workings of an automobile. I talked to him about the brakes, gears, clutch, oil, gasoline and motor. Then, we went to the side of the house where Mabel was parked. I poured water into the radiator and explained to Jason why it was important for Mabel to have plenty to drink. I always carried a large can of extra water with me. She needed to get watered about every thirty to forty minutes. Then, I got into the jeep and Jason pushed us down the little hill and I popped the clutch. Mabel heaved a couple of times and roared to life. Jason came puffing up and slung himself into the seat beside me.

The dry road left billows of dust behind us as we snaked our way through the hills to the spot I had chosen for the driving lesson. I continued to explain to Jason the mechanics of driving as we roared down the road.

The sun was blistering hot that day and beat down on us. We were both sweating profusely. I squinted as I looked out over the flat plain in front of us. There was nothing to hit. "This should be an ideal spot to teach Jason how to drive," I said to myself.

The road ran straight as an arrow for several kilometers before it began a gradual curved decent into the valley below. I pulled Mabel over and invited Jason to take the driver's seat.

"Look," I cautioned, "driving is serious business. I'm going to stand on the running board next to you. If you get into trouble all you have to do is move over and I'll jump in and take control."

"Righto!" Jason said as he eagerly scooted over into the driver's seat.

"Now, let's just sit here for a few minutes and look things over a bit. Let's do a dry run, Ok?

"Ok."

"So, put your foot on the brake. Remember you have to pump it hard up and down to stop. Ok, good. Now, push in the clutch. Give it just a little gas."

At this, Jason shoved the gas pedal all the way to the floor. The next second, Mabel just about came unglued. Fortunately, Jason still had her clutch engaged, so she didn't leap forward. I shouted at the top of my lungs, "Let up, let up! You're going to blow her engine all to pieces! You've got to handle her gently. Now let out the clutch slowly and, at the same time, push down the gas pedal just a tiny little bit."

For the next twenty minutes or so we tried to drive down the road. The first eight or nine starts made us look like a Texas jackrabbit trying to outrun Wylie Coyote. We would jump and zigzag down the road and then stall. However, we did finally succeed in going fast and smooth enough to put Mabel into second gear and then, even into third gear.

Of course, steering was an entirely different problem. With all the play in the steering wheel it was very hard for Jason to anticipate the apparently random directions Mabel would decide to take next. We drove into one ditch and then headed for the other ditch on the opposite side. Using the windshield for a brace I leaned over and helped Jason roughly stabilize Mabel in the center of the road.

Finally, he seemed to catch onto it and I began to relax a bit. We were actually doing fairly well there for a while - until the road began its serpentine descent into the valley below. At this point, Mabel began to pick up speed at an exponential rate.

I screamed, "Jason, push on the brake! Push on the brake!"

Sweat was pouring down Jason's face. This was a little more difficult than he'd ever anticipated. He pushed on the brake but nothing happened.

Alarmed, I yelled, "Pump it up and down! Up And Down!"

Mabel kept going faster and faster. Not too far in the distance loomed a sharp curve. Things were getting out of control.

"Move over Jason! Move Over!" I shouted right in his ear.

Jason didn't flinch. He sat there frozen in place. His white-knuckled hands were glued to the steering wheel. His eyes were wide and glazed over in fear. I was desperately trying to shove him over. Soon, I knew it was too late. We were going far too fast to make it through the curve. I grabbed the windshield and the seat and hung on.

We left the road at breakneck speed and leaped over a ditch. Mabel teetered for a moment and righted herself as we sped along through the brush. Right in front of us loomed the protective fence surrounding several large huts. We smashed right through it as if it wasn't there, plowed through dozens of chickens as feathers went flying all around like snow, and then ripped out the side of a hut, exposing a family who'd just settled down for an afternoon nap, before destroying half a dozen banana trees on the other side of the village. Finally, Mabel came to rest in the middle of the banana grove. As we sat there in stunned silence for a moment, chicken feathers came floating down softly on us. As I blew one off my nose, I noticed that dead chickens were scattered all along our path. It was a chicken massacre.

Jason sat in absolute silence for several minutes. Finally, he spoke just two very emphatic words, "You drive!" During the remainder of my stay there at Heri Hospital, Jason never asked to drive again.

Jason and his family

An Unforgettable Bus Ride

My mom and I were finishing up our stay at Heri Mission Hospital in Tanzania and were ready to return back home to the States. She suggested that, on our way back home, we take a detour through Egypt.

"Wasn't it fun the last time we were there together?" she smiled as she reminisced.

I nodded my head, but really, I only vaguely remembered Cairo. After all, I was only six years old when, in 1948, she took my sister Linda and me on a "detour" to spend a few days in Cairo on our way home from Bolivia. I did, however, remember one particular incident that happened on that trip. Elder Neal Wilson, who was the president of the local mission at the time, met us when we arrived in Cairo and put us up in a room at the mission headquarters. He told us that the next morning he would personally take all of us to see the pyramids.

That night we heard gunshots in the neighborhoods nearby. Egypt was in the early stages of a revolution in the 1940's (some things never change), but we didn't really understand what was going on at first. I remember getting up early in the morning just as the sun was rising. I went and sat down on the mission's front steps and looked down the street. As I watched the people and traffic, I soon noticed that a rather unique truck was coming toward me down the road. I still remember that truck very well because it had no cab cover. The front end was just open, with an exposed seat. An old man was driving. He was looking straight ahead with kind of a blank expression as he drove the old truck slowly along. Suddenly, the truck backfired like a rifle. At least that is what I thought had happened at first. However, at that very moment, the old man slumped over and tumbled off into the street and lay very still. The truck careened slowly toward the opposite side of the road and hit the building right across from me. Just then, I looked up the street and happened to glimpse a man with a rifle disappear into an alley.

For a moment I sat there in shock. Did I see what I thought I saw? I shook my head, jumped to my feet and ran into the mission yelling, "Mom, come quick! Mom, come quick! Someone just shot an old man outside!"

When she heard me she quickly ran and locked the door.

"Don't go out there!" she said with a very worried look in her eyes and a sharp sternness in her voice.

I don't know what she told Elder Wilson, but we did not get to see the pyramids – and the very next day we left for Europe.

Of course, that was many years ago. I'd grown up since then and was now a twenty-year-old college student who was very interested in history. What a unique experience it would be to visit the cradle of civilization and this time be old enough to appreciate Egypt's ancient history. So, we went.

When we arrived, we found a modest hotel several blocks from the main plaza to save money, but decided to live it up just a little by going down to the Cairo Hilton to eat our meals – since the preparation of the food there was up to American standards and we wouldn't have to worry as much about coming down with some local bug.

On the other side of the plaza was the Cairo Museum. I spent all of my first day in Cairo in that museum looking at the treasures from King Tut's tomb.

The next day my mom had a meeting to attend so I decided to go off and visit the pyramids very early in the morning. Since my financial resources were rather limited, I decided to take a bus instead of a taxi. The doorman at the Hilton told me that buses were less expensive than taxis, but were generally very crowded. He explained to me the routes that the different buses took and how to tell which buses would end up at the pyramids.

The sun was just coming up as I walked across the plaza to wait at the bus stop. No one else was there. I was the first one on the bus and made my way to the back.

I thought to myself, "This isn't going to be bad at all. That doorman didn't know what he was talking about."

However, my opinion of the doorman quickly changed as the bus began to winding its way through the city. About every other block it stopped to pick up more and more people. All kinds of people, and animals, were crowding in and almost no one seemed to be getting off. In a very short time, the bus was jam-packed with people, chicken, goats and assortment of bags and cages. And, dozens of people were hanging onto the back of the bus on the outside, blocking the doors and sitting on the fenders. Produce and luggage were also piled high on top of the bus as well.

"Ok," I thought, "now that the bus is full the driver will make no more stops until people start getting off to make some room."

Wrong! The bus seemed to sway and lurch much like a drunk heading home after a long night at the bar. The driver continued to make his stops. There was an ebb and flow to the crowd. More like tidal waves of people beating against a living wall of people. People were shoving and cursing, babies were crying and animals were bellowing. I wasn't too sure of the exact nature of the cursing because I didn't understand Arabic, but by the tone and expression I was pretty sure it was some kind of cursing, or close to it, occasionally interspersed with the word "Allah". I assumed it was either curses or blessings and by the looks and gestures I didn't think there were very many blessings going on.

Then, we made another stop that will always be etched in my memory. On the curb near the back door of the bus stood one of the largest ladies that I have ever seen trying to use public transportation. She must have weighed over 350 pounds. For the life of me, I could not believe that she was actually planning to get on the bus. The door in front of her was jammed tight with people and no one could move an inch. Yet, she clearly intended to give it a try. I watched in amazement as she took several steps back hiked up her skirt a little and adjusted her belt, which she didn't really need. Then, she charged at the door like a steam locomotive, pistons pumping. She hit like a professional linebacker playing with grade school kids. The impact shook the entire bus and people flew around like bowling pins – falling all over the sidewalk and on the floor of the bus. Now that she had a foothold, she again adjusted her skirt, smiled sweetly and bulldozed her way to the center of the aisle amid a chorus of protests.

As for me, I was just glad that I still had a seat, but felt a bit guilty that several little old ladies were standing while I was seated. I would have loved to give up my seat to some little old lady but I knew the moment I moved the men who were eyeing me like vultures would have descended in mass confusion to take over my place and the poor little ladies would have been plastered along the aisle of the bus. Besides, once I left the safety of the seat there were no assurances that I would not be pushed right out of the bus with the mass of people who were being shoved toward the exit door at each stop.

In the mass of this confusion a young woman who was overburdened with bundles and the burdens of life in general suddenly set her naked baby girl right on my lap. The baby must have been a little over a year old and from the look and smell of her it seemed to me like she'd never had a bath in her life. Her little eyes were infected and she had a runny nose and a club foot. When my eyes focused on her wispy black hair, there were dozens of fleas playing chase with one another. I didn't know what to do, so I just held her there on my lap for a while. Then, after a few minutes, I began to feel a kind of warmish wet sensation. I instantly realized what was happening and quickly lifted her off my lap and held her as far out in front of me as I possibly could her while she finished her business. But, she didn't like being held up in the air, so she immediately began to cry at the top of her lungs. I tried to comfort her but she would have none of it and continued crying very loudly even after I put her back on my lap.

Meanwhile, her mother was being pushed by the crowd farther and farther away from us. Then, before I could do anything about it, she was shoved right off the bus with half a dozen other people. I saw her through the window as the bus took off. She started running behind the bus yelling and crying for her baby. I jumped to my feet and tried desperately to push my way through the crowd, but it was pointless. I couldn't move a foot in any direction under my own power. I could only move when the crowd moved. The bus driver couldn't possibly know what had just happened, so he kept driving and stopping as usual.

Several blocks later the crowd moved me close enough to the exit door so that I too could get shoved out with the baby, holding her in both arms like I was carrying a football through the defensive lines for a touchdown. Then, I put her over my left shoulder and raced back down the street as fast as I could go to see if I could find her hysterical mother. After several blocks, I turned a corner and saw a large crowd gathered around the mother. I have no idea what she was telling them. She may have been telling then that this ugly American had kidnapped her child. After a brief pause, I ran up to the crowd and worked my way, red-faced and panting, to face the sobbing mother. I handed her back her little baby girl and then looked up at the crowd that now surrounded me. They seemed just a little bit hostile and didn't just let me walk away easily. I kind of had to work my way through the crowd rather slowly to get out of there, but, thankfully, they did eventually let me leave unharmed.

Right then and there I decided that maybe the extra expense of a taxi was worth it. So, I flagged one down and the driver happened to speak English!

"To the pyramids!" I said as I laughed a little to myself and leaned my head back to catch my breath.

I must have only been a couple blocks from the pyramids by then, but I didn't argue when we pulled up and the taxi driver said, "Ten dollars please." I was just relieved to still be alive after my harrowing bus ride.

Early Adult Years

Early Adult Years

After I graduated from college I faced an uncertain future. I lost an opportunity for a job as a pastor in Florida because, at that time, a young pastor had to be married to be offered a job. Of course, at that point in my life, I had yet to find someone I wanted to marry. So, I decided to go to California and find a job, any job, to support myself as I worked on my post-graduate degree in history.

When I arrived in California, I moved in with my mom who was working at Loma Linda University Medical Center and enrolled in the Masters program at the University of California at Riverside. I also took some classes at La Sierra College so I could at least run into a few Adventist girls. Frankly, I was more impressed with some of the young women I met at UC Riverside than the ones I ran into at La Sierra. However, regardless of how attractive they were, I refused to date any non-Adventist girls. I still felt called to the ministry and knew that I needed to find a good Adventist girl. I thought to myself that if ever I found a good Adventist girl who would actually consent to marry me, I would then go off to the seminary, get an advanced degree in theology, and then pastor a church. Of course, in the back of my mind, I also planned to go back to Bolivia and continue the dream of my Father where he left off when he was killed.

Until then, I worked in the cafeteria at La Sierra College washing dishes. I was astonished at the amount of waste. A lot of the students would push their trays through the window with much of their food completely untouched. This was especially true of the girls. Their eyes were often bigger than their stomachs. We were forced to throw away tons of perfectly good food. I just could not stand to see all this food go to waste. I thought about so many children I had seen on my travels who were starving. All that food would have fed hundreds. But, the California health laws at the time said that we had to put it all into the trash and throw it away. None of it could be used for soup kitchens to feed the poor or anything like that. However, it wasn't all bad. Nothing was said about me eating the leftovers. So, for six months I ate delicious lunches and dinners in the washroom thanks to the generosity of the La Sierra students. I never had to purchase any food while I was there. This was a real bonus because back in those days I had a very healthy appetite and it normally cost quite a bit of money to keep me well fed.

Still, I didn't really enjoy washing dishes. So, after about six months of it, I decided to take the civil service exam and became a juvenile probation officer for the county of San Bernardino. Working for the probation department meant I had to take a lighter load in school. But, it was worth it. Being a probation officer was exciting and even a bit dangerous. Not everyone was suited for the job. I watched one retired military officer, a full bird colonel, have a complete meltdown when one of the kids in his charge refused to follow orders and yelled and swore at the colonel. The colonel, who was simply not used to having his orders disobeyed much less ridiculed, lost his mind, jumped on the kid, and started punching away. Several of us had to pull the colonel off the boy and re-explain to him why he was there and how to handle the kids.

I became very attached to many of my boys. Almost all of them came from terrible backgrounds and home situations that were very abusive. Many of them had never been cared for by anyone who really loved them. The only real security and genuine care that they had ever known in their short lives were given to them by their probation officers at Verdemont Boy's Ranch (located just outside of San Bernardino). At the ranch, they were given clean clothes, a bed and good food. They were also forced to attend a school and to work, but soon learned to appreciate the opportunity that both school and work afforded them. While I was there I even set up a program where the Loma Linda School of Dentistry would provide free dental care to the boys at the ranch. It gave the dental students an opportunity to practice their skills and helped many kids who had serious dental problems. Also, Loma Linda University Hospital set up a medical clinic to provide free health care for our kids.

So, it was really a nice setup and many of the boys thrived under these conditions. Yet, it was not without its risks and dangers. For example, on several occasions, it was me rather than my delinquent boys who had to visit the medical clinic. One week I was stabbed in the arm trying to break up a knife fight between a two of my boys. I went to the clinic and they stitched up my arm for me, but two days later I was back at the clinic needed more stitches. One of the bigger boys had punched me right in the same arm when I was trying to break up a fight and tore apart my stitches.

My boys and I getting off the Verdemont Ranch bus

The doctor joked, "Why don't we just put a purse

string on your arm so we can just pull it closed each time you come back?"

It wasn't a bad suggestion because I did come back, again and again. A few days later I was walking through the dorm there at the ranch when I was stopped cold in my tracks by a powerful impact to the left side of my face. I didn't know what had hit me. The force of the blow dropped me to my knees. I did manage to maintain consciousness and held my face in my hands. I felt something warm running down my arms and when I pulled back my hands to look at them, they were covered in blood. Robert Santos, one of the older boys, had blindsided me. When I recognized what had happened, I reacted instinctively. I jumped up, clenched my right fist, and swung with all my might. My fist landed squarely on his jaw and he went down with a thud holding his own face. We found out later that his jaw was actually broken! – as was my own nose. So, we both ended up going to the hospital and spent several hours together in the emergency room talking.

When we got back to the ranch the director of probation called me into his office.

"I want you to understand that that what you did was not according to policy. I can sympathize with what you did and it may accomplish what years of talking could not have. I probably would have done the same thing in a similar situation. But, at my age, I probably would have never made it off the floor. However, if you do it again, you're fired! You understand Tui? The legal risk is just too great. The fact that he attacked you first would probably be in your favor if

Robert Santos and the new boy

this thing went to court, but I can't take that chance."

However, for that particular case, it was probably the best thing that ever happened to Robert. Robert was a very large boy of seventeen who had been through juvenile court for assaulting his father. He'd almost killed his own father when they'd gotten into an argument. During the argument, Robert had gotten so angry that he picked up a piano bench and hit his father over the head with it with all of his might. He then jumped on his father and was pummeling him with his fists over and over again when the police arrived – saving his father's life. Of course, Robert was arrested and, as part of the plea agreement, was sent to our ranch to see if he couldn't be reformed. Nothing worked, however. No one could get through to him. He was simply angry at everyone and everything all the time. He intimidated everyone - especially the smaller boys. I was constantly having to reprimand him and talk to him, but nothing I did seemed to help at all. It only seemed to make him more and more angry at the world.

Yet, from the day that I broke Robert's jaw onward, he became a model young man. I never had to ask him more than once to do this or that job. He followed my every direction without question and was nice to the other boys. He began to seek me out to talk to me about his troubled home life.

His father was a legalistic Seventh-day Adventist who physically abused his children if they did not immediately obey his demands. When Robert reached the point that he was physically stronger and bigger than his father he decided once and for all to end his father's abuse. Robert also told me that his father, who was a leader in the local church, was leading a life contrary to the church's teachings. At the church, he was a model of righteousness. But, at home things were very different. He drank, smoked, yelled and cursed as only a sailor could, and was physically as well as verbally abusive to his wife and children.

After hearing all this I asked Robert if he would mind if I asked his father to come for a family conference, where I would lead out? Robert wasn't so sure that this would be helpful, but reluctantly agreed. So, I invited Mr. Santos to meet with Robert and me and he actually agreed to come.

During the conference I asked Robert, "Do you ever remember your father telling you that he loves you?"

Robert stared at the floor for a long time. Finally he answered, "I've never heard that word in my home."

Then, I turned to Mr. Santos. His face was hard and the muscles at the side of his jaws were clenched. His eyes blazed with a certain fierceness as he glared at the top of Robert's head.

"Do you love your son Mr. Santos?" I asked.

His eyes darted toward me and we looked at each other, square in the eyes, for just a moment. Then, something strange happened. He slowly turned his gaze from me toward the floor, then toward his own shoes. His hardened face began to soften and he finally spoke in kind of a horse whisper.

"Of course I love my son."

"Why don't you tell him? right now? Come on, why don't you tell him directly to his face?" I encouraged.

Tears began to flow between father and son as the Mr. Santos sobbed out the words, "I love you Robert my boy! I really do love you so very much!"

A few months later Robert went home, arm-in-arm with his dad. A bit later, he came back to visit me and to thank me. As he walked through the door, I notice that he looked just like me. I always wore black wing-tipped shoes with dark blue pants and a light blue dress shirt to work. And now, here was Robert with black wing-tipped shoes, dark blue pants and a light blue shirt. It was a great honor.

Sometime after that, I decided to visit their church one Sabbath. When I walked in, Mr. Santos was on the platform leading out. He noticed me as I walked in and gave me a big smile. After church he asked me, "What are you doing here? Why did you come to see us today?"

With a big smile I said, "I am a Seventh-day Adventist too! I grew up in South America speaking Spanish and I thought I'd check out your church and see how much Spanish I remember."

He laughed and shook my hand and patted me on the back and told me how happy he was to see me. He thanked me again and again for helping him change his ways. He'd stopped drinking and smoking and had learned to be much more sympathetic with other people and to really love God and live like Jesus. Robert was also much happier and he and Robert were very good friends now.

Now that I look back on this experience with Robert and his dad, I'm so glad that they were able to experience this time of reconciliation and forgiveness. After all, they only had a few months with each other before they were taken away. A few months after my visit, Robert and his dad were killed on the San Bernardino freeway. They had run out of gas and were pushing their car off the road when a truck hit them from behind, instantly killing them both. I fully expect, however, to see them both in heaven someday, picking up right where they left off. I don't know if anyone wears dark blue pants, light blue shirts, and wing-tip shoes in heaven, but don't be surprised one day when you see the three of us coming down the golden streets each wearing this outfit – just for old time's sake.

The Girl of My Dreams

My dream had always been to go back to Bolivia and pick up where my dad left off. To that end, I signed up for every practical course at Southern Missionary College that I could get my hands on. I had so many credits in the industrial arts that it could have been my major. Of course, I had started out with a pre-med major and a goal of becoming a medical missionary like my parents. However, during my senior year I decided to add a theology major. That meant staying in college for an additional year. In the middle of my extra and last year of college, I received a call from the president of the Florida conference, Elder Schmidt. He wanted to invite me to join his conference as an intern pastor after I graduated – my first job offer!

There was just one problem, however.

"You need to be married," Elder Schmidt informed me.

Of course, I wasn't married and, as noted in the previous chapter, had no immediate prospects along these lines.

The last few months of my final school year Elder Schmidt was so concerned about my social status that he called me several times inquiring about my prospects.

"Surely, he suggested, "there must be one girl out of several hundred that will have you." He even threw out a few names for my consideration.

Still, despite all of Elder Schmidt's "help", the end of the school year came with no prospects in hand. So, I had to regretfully call Elder Schmidt and inform him that, until I located a wife, I would be turning down his call due to the fact that I was unattached. He asked, in a fatherly way, "Have you tried praying for a wife?"

Not a little taken aback I said, "Of course. I pray every day for a wife! My poor mother has been praying for my future wife since I was born. Unfortunately, however, my social graces have made God's job a little harder than usual for a theology major, I suppose. As far as I can tell, there's a very good chance that I may be in my eighties before my prayers are answered!"

There was a long pause on the other end of the line. Then, Elder Schmidt cleared his throat, wished me luck, and told me, "Probation's door for your call is still open, but I can't keep it open much longer."

That was when I decided to head for California to do graduate work and live with my mom and, in the meantime, look for a wife.

One day after I came home from the San Bernardino boy's ranch where I worked as a probation officer, I went up to the Loma Linda University Hospital to wait for my mom who was teaching pediatrics there.

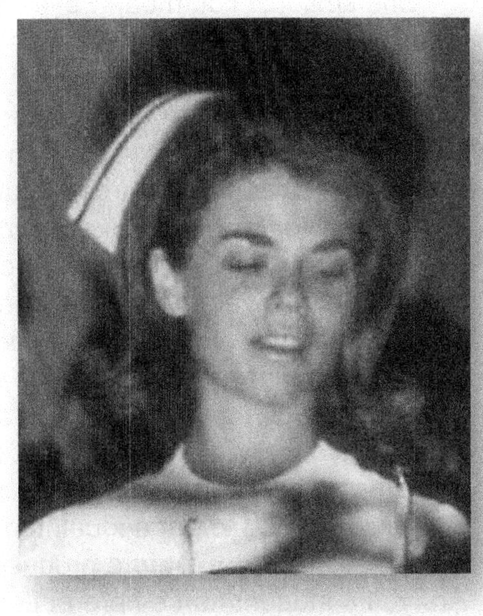

"As soon as I check on a couple of patients we'll go eat," she apologized as she stuck her head into the waiting room to see me. So, I sat there for a while reading a magazine as I waited. Then, out of the corner of my eye, I glimpsed the most gorgeous little nurse I'd ever seen. She came toward the waiting room and walked right through, right in front of me. I nearly dropped my magazine. I'm sure a fly could have flown in and out of my mouth without me noticing as I turned my head to follow her as she moved across the room in what seemed like slow motion. Before I could regain my senses, she was gone, vanishing down the hallway. I shook my head and stared blankly at my magazine trying to figure out how to meet this girl when, all of a sudden, there she was again. This time she had a stack of towels piled on her arms in front of her as she walked briskly past me.

Later she told me that she had noticed me in the waiting room as well, but not for the same reasons that I had noticed her. She thought that I was some dirty old man who was checking out all of the young nurses while waiting to see the doctor about his child. She had deliberately carried that big stack of towels in an effort to try to keep me from checking her out.

At the time, however, I didn't know that she even saw me. I began thinking to myself about how I might be able to be introduced. So, when my mom finally finished checking on her patients and we were in the car headed for the restaurant, I turned to her and asked as casually as possible, "Who is that cute little nurse working on the pediatric floor?"

She smiled, "You mean Faye? Faye Heath? You don't want to get involved with her. I am sure she's just a high school volunteer - every bit of fifteen!"

"Oh, come on Mom," I protested. "I am serious about this. Check her out for me will you? I am sure she's a nursing student. She has got to be the most beautiful girl I've ever laid eyes on!"

So, the very next day mom summoned Faye to her office on the pediatric floor. My mom was known for being a no-nonsense doctor. She was very gentle with the patients but tough on the nurses. Faye was absolutely petrified.

"What in the world have I done wrong that Dr. Pitman has to talk to me?" She thought to herself as she walked into the office.

As Faye walked into her office, mom got up from behind her desk with a smile and asked her to sit down.

"I just wanted to get acquainted with the nurses that work on this floor," she began before proceeding with a series of questions. "Are you a student nurse here at Loma Linda? What year are you in? Do you have family here? Are you married? What are your plans for the future?"

After the little question and answer session, Faye left my mom's office trying to figure out why Dr. Pitman had suddenly taken such a special interest in her?

That evening at supper mom told me the results of her inquiry – which was quite positive. As it turns out, Faye was, in fact, a senior nursing student, she came from a good Seventh-day Adventist family, she liked to sing and play the piano, *and* she was single. Mom also gave me her phone number.

So, over the next few days, I tried over and over again to call her to arrange a date. She kept putting me off, telling me that she already had dates with this guy and that. At first I thought that she was just making excuses to brush me off. However, I soon discovered that Faye was very very popular and that if I wanted to even meet her I'd simply have to get in line with all of the others. In fact, in the last couple months she had gone on no less than seventeen dates, each with a different guy! I don't know how she kept up such a schedule?

The fact is that she had so many guys vying for her attention that she really had serious scheduling problems. On one occasion she was just a bit late getting back to the dorm from a lunch date with one guy when she ran into another guy who was her dinner date. He had arrived just a bit early and was waiting for her in the lobby of the girl's dorm. Of course, he had to wait a little longer while she rushed up to her room to change her clothes to dinner attire. I was told that this wasn't an uncommon occurrence with Faye and that I would just have to get used to it.

So, I decided to give up on the idea of a date with Faye and just put her out of my mind. Then, about a month later, I received a request to play my saxophone at a radio station in Riverside. On Sunday afternoons they broadcast an hour of live religious music and they invited outstanding musicians in the area to perform at their station. An organist who played at the station every Sunday had heard me play and invited me to perform live on the radio. I was honored and practice very hard on the music I was to play. I had it all memorized and smoothed out to perfection. Then, in the middle of my performance, who should walk into the studio and sit down right in front of me, but Faye! My fingers suddenly felt all stiff and sweaty and I lost all concentration on what I was playing. I was fumbling all over the place for the notes. I couldn't remember where I was in the piece. It was a complete disaster! Faye did not remember me since I wasn't dressed in my dusty ranch clothes this time. She leaned over to the girl who was sitting next to her and whispered, "Where did they find this guy?"

"I was told he plays the saxophone very well?" she said.

"It sure doesn't sound that great to me!" Faye smirked.

I easily overheard them since they weren't more than a few feet away, just outside of the sound booth. So, their conversation kind of took the wind out of my sail. After I finished playing, I meekly made my way out of the sound booth and walked over to my case to put away my saxophone.

"Oh boy," I muttered to myself. "I really blew it! She must think I'm the worst sax player in the world. What a great way to leave a good impression. This was my one chance."

The strains of the organ filled the air and Faye walked into the sound booth and began her song. I stayed to listen. She had a beautiful sultry voice – and she wasn't distracted by me at all.

When Faye finished her first song, the girl who had been talking to her when I was playing stood up a said to the group who was there to listen to the performances, "Can anyone take Faye to La Sierra when she's finished here? She wants to go to the wedding of one of her classmates, but doesn't have a way of getting there. Her boyfriend dropped her off here, but he had to leave."

Bucky, a good looking Casanova type, was very quick on the draw and immediately volunteered. I decided that if I was ever going to get acquainted with Faye that this was my golden opportunity. So, I walked over to Bucky and took him by the arm.

"Listen Bucky boy," I said through gritted teeth, "you and I need to have a little talk." I guided him over to the corner of the room. Then, while squeezing his arm a little harder and looking him straight in the eye, I said, "This one is mine. You need to back off! Do we have an understanding here?"

"Ok, Ok," Bucky said as he tried to shake his arm free. "You can take her! You can take her!"

So, when Faye finished her last song and came out of the sound booth I immediately went up to her and announced, "I'll be taking you to La Sierra and escorting you to the wedding of your friend. I happen to know the couple getting married too, but first I have to run by my house and change clothes – if you don't mind."

"Great," she smiled. "I hope we're not too late!"

When we walked into the house, my mom

looked up to say hi and was very surprised to see Faye there with me. Faye looked rather shocked herself! "Dr. Pitman is *your* mom?!" she gasped.

"Yep," I answered. "She's my mom. I'll let you two chat while I go get changed."

So, my mom and Faye sat down in the living room to talk a bit as I went to my bedroom to change clothes. A few minutes later I was ready and we headed out the door. As we were leaving mom grabbed my arm and said, "I heard you on the radio. You sounded a little sloppy. What happened?"

I smiled, rolled my eyes, and looked at Faye. She smiled up at me and shook her head a little. She knew.

The wedding was great! Both of us had a great time. Afterward, I took her back to the dorm but, instead of going in, we sat in the car and talked for more than an hour before she finally said, "I do have to go. I had a really great time though."

The next day I called her up and said, "Do you like ice cream? How about going with me to get ice cream this evening?"

"I think I can arrange it," she laughed.

So I picked her up and we spent an hour or two talking as we sat out on the outdoor patio of the ice cream shop. The time just flew by, for both of us. The more I was around Faye, the more I liked her. She was full of energy, smart and extremely good looking. She was everything I had dreamed about, but she still seemed to have a crush on a young doctor and was not at all interested in getting into a relationship with anyone who was headed into the ministry. She just wasn't interested in ever becoming a "pastor's wife." I soon began to worry that I wasn't making any real progress with her. It seemed fairly clear to me, at that point in our relationship, that we weren't going to be much more than "just friends." Of course, I was also in kind of a relationship of my own. Her name was Margaret.

The previous summer I had gone on a trip to Africa with my mom. She was doing studies on children's nutritional needs and invited me to go with her. On the way home from Africa we decided to drop by Italy. While in Rome, a South African lady and her eighteen-year-old daughter joined our tour group. The girl was very beautiful. She reminded me a little of a young Elizabeth Taylor. And, she was set financially. Her parents were wealthy farmers in South Africa. She and her mother were on their way to live in Long Beach, California. For the next couple of days we were with each other constantly. When we left she gave me her address and asked me to call her when I was in California. As soon as we arrived at Loma Linda I called Margaret and we began dating. I even took her up to meet my grandparents in Santa Cruz. But, I could tell that my grandfather, in particular, was not pleased with Margaret. My grandparents were very conservative Seventh-day Adventists and Margaret was a practicing Catholic who smoked little Mexican cigars and liked to drink a few alcoholic beverages on occasion. She wore jewelry and her clothing was a bit revealing. Yet, even though they disapproved of my dating her, they were very kind and courteous to her and she liked them very much. Of course, I knew that, because of our religious differences, we should not be dating. However, she was so very good looking, witty, and fun to be with. I was very conflicted. And, after meeting Faye, I was even more conflicted.

Finally, I made my decision. I went to Margaret's house for the weekend to break up with her. I told Faye that I had a date that weekend, but I didn't tell her what kind of date it was. But, she wasn't born yesterday. In short order she had it all figured out and was very upset with me. She seemed to be pretty jealous of Margaret, which, in a way, made me feel pretty good because it was the first clear sign to me that Faye really did have feelings for me beyond mere friendship.

But, it wasn't all fun and games. While I was gone to Margaret's house for the weekend, Faye decided that it was time for her to turn the tables on me. She called up her cousin, a very handsome medical student, and asked him to escort her to church that Sabbath (of course, few in the area knew that he was actually her cousin). She put on a beautiful blue silk dress that I was told by many looked absolutely stunning. Then, she and her cousin strode down the long aisle to the very front of the church. She wanted my friends to send me the news that my absence that weekend was not about to cramp her style.

Needless to say, the news did get back to me in force and I wasted no time in calling Faye as soon as I got back in town that Monday night.

"You got anything planned for tonight?" I asked, very innocently.

"Well, I was pretty busy this weekend," she coyly remarked. "But, maybe I can work you into my schedule."

We talked for hours that night. I told her that I had completely severed all ties with Margaret. I explained that she simply wasn't the kind of girl that I was really looking for. "What are you looking for?" Faye asked as she played with her hair.

"I am looking for a girl who is primarily interested in God and wanting to serve Him and others more than she's interested in me. Now, I'd also like a girl who is intelligent and has some musical talent. And, of course, it wouldn't hurt if she happened to be beautiful and a great lover on top of it."

"Wow!" Faye laughed, cocking her head to one side, "Do you think you'll ever find anyone that will meet all your criteria?"

"Yes, I think I can. In fact, I'm positive I can." I looked over and grinned at her, "You know, I think she's sitting in the front seat of my car right now!"

She smiled as she scooted a bit closer to me. Then, she leaned over and kissed me and said, "I think you're right."

We began to spend more and more time together. Every little break we could work out we spent it together. Then, one evening while we were sitting in the driveway talking, I took her by the hand and said, "Faye will you marry me?"

"Are, are you crazy?!" she stammered. "We've only been dating for six *whole* weeks!"

What happened next I really can't explain. I really don't know what came over me or why Faye didn't just dump me right then and there? However, this is what actually came out of my mouth next:

"Well, I really don't want to waste my time here. If you don't want to marry me I don't want to ever see you again."

"Are you serious?!" she said as she looked over at me in shocked disbelief.

"Yes! I'm very serious!"

Then, there was a long period of silence in the car. We just sat there, but still holding hands. Finally, the silence broke. "I am scared to death but ok," She said with a very serious tone in her voice, tightly gripping my hand.

I was absolutely ecstatic! I couldn't believe it! Forget about my fumbly completely unromantic proposal. She said YES!

We held the wedding at the Hill Church there in Loma Linda, California. The place was packed with friends and classmates. Three busloads of my boys from the ranch took up the last few rows of the church. And, at the end of the service, they all lined up to kiss the bride.

Faye whispered to me, "They all want to kiss me on my lips! What should I do? They're your boys. Cool them off a bit!"

"Ok guys," I announced. "Just kiss her on the check. Those lips are sacred and are reserved for just me - you understand?"

They all laughed and one of them said, "Awh man!"

Faye and I spent our first night after the wedding at the Mission Inn in Riverside. It's an old Spanish-style high-end hotel and everything was set up for us when we got there. It was all very romantic. That entire day I was so overwhelmed with it all, with the joy and love that I felt for my new beautiful bride, that it seemed like a dream. I had to pinch myself a few times to prove this was all real. She was really my wife. She had really chosen me – me!

After the wedding, Faye changed into a beautiful blue suit and put on a big corsage and I put on a new gray suit. When we walked into the lobby we might as well have had a huge sign around our necks that read, "Newlyweds!" We walked right into the middle of a French chef convention and were greeted with cat calls and whistles and "Oh la la!" and "Bellisimo!"

I turned bright red and tried to make it through the lobby as quickly as possible. The next morning we drove along the California coast to Carmel.

Faye and I spent the rest of our honeymoon on Fifer Beach on the coast. My uncle and aunt had a cabin there and had stocked it full of food for us. We spent an entire glorious week there seeing the sights and going on different outings. One evening we visited Monterrey Bay and went to a restaurant that offered great pizza and showed old time movies. The restaurant was located in a warehouse toward the end of the wharf. There was no door to get in. Instead, at the side of the building was a telephone booth. The whole restaurant was based on the speakeasies of the roaring twenties. So, we stepped into the telephone booth and lifted the receiver. A little slat opened and two eyes looked at us through the slat.

"May I help you?" said the woman's voice on the other side.

"We hear you serve good pizza here," I said with a smile.

"Ya both at least twenty-one?"

"Yes," we both said as we looked at each other.

It just so happened that this place also served beer and liquor, so you had to be at least twenty-one to eat there. The problem was that Faye had left her driver's license back at the cabin.

"Let me see some I.D." the woman demanded.

"Look," I tried to reason with the lady, "We're on our honeymoon and have traveled all the way from Carmel to eat here tonight. My wife left her I.D. in our cabin. But, we really are both older than twenty-one! Can't you help us out here?"

After looking Faye over she replied, "Sorry honey, you'll have to come back when you grow up. By the way, that boyfriend of yours is older than dirt. You should pick someone who's more your own age."

I was angry. Just because I was losing some of my hair didn't mean that I was "older than dirt!"

But, Faye just laughed and said, "Don't worry about it Tui. I'm the one who looks like I'm fourteen!"

In any case, there was no changing the lady's mind. So, we didn't get to eat at the speakeasy that night and had to find somewhere else to eat.

Throughout our marriage Faye continued to look very young. Even after I had been a pastor for a number of years, Faye's youthful looks put me in numerous interesting situations. For example, after I finished my sermon one Sabbath, a visitor came up to us while we were greeting everyone at the door of the church. He spoke to Faye and said, "Your father preached an excellent sermon today. I really enjoyed it!"

It sometimes bothered me to know that many people looked at me as an old man carrying my daughter around. However, as I grew older it didn't bother me so much. In fact, I began to enjoy it. It was rather entertaining actually. I remember one time when my boy Sean was in his late teens it happened again. A group of young people went with us to New Orleans to visit the aquarium there. A lady approached us trying to interest us in time shares. Looking at Sean she said, "Bring your girlfriend (referring to Faye) and your dad (referring to me) and listen to our ten-minute presentation and you'll get free tickets to the aquarium."

Of course, Faye loved every minute of it . . .

Andrews University

At the end of the summer when Faye and I were first married, we packed our things in a small trailer and headed for Andrews University in Berrien Springs, Michigan. It was a beautiful campus and we found a small apartment not too far away. I was full of enthusiasm, more than ready to start my graduate studies in theology. Usually, a conference will sponsor a seminary student through school and then pick him up afterward to pastor one of the churches in that conference. However, I had started school without first obtaining a sponsorship. So, we had to meet all of our expenses on our own hoping that some conference would eventually sponsor us.

In the meantime, it did help that Faye was able to get a nursing job at St. Joseph's Hospital, which was only about half an hour away from our apartment. I also found some work cleaning the library in the evenings. Unfortunately, our work schedules conflicted with each other. Just when Faye was coming in early in the morning after working all night at the hospital, I was heading out to school. And, the work at St. Joseph's was brutal. Faye was the only RN on her floor and was expected to do everything. It was scary having so much responsibility. Many nights she would come home sobbing and tell me through all the tears, "I hate my job! I don't want to work there anymore!" But, at the time, we really had no choice. So, she kept her job and I kept mine and we tried to make the best of it. Then, winter came.

That first winter brought one of the biggest snowfalls in years. We still had the hopped-up Mustang that I'd bought when I was still single. It had wide slick racing tires on it. Of course, when the road was wet or icy, these tires offered absolutely no grip to the road. We couldn't afford new tires, so Faye had to drive that car on icy roads back and forth to work. Several times she lost control of the car and ended up in the ditch and had to be towed out. She was a member of a carpool, but when it was her turn to drive the other girls, they decided that it was safer to skip Faye's turn and simply use their own cars instead.

One afternoon I was actually driving the Mustang, with Faye in the seat next to me, when we found ourselves on an extremely icy road near our apartment. As we approached our street we noticed a lady in a car up ahead trying to turn onto our road right in front of us. As soon as she turned onto our road, her tires started spinning and her car stopped making progress. She was blocking most of the roadway and there was no way to drive around her. So, I put on the brakes, but our Mustang, with our slick tires, didn't even slow down. We slid along the road as Faye yelled at the top of her lungs, "Stop! Stop!"

When the lady realized that our car was sliding down the road towards her, she shoved her accelerator to the floor. Her tires spun furiously on the ice, but her car didn't budge an inch. As we approached, her eyes grew larger and Faye's mouth grew wider and my praying got louder.

"Lord, get us out of this!"

Our Mustang finally came to a halt just inches from her front door.

Soon after that, the Mustang died on us. The engine just quit running. So, I made arrangements with a friend to borrow his garage. I backed our Mustang in, and, in the freezing cold, overhauled the engine. We wore sweaters and heavy coats, but we were still freezing in that brutal Michigan winter. Faye washed parts in gasoline using some rubber gloves. Unfortunately, her gloves ended up melting in the oily gasoline. Her beautifully manicured hands were terribly stained and there was no way to remove the stains until they eventually wore away. However, in a few days, we did manage to get the engine overhauled and back together. Despite having a few nuts and bolts left over, it cranked right up and purred like a kitten.

We finally made it through our first winter and were coming up on spring break. We decided to head back to California to visit family. One of my seminary friends asked if he could ride along with us. He was scheduled to get married in Loma Linda. He would finish his last exam on Sunday morning and his wedding ceremony would begin Monday night at eight o'clock. In order to make it on time, we'd have to drive in shifts all night long.

So, Faye pulled our mustang up to the back of the seminary building and, as soon as we finished our exams, we climbed into the car and headed for California for spring break. The only time we stopped was for gas. While we were filling the tank, Faye would be getting our food together. We'd make a quick bathroom run and then we'd be off again, eating our meals in the car as we drove. Of course, when we got to some of the western states we really made good time because, on some of the isolated roads, we could hit speeds of 90 or even 100 miles an hour without fear of being pulled over for speeding.

Finally, we made it. We pulled into Loma Linda at 7:40 p.m. - twenty minutes before the wedding began. The bride was very anxious as we pulled in, but was ecstatic when she saw her man.

As far as the Mustang was concerned, she performed wonderfully for most of the trip. However, just before we arrived in Loma Linda, I noticed a small knocking sound in the engine. After a couple more days of driving around without getting it looked at, our Mustang suffered a catastrophic breakdown. So, we decided to sell the car to a mechanic and purchase a more sedate four-door sedan. We invested in studded tires in preparation for the next brutal Michigan winter.

After spring break, we spent our summer months back in Michigan picking cherries and other fruit and making canned preserves during our free time on Sundays (in order to cut down on the food bill for the following year). We also made friends with Archie and his wife Sarah. Archie was a used car salesman, and they didn't have much money either. They lived in a back alley behind a filling station in one of the worst sections of town. They were like us, just trying to make it from week to week. We hit it off and used to enjoy going over to their house to pop some popcorn, grill some cheese sandwiches and talk or watch TV, but mostly we just sat around talking and telling stories. However, one night when we were visiting with Archie and Sarah, things got a bit exciting. We were all in the kitchen helping get supper ready and talking up a storm when we heard gun shots.

"Ah, it's just the TV!" Faye laughed.

"Oh, no it's not!" Archie shot back over his shoulder as he grabbed his handgun and ran for the door and then out into the alleyway.

I followed right behind. The girls were screaming at us, telling us to get back into the house, but we didn't listen. Both ends of the alley were blocked by flashing police cars. Several police officers were crouched behind one of the patrol cars firing their guns into the service station where several men were firing back. They had broken into the filling station and were in the process of stealing tires and batteries when the police showed up. The police were swearing and yelling at us telling us to get back into the house. Then, I heard one of the men in the station yell, "I give up! I give up! You shot me!" It did not take long for the police to subdue the rest of the thieves.

It all seemed very exciting at the time. I didn't think much of it until a few weeks later when I went to visit Archie and Sarah on a Saturday night by myself. Faye had to work so she couldn't come with me. We sat and talked and watched TV until late in the evening. Finally, I told Archie that I just had to get back home if I wanted to be functional the next day. I took off in the car and, after a few blocks, pulled up to a red light and stopped. While I was waiting for the light to change, a car pulled up beside me on my driver's side. I looked over my shoulder at the young men in the car. There must have been six or seven of them in there, all laughing and drunk and probably high on something. They were playing their stereo so loud that my own car was vibrating. The streets were deserted except for our two cars. As I looked at them, the guy in the front passenger seat raised his hand and pointed a .44 magnum right at my face – just a couple feet or so away. He was smiling at me with his gold-capped teeth gleaming.

Someone yelled, "Shoot the honkie! Shoot him!"

"Lord," I prayed to myself, "Save me!" The light changed and I slowly pulled out and they pulled out right along beside me and followed me down the street, keeping right abreast of my car. Out of the corner of my eye, I saw that the .44 was still pointed right at my head.

I continued to plead with the Lord, "I know this is stupid to be out in this neighborhood at this time of night, but please, please help me!"

Then, out of nowhere, a patrol car appeared behind us. The gun quickly disappeared and, at the next corner, I stopped and they turned left and the patrol car followed them.

To this day I'm not sure if that was an angel in that patrol car or not, but I have my suspicions. In any case, I breathed a prayer of thanks to God for saving my life and headed for home. The next day I told Faye what had happened and then explained to Archie and Sarah that we simply couldn't take the risk anymore. We couldn't visit them in that dangerous neighborhood. They understood and, not too long after, they moved to a better location.

So ended our exciting summer and fall months before our next winter in Michigan. During our second winter, we seminary students were assigned to preach in different churches twice a month to get some experience speaking in front of an audience. I was initially assigned to Battle Creek church and was really looking forward to the opportunity. However, I ended up being reassigned to preach at the local psychiatric hospital, where I learned, like Moses tending sheep in the wilderness, a great deal of patience. I remember one occasion when someone raised his hand right in the middle of my sermon. "Finally," I said to myself, "here is someone that is paying attention to what I am saying." I stopped my sermon to answer his question. "Yes," I motioned to him, "What's your question?"

"I, I, I, I am getting a n-n-n-new checkerboard for my b-b-b birthday," he blurted out.

I quickly learned how to adjust my sermons and my pastoral work to the needs of my congregation – to "keep it simple" and use a lot of stories and illustrations, which seems to work for a very wide variety of audiences – as it did with Jesus when he spoke about the Kingdom of Heaven and the good news of the Gospel.

During my last year at the seminary, I became close friends with Jim. He had grown up in the Baptist faith tradition and had thought about becoming a Baptist minister before he was drafted into the army. So, I asked him why he'd decided to become a Seventh-day Adventist?

He smiled as he explained, "It's most interesting how God works with people. You see, I had a group of buddies in the army who always invited me to go with them when they went bar hopping. I wasn't into drinking myself, but I went along because I knew that none of them would be in any condition to drive back to the base when they finished their drinking for the night. So, in this way, I managed to keep most of my group out of trouble and get them safely back to camp. Now, there was one guy in particular who was very much anti-religion and God when sober. However, ironically, when he got drunk he became a saint and would want to give me Bible studies. You see, this soldier used to be a Seventh-day Adventist and he really knew his stuff."

At this point, Jim sat back in his chair and laughed as he remembered the irony of it all.

"I could hardly wait for the next night of drinking to learn more. We went through most of the fundamental beliefs of the Seventh-day Adventist church and by the time we were transferred I had decided to join the Seventh-day Adventist church. It's amazing, isn't it, that God can use a drunken atheist to give someone Bible studies and explain the true meaning of Scripture?"

How to Be an Evangelist

Part of our training at the Seminary involved assisting an evangelist with a series of meetings. So, after looking at all the available options, I decided to attend the Azure Hills evangelistic series in California. Pastor Harmon Brownlow would be leading out in this particular series. He was especially noted for his flamboyant style of preaching. I had been told that my own personality was more like a banker than a preacher. So, I thought that Harmon's more open style might show me how to loosen up a little.

Harmon had a unique way of evangelizing. For example, he

viewed the game of golf as an evangelistic tool. He was better than the average golfer. In fact, he played like a pro but didn't let on that he played so well. He would pretend to be a beginner or just average. You could say that Harmon was a bit of hustler. You see, when he would go to a town to hold meetings, he would first go and check out the nearest golf course and invite the course professional to give him a couple of lessons. Harmon would complain about having difficulty controlling his drives. Then, after assessing his teacher's abilities, Harmon would challenge him to a game. After the first couple holes, Harmon would suggest a wager.

"If I beat you you'll have to attend my meetings that open next week."

As he told of his methods, he would add with a grin, "You'd be surprised how many golfers I have converted with my game!"

Unfortunately, golf was not one of my talents. Although Harmon tried to teach me the finer points of the game, I never mastered the game sufficiently to challenge anyone. My redemption, in his eyes, was my musical ability. I could play the saxophone better than average and did a decent job of leading the song service. However, with my banker personality, I lacked the appropriate level of enthusiasm.

Harmon, on the other hand, was very enthusiastic and exuberant in everything that he did. When it was his turn to lead the song service, he would run up to the stage playing his trumpet with one hand and leading the congregation in song with the other as he moved rapidly back and forth across the stage.

He would always say, "If you want to be impressive, be enthusiastic!"

Of course, his enthusiasm was a bit risky. On several occasions he narrowly missed falling off the platform while leading the song service and while preaching. I asked the lady that accompanied him on the piano, "Has he ever actually fallen off the stage?"

"Oh," she replied with a giggle, "He has fallen off several times during the time I've known him. One time he was leading a song service just before a baptism and forgot that there was an open baptistery on stage. He was so engaged in the song service that he stepped back and fell right into the baptistery! - trumpet and all! He made a big splash. It was spectacular! As he climbed out of the tank, water pouring out of his trumpet, he announced, 'Be back shortly folks!' Needless to say, it brought the song service to a sudden conclusion. But, no one ever forgot it."

Harmon's counseling sessions for young pastors were very entertaining as well. One day, the subject of baptism came up.

"Boys," he said, "you need to know the fundamentals of conducting a successful baptism. The size of the person you plan to baptize is very important. Large people need very special handling."

To stress this point he told us about an experience he'd had baptizing a rather large woman. With a big smile he said, "When I saw the deacons struggling to get her into the tank and the water beginning to pour over the edge of the baptistery I should have known then and there that I faced a colossal problem. You see, when I finally finished with my comments and tried to put her under, she kind of fell over on me. Her weight was far more than I could handle by myself. She slipped from my arms and slowly began to sink beneath the waves and then settle at the bottom of the tank. The euphoria of the baptismal service changed dramatically. I did the only thing I could do. I dove down to the bottom of the tank and tried to raise her. It was a real struggle, but, with the help of several stout deacons, who'd also plunged into the tank to assist me, we managed to bring her back to the surface. As she sloshed up the stairs with heavy breathing she muttered, 'I do believe that he almost killed me!"

He laughed as he thought back before getting serious again.

"Now I want to emphasize the point of this little experience. If the person you're about to baptize is large, then show him or her how to squat. And, just in case, get some stout deacons to help you dunk them under the water. Otherwise, you could find yourself in very deep water really quick – if you know what I mean."

Harmon was always getting himself into interesting situations like this. At the end of our final night of meetings, he rushed to the foyer to greet the guests. As he was shaking hands he happened to look down and notice, to his horror, that his pants were unzipped and that part of his shirt was sticking out of the opening.

"Well," he thought to himself, "I can solve this problem very quickly and discretely. "I'll just step behind this rather large lady and tuck my shirt in and zip up in a jiffy before anyone notices anything."

Quickly all was in order but, as he started to head back to the door to shake hands, he was shocked to discover that the lady's dress was caught in his zipper! After frantically trying to extract the dress for a few moments without causing a scene, he gave up and gently tapped her on the shoulder and whispered in her ear.

"Excuse me ma'am. I believe you and I have a bit of a problem. Somehow I managed to get your dress caught in my zipper. Can we slip down the hall quietly and see if we can solve our problem? And please, you lead the way."

I learned a lot from Harmon, but mostly I learned that the Gospel story has a very broad appeal regardless of the style in which it is told. The story of Jesus and all that He has done and is planning to do for us is powerful to convert those honestly searching for truth, regardless of if the story is told by an energetic outgoing evangelist like Harmon or by someone with a more quiet and deliberate banker-type style like me.

Our First Church

When we first arrived at the seminary, we had no one to sponsor us or support us financially. We were there all on our own and had real struggles financially during those first few years of our marriage. It was hard, but we did manage somehow and, now that we look back on it, remember those days with a certain fond nostalgia.

However, during our last year at the seminary, the President of the Illinois Conference, Elder Nelson, came by for a visit and invited me into the dean's office for a chat. I was not expecting him and I didn't really know why he wanted to talk to me, so the interview was very informal. Elder Nelson was a kindly old gentleman and he talked to me much like a grandfather would talk to his own grandson. He asked me about my background and my interest in ministry and then asked me about my wife. He wanted to know how she was adjusting to the life of a preacher's wife and if she was an asset to my ministry?

"Oh yes", I explained, "Faye loves the Lord and is very helpful to me. She's extremely talented you know. She's little, but very energetic. She can sing and play the piano beautifully and she works in the local hospital as a nurse. Oh, and she's very cute!"

At this, his eyes lit up and with a smile he said, "I'd really like to meet Faye. Is she available this afternoon?"

I shook my head. "I am sorry. She is at work and won't be home until after midnight."

"Well then, do you have a picture of her?"

"I sure do!" I said as I quickly reaching for my wallet without a second thought. However, I only had one picture of Faye in my wallet – one of her in a little lace bikini sitting on a rock in the ocean. I'd taken it on our honeymoon at the beach in Carmel. As soon as I pulled it out and looked at it, I thought, "I can't show *him* this picture!"

But, before I could react, Elder Nelson reached over and snatched the picture right out of my hand - and then carefully studied it for a moment. Once again, a smile broke out on his face. "She's a real stepper isn't she?"

My face flushed a bit as I reached for the picture and said, "Yes sir, she sure is!" As I replaced my picture and slid my wallet back into my pocket, I thought to myself, "Oh man, I've really blown it this time!"

However, a few weeks later I received a letter from the Illinois Conference Office informing us that they would sponsor us during our final year at the seminary.

I told Faye, "I think it was the picture of you in the bikini that got us this job!" She laughed and then looked at me with a serious expression.

"You know, I've been praying for God to lead us to the right place, and I think this is an answer to prayer."

"I've been praying too and I think you're right."

We both felt that God was calling us, and bowed our heads and thanked God for his leading in our lives as we looked forward to our work in the Illinois Conference.

At the end of that year, we were informed that I would be an assistant pastor in the Donner's Grove district of Chicago working under the direction of Elder Matthews. My primary responsibility would be the Villa Park Church – a church that came with a number of perks. For example, this church was composed mostly of Italians, many of whom were among the best cooks in the entire city of Chicago. All I have to say is that visiting those church members was always a blessing. Everywhere I went the most magnificent Italian food one can imagine would be pretty much forced upon me – and I never got tired of it.

The Sabbath that they introduced us to the church was an exciting day. We were a bit nervous, of course, and hoped that our first church would be happy with us. To our immediate relief, the elders of the church were most kind and the people were very friendly. But, we didn't see anyone that we knew. It was going to be an entirely new experience for both of us.

Finally, it was our first Sabbath at our first church. Just before I got up to preach my first sermon, there was an offering appeal and the deacons were asked to come forward. As the deacons walked to the front I almost fell out of my chair. One of the deacons was Eddie, my old childhood friend!

I couldn't believe it! I never expected to see Eddie, of all people, in church! Eddie, you understand, was as wild a kid as you would want to meet. The last time I'd seen Eddie he was so drunk that he could hardly walk. He and a couple of my friends were trying to get on a motorcycle to ride home. All three of them were trying to ride on one motorcycle. I had stopped at a phone booth to make a call before heading back to college when I saw them staggering out of the bar, and hadn't seen Eddie since.

After the service, I went to the foyer to greet the members of my new church. Eddie came up to me and gave me a big hug.

"I never expected *you* to be my preacher! You sure were wild back in the day!"

I laughed and, with a big smile and a slap on his back, I said, "I too am so surprised to see you in church! much less my head deacon!"

Of course, Eddie turned out to be the best friend and supporter that I have ever had in my ministry.

After we were there a while, I went to visit Eddie at his home and asked, "What caused you to change the direction of your life?"

"God did!" he answered without hesitation. Then, he looked at me, shook his head and said, "Tui, you know that I was living a wild life. I'd work hard during the week and on the weekends I'd go out and party and get drunk. I thought this was really living, but I was falling apart. One day I got so sick that I thought I was going to die. I ended up in the intensive care unit of the local hospital. Laying there in that hospital bed I began to worry about what would happen to me if I died. Right then and there I made an agreement with God. If you let me live I'll quit this foolishness and serve you. And, He let me live. So, I am keeping my part of the bargain."

I'd like to say that everything in the Villa Park church always ran smoothly. But every once in a while, there were a few bumps in the road. As a young pastor, I had a lot to learn. Our congregation was renting the church building from the Church of the Brethren, and I thought that we were on good terms. But one day, the pastor of the Brethren Church decided that he wanted to terminate our lease agreement. However, rather than talking to us about it or telling us of his wishes, he began to crank up his lawn mower on Sabbath mornings at 11:00 a.m. To make things worse, he took the muffler off his mower. His mower was so loud that it drowned out our service. After the third week of lawn mowing I went and talked to him.

"I'm getting the idea that you may not want us around?"

"Yep, that's right!" he shot back, without further discussion.

So, we had to quickly scramble to find another church to rent.

Ingathering was also a unique adventure. It was a slash and burn situation in Chicago. There were too many churches competing for dollars in overlapping territories. Some neighborhoods were solicited five or six times for funds to help the "poor and needy." Since I was the young pastor and naive I was told by the ministerial director, "You get your ingathering goal for your church or there's no vacation for you!"

"Yes sir! I'll do my very best!" I answered as any good Gospel soldier.

Of course, no one told me that the church had never ever met their ingathering goal since anyone could remember – at least not during the past ten years or so that ingathering collections had been recorded. Not knowing this, I stood up before the church that next Sabbath and enthusiastically announced our ingathering goal and encouraged everyone to come out on Saturday night and join in the ingathering effort – to go out in groups to solicit donations door-to-door in our district.

"If we all work together, we can meet our goal in a matter of days!"

Now mind you, this was in the dead of winter in Chicago and it was extremely cold. It seemed to snow every night. We should have known better, but when our first Saturday night of ingathering arrived we really did expect a large crowd to show up at our house, ready to get the job done. Faye and I had prepared soup and crackers for a multitude, but only two little old ladies showed up. So, Faye and I had leftover soup, every night, for the next two weeks.

Rather than the quickie campaign that I had imagined, our solicitation efforts drug out for weeks on end. Most nights it was just Faye, who was heavy with child, and I who were trudging down the snow-covered streets knocking on doors asking for donations for the poor and needy. Of course, the ministerial secretary would call me every single morning to check up on how we were progressing with our campaign. But, we did finally reach our goal! - a first for that church. And, I promised Faye that she would never have to go ingathering ever again. And, she never has!

There were also those events where pastors are called upon to be involved in situations for which we received no or little training in the seminary. For instance, late one evening I received a call from a very distraught woman. She wasn't one of my church members, and she wasn't even an Adventist, but her husband, we'll call him George, came from a very prominent Adventist family and was a leader in my little church. She explained to me that they'd been in a verbal fight that ended up getting physical. He'd punched her in the face repeatedly, giving her a split lip and a black eye before walking out the door.

"I am going out to get drunk!" he yelled back over his shoulder as he slammed the door.

"How long has this been going on?" I asked.

"For many years," she cried on the other end of the phone.

I don't think anyone in the church knew about George's secret life. While in church, he portrayed an image of perfect sweetness and great piety. In any case, when I got off the phone with his distraught wife, I told Faye that I was going to go bar hopping until I found him.

It didn't take me long. I found George in the second bar I entered. He was sitting at the far end of the counter, smoking a cigarette and slowly nursing a drink. He was so absorbed in his thoughts that he didn't look up when I sat down in the seat beside him. A pretty little bartender came over and asked me, "What will you have sweetie?"

"I'll take a Seven-Up."

"You want Vodka with that?"

"No, I'll just take the Seven-Up straight."

Suddenly, George recognized my voice. He looked over at me with his bleary bloodshot eyes and slurred, "What you doing here preacher?"

"I've come to take you home."

The following weeks I met with George and his wife regularly. I explained to George that he really should resign from his leadership positions within the church until he could get his life in order. While he did voluntarily resign his positions within the church, he never did get is life back in order. A few years later, his wife finally had enough and left him.

I found out very quickly that you can't always tell a book by its cover. Things can look so good on the surface and yet be boiling over underneath the façade. I also found out that it's impossible to get a person to change against his or her own will. Not even God will overrule the will of a person who is bent on self-destruction.

Elder Nelson came to visit me one day and I began to unload on him some of the frustrations I faced in my church. He listened to me for a long time before pointing out something fundamental to the life and success of a pastor.

"There are no perfect churches, only a perfect Savior."

Then he looked at me for a moment, put his hand on my shoulder and furrowed his eyebrows as he continued, "Churches have personalities like people you know. You really don't know your congregation until you've been there for a while and visited, cried and prayed with your people. Only then do the real issues begin to surface. These are the times when the Lord can really use you to minister to your congregation."

His words proved true. I had so many good and bad experiences during those few years at my first church. We grew to love those people like family, and they loved us too. And, this early training prepared me for my next calling – the mission field of Bolivia in South America. Little did I realize what was in store for us, but I had learned to trust God more and more, which prepared me for the things to come.

What an Ugly Baby!

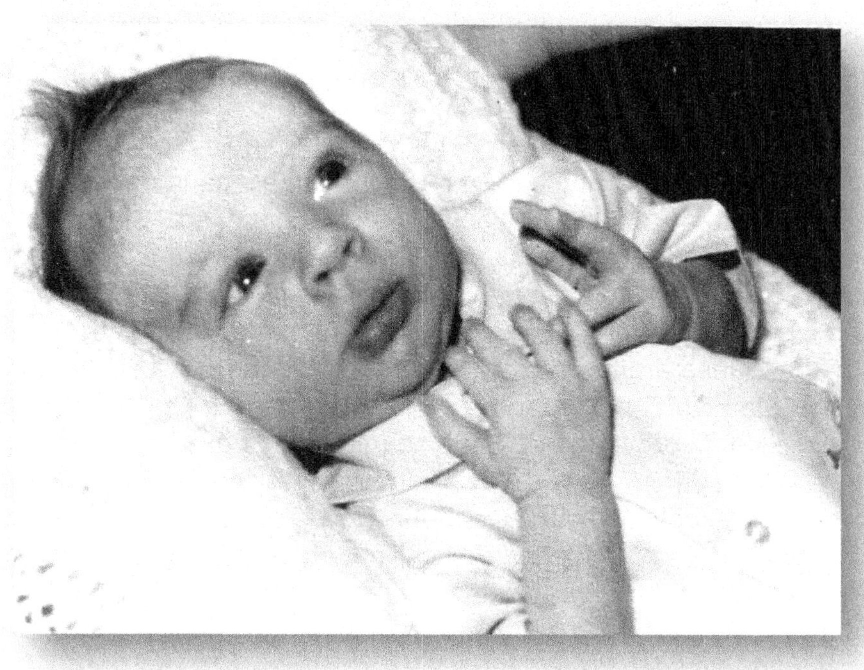

When Faye and I first got married we talked things over and planned to have three children. However, even after several years of married life and a lot of praying and trying every trick in the book, we still had no children. I thought I knew what it took to have children, but I was beginning to doubt myself. Finally, Faye suggested that we visit a fertility clinic and get things checked out.

I was embarrassed. Just to enter the door of such a place was difficult enough for me and my male ego. Then to make things worse, the doctor jumped right in with, "Let's see if the good Reverend is fertile." There was no "Good morning pastor Pitman. How are we today?" Oh no, none of that chit chat stuff.

As you can tell, I had a hard time liking the fertility doctor. Faye, on the other hand, thought he was great. She liked his "no-nonsense style." I would have preferred at least a little bit of nonsense – to break the ice you know.

After we'd gone through a series of tests, the doctor ushered us into his office and confided that our chances of having children were about as likely as the Pope converting to Adventism. He took his glasses off and began to slowly clean them with his tie.

"Faye has several complications that we will discuss later and conception is absolutely out of the question."

We both felt horrible and went home absolutely dejected. However, after a few days of talking and thinking about our options, we decided that perhaps it wasn't the end of the world – perhaps adoption was the answer?

So, a few weeks after our visit to the clinic we set up an appointment to meet with a beautiful young girl who'd come home from boarding school when she found out that she was pregnant. She'd become involved with one of the teachers there. At seventeen she felt that she was simply too young for the responsibility of a child and asked if we could find someone who would be willing to adopt her baby. I asked if her family had agreed to her decision and she said that they were aware and had agreed. So, Faye and I secretly made arrangements to adopt her baby once it was born. Then, we anxiously awaited the day when our new baby would arrive.

As the time grew near an amazing thing happened. Just a few days before the baby was due, Faye got sick going to work. She pulled the car off the side of the road and threw up. That night she told me, "I've been feeling sick the last couple of mornings going to work. Do you think it might be the flu?"

The next morning she went to the doctor to get something for her infection. After his exam, he explained, "You don't have the flu. You're pregnant!"

We were overjoyed with the news. I could hardly wait to tell the fertility doctor that I was awaiting the Pope's conversion. When I told him his response was, "You've experienced a true miracle. It is almost like the Immaculate Conception. Only when the Russians give up Communism will it ever happen again."

We gave up our plan to adopt. It would have been too much for Faye to be pregnant and have to take care of a newborn at the same time. So, another Adventist couple adopted the baby that we were planning to adopt. However, I did go to see the baby once it was born. As I looked into the nursery I had just a tinge of regret.

Her baby was an absolutely beautiful little boy, perfect in every way. But, we were going to have our very own baby.

By the end of June 1970, Faye was almost a month overdue and still hadn't gone into labor. I had been away at campmeeting for a couple weeks expecting any minute to get the news to rush home for the birth of our firstborn. But, nothing happened. Finally, campmeeting was over and I took the train home to see Faye. She drove our car down to the train station to pick me up. I saw her struggle out of the car. Then, she waddled over to where I stood and gave me a kiss. As we walked over to the car, Faye insisted on driving me home. Reluctantly, I agreed, but when I looked over to where she sat all squashed under the steering wheel I said, "Don't you think I'd better drive?"

"Heavens no!"

"Why can't I drive?"

"Because," she laughed, "You don't drive well under pressure."

"What pressure?!" I was beginning to get a little upset.

"I am in labor," she said calmly.

"What?! Why aren't you in the hospital?! Stop this car immediately! You're in absolutely no condition to drive! I have to get you to the hospital right away!"

So, Faye stopped the car and looked at me with an exasperated expression.

"See what I mean?! You are getting all excited and we are going to have a wreck getting to the hospital. Do you really want that to happen?"

I fumbled with the door handle. I tripped over the edge of the door and fell to the pavement. Faye struggled out of her side of the car with a bit less difficulty and waddled over to the passenger side of the car where I lay sprawled out on the ground. In her oversized yellow dress, she looked like the canary that had just swallowed the cat. Faye was a little thing and there just wasn't a lot of room for a normal size baby. Everything seemed to be sticking straight out in front of her. Just then a contraction hit and Faye winced as she stuck out her hand to hang onto the car. I looked over at her with wild eyes and exclaimed, "You're not going to have the baby right now?! Are you?!"

She laughed again, "Tui, we've got plenty of time. Let's go home and get my things." Then, with a smile she added, "Please drive slowly and carefully dear."

The doctor thought he could deliver the baby normally but Faye was in labor for most of the day and into the night. Our baby was just too big and wouldn't come out. So, eventually, the doctor gave up waiting and decided to operate and perform a C-section to deliver our baby.

I was a nervous wreck. The doctor had been gone in the operating room for over an hour. With me in the waiting room was another man waiting for his wife to deliver. He was an old pro at this since he'd already had four other children. He'd been sleeping on several chairs that he'd grouped together. At one point he yawned and said to me, "Why don't you try to get some sleep? There's not much you can do about any of this anyway."

But, I just couldn't relax. I was pacing back and forth in that room, wearing out the carpet.

Finally, after what seemed like an eternity, the doctor came in to see me.

"You have a new baby boy," he said in a rather somber tone.

I didn't like his tone of voice and asked, "What happened? Is everything Ok?"

"Well, we did have a few complications. We had put Faye under heavy sedation during the surgery and it affected the baby as well. We had some difficulty getting him to breath."

The doctor stopped to scratch his nose and continued.

"Now, just to warn you, he also looks a little beat up because Faye was in labor for so long and he was face presentation. His face was continually being shoved against her pelvic bones for days, so his face is all swollen and bruised. We also have some concerns because he seems to be a little spastic with poor muscle tone and control. He may have some brain damage and some mental retardation. Only time will tell."

This wasn't at all what I was expecting. I was in a state of shocked disbelief. My mind was all foggy. In a daze I asked in a trembling voice, "Is Faye alright?"

"Oh yes! She's one tough little cookie! It will be about an hour before you can see her. In the meantime, why don't you go down to the nursery and take a look at your new boy?"

"Thanks doc," I said as I hung my head and headed for the nursery. The father of five snored on.

When I arrived at the nursery there was a sizable crowd of people all gathered by the nursery windows looking at the new arrivals. I walked over to them and looked through the window at the triple row of cribs. My eyes quickly scanned down the name tags attached to the heads of the cribs, looking for "PITMAN". Two matronly ladies to my right were cooing over an assortment of babies. Suddenly, one woman put her hands to her mouth and gasped, "Oh my! What an ugly baby!"

I looked in the direction she was pointing and there, stenciled in neat black letters, was the name "PITMAN". There lay my new baby boy, my son Sean. And indeed, he was ugly! His face was red, swollen, and distorted and part of his head was caved in from the struggle he had been through to be born. But, despite his ugliness, I felt something strange happening to me at that moment. My heart felt like it was going to explode with pride. I was his father and he was my little boy. I didn't care what those silly ladies thought. I had tremendous plans for him. I suddenly began to realize the tremendous worth that God places on each one of us. It doesn't matter what we look like or who we are. God loves us just the same. He sees us not for what we are, but for what we might become.

Looking over to those ladies I pointed to the crib and said, "That's my boy."

They looked at me and slowly shook their heads with pity.

We took Sean home and, as the swelling and redness went away, he perked up and did quite well. It was hard to believe that he had serious brain damage or that he would be mentally retarded. In fact, he eventually grew up to be a very handsome man, a strong Christian who loves God, and probably one of the smartest mentally retarded doctors I know (He's now a pathologist practicing in Northern California).

Uncle Beaman's Demise

During the early 1970s, while my mom was still teaching pediatrics at Loma Linda University, she heard that her favorite brother, Beaman, was hospitalized with serious complications. He was the last survivor of her twenty-three brothers and sisters, but now his prognosis was very grim. She quickly canceled all of her appointments and went to be by his side during his last days.

He told his family that he didn't want anyone taking any kind of extraordinary measures to prolong his life. The last few months had been very difficult for him, and he felt that it was his time to go.

Beaman had been a minister and a church administrator for many years and he felt that he deserved a little nap until the resurrection morning. He was a very strong-willed man who wanted things to be done in an orderly manner - according to a well-considered pre-ordained plan.

When he heard that his chances of making it through the next night were slim to nil, he called each member of his family to his bedside and whispered his blessings and good-byes. He told them all that he planned to meet them on the resurrection morning and to keep the faith till then.

Having done his duty, he lay back on his pillow, closed his eyes, and waited for the sleep of death. He expected that in the unconscious state of death time would pass very quickly. In just a moment, an instant of time, he would be awakened out of his sleep by the melodious voice of his guardian angel and the command of Jesus. Then, with all of the redeemed, he would be escorted past the clouds for the majestic trip to heavenly courts beyond.

It was quite a shock, then, when the next thing he heard was a gruff gravelly voice saying, "Wow, you made it through the night!"

Beaman, still with his eyes closed, never imagined that his angel would sound like this! He cautiously cracked open one eye and looked for the face of his angel. The being that stood over him was short, overweight, rather homely, and smelled of stale tobacco. She was hardly angelic to be sure . . .

Uncle Beaman was very upset once he fully realized that she wasn't his guardian angel after all. She was the head nurse!

"Why did I not die on schedule?!" he demanded to know in no uncertain terms. He was most perturbed to still be alive in the hospital. "Saying goodbye is just so emotional. I just can't do it all over again! I just can't!" He lamented.

However, he didn't have to wait too long to meet his real angel. Later that same day Uncle Beaman slipped into unconsciousness and quietly passed away. I wonder though if, on Resurrection Morning, uncle Beaman will again carefully crack open one eye to see if his homely head nurse might not still be looking after him.

I for one though am really looking forward to being there to meet my own guardian angel and see all my family and long-lost friends – and to walk up to Uncle Beaman and laugh with him a bit about his unscheduled demise.

Bolivia

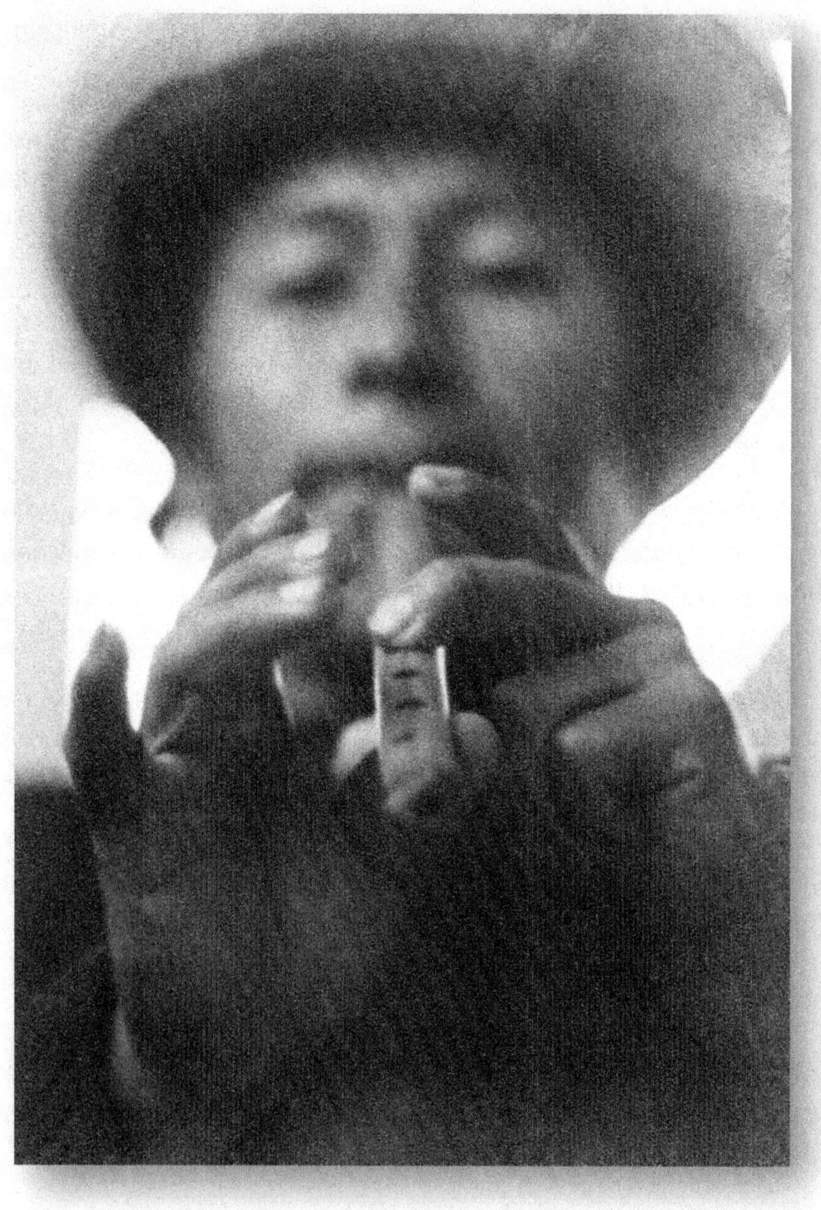

Bolivia

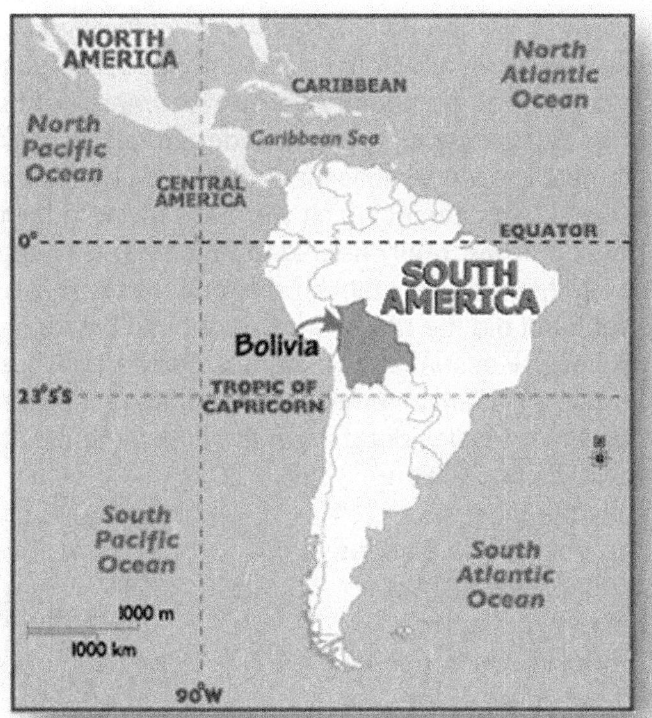

My parents had a huge impact on my life. Even though my father died when I was just a little boy, his influence was always with me. I grew up hearing many stories about how he and my mother helped so many people and had such great plans for their work in the mission field – plans that were cut short when my father was killed in a plane accident. I knew of the danger, as well as the excitement, adventure, and sense of fulfillment and a worthwhile life that the mission field offered. So, from childhood, I had always determined in my mind to go back to South America and take up where my parents left off.

The Republic of Bolivia has been called "The American Tibet" because of its high elevations. It is one of the world's poorest nations and has also been called, "El Pueblo Enfermo" (a nation of sick people). Bolivia is a fairly large country, roughly the size of Texas and California combined. Despite its poverty, there are few places in the world as beautify and as rich in natural resources as Bolivia. However, political turmoil over many decades absolutely ruined the economy of the country. About 150 years before I arrived, Simon Bolivar gave Bolivia its independence. However, during that time there were more than 70 full-scale revolutions and around fifty presidents, ten of which were assassinated while in office. No one in power really helped to fundamentally change the country or help the poor or establish a strong middle class. All the politicians said and did the right things to get into power, but once in power, they were all essentially the same. Bolivian politics was and is an inglorious saga of rival families in a struggle for power and profit without any real consideration of the impoverished state of the vast majority of its population.

Probably the most incompetent president in a series of incompetent presidents was Mariano Melgarejo, the 18th President of Bolivia. Although he was elected president of the country, he could neither read nor write. His aged mother once commented, "If I'd known that he'd one day become president I'd have sent him to school!" Regardless of his own inability to read or write, he liked to impress people with his huge library. He'd walk over and pull out one of the many volumes and pretend to be reading through the pages. The problem was he could never tell if the book he was holding was right side up or not.

Primarily, Melgarejo spent his presidency devoted to wine, women and general debauchery while the business of the country was completely ignored. Well, for the most part anyway. He did occasionally dabble in political affairs, unfortunately.

For example, shortly after taking over the country, President Melgarejo held a lavish banquet and invited the recently appointed British ambassador to attend. During the party, the President introduced his mistress to all of his guests and proposed a toast in her honor. So, all of the guests toasted the President's mistress with their glasses of wine held high – all except for the British ambassador that is. He refused to salute a woman who was well-known in the area as a gifted prostitute. Of course, Melgarejo took this as an insult and had the ambassador arrested. The next morning they stripped the ambassador of all his clothing and mounted him on a donkey. Then, they paraded him through town, stark naked, while thousands watched.

When Queen Victoria heard about the shameful treatment of her ambassador she ordered her navy to steam over to Bolivia and sink all Bolivian ships. When the British admirals cautiously pointed out to Her Majesty that Bolivia was a landlocked country, that it had no navy, she was furious and ordered that all the maps in the entire British Empire exclude Bolivia as a listed country. As far as she was concerned, Bolivia ceased to exist.

Unfortunately, this had little effect on Melgarejo. He kept right on as usual. For example, not too long after the incident with the British ambassador, the president of Paraguay sent Melgarejo a pair of dueling pistols as a gift. Of course, Melgarejo was very happy with such a fine gift and was anxious to try them out as soon as possible. So, he stepped out on the balcony of the presidential palace and shot dead the first person who crossed the plaza.

On another occasion, the Brazilian president gifted him with a beautiful white stallion. He was so pleased by this gift in particular that he pulled a map of Bolivia out of his desk, traced the horse's hoof print on the map, and seceded all the territory within this tracing to Brazil. His tyranny was understandably terminated, on January 15, 1871, by an uprising under the command of General Agustin Morales and was assassinated later that same year.

Still, nothing changed over the next 70 years or so. By the time my parents arrived on the scene only three to four hundred people in a country of three million could read or write. A few hundred families were very rich and the rest of the population lived in misery.

The death rate was appalling. Infant mortality was the highest in the world. Tuberculosis, malaria and parasites all took their toll. The illiterate masses took their sick to curanderos (witches). Dried llama fetuses were said to cure most any illness. There were few schools and the only rural schools were run by Seventh-day Adventists – not the local government. Roads were few and, where present, were in very poor condition. Electrical power was rare, even in the major cities, and was very inconsistent. The country at large had little capital and few professionally trained men and essentially no professional women (my mother was a real oddity as a professional doctor there in Bolivia in those days). Things were so bad and so desperate that even the casual visitor could not escape the overwhelming feeling of hopelessness that was ever present.

Yet, in the mid-1940s, my parents decided to go and work as medical missionaries in Bolivia – despite the general hatred and distrust for Americans. Just before my parents arrived, yet another revolution brought Major Villarroel to power. Among his supporters were the Nazi sympathizers and supporters of the Peron regime in Argentina. However, shortly thereafter Villarroel was lynched by a mob and his body was hung on a lamp post in front of the national palace. And, of course, his death was blamed on the Americans.

Still, my parents felt called to go to Bolivia. It wasn't that they weren't given other enticing options. My father had been offered the position of Chief of Surgery at a large hospital in Fresno, California. It was tempting, but both he and my mom felt a very strong desire to go somewhere in the world where there was a truly desperate need for medical as well as missionary services. Clearly, Bolivia met these criteria.

Then, some 25 years later I was back to take up this same challenge. Little had changed during that time. The people still desperately needed medical and missionary help just as much as ever before, if not more so. My mom came to visit us in Chulumani. She walked around the town and through the hospital and remarked, "Things haven't changed a bit since your father and I were here."

Disease and poverty continued as before and there was still a great deal of political instability. However, the church was growing and making inroads to solving at least a few of Bolivia's problems.

Pepe

Chulumani was a poor town in a poor country, but had a fantastic view of the surrounding garden paradise. We lived in a white two-story stucco house (pictured above on the left). People did what they could to get by, but were in desperate need of basic things – especially basic medical and dental care.

Our neighbor, a bachelor who went by the name of Pepe, ran a barber shop on the first floor of his two-story home. He had a way of carrying on an animated conversation with his patrons while looking out the door at whatever was happening outside of his barber shop, instead of paying attention to the head of hair that he was actually cutting. His prices were very reasonable though. At ten cents a cut, it seemed like a great deal. However, you got what you paid for. His haircuts were awful! Those walking out of his barber shop looked like they got hit by a driverless lawnmower. But, it didn't really matter. In a town like Chulumani nobody cared what anyone else looked like anyway. No one was out to win any beauty contests there. And, Pepe was a great guy. People liked to get their hair cut just for the conversation. His place was kind of the town meeting hall where the men of the town would get together and hang out. And, Pepe loved his job because he loved people. He was always very friendly and had a great big smile - but the worst set of teeth I'd ever seen.

So, one day while sitting in his barber chair I mentioned that if he fixed his teeth he might get himself a good wife. He grunted and nodded in agreement, but explained, "I thought about that, but I can't afford the prices the dentists charge in La Paz. And, there are no dentists here."

"Well," I grimaced as his rusty scissors pulled at my hair, "I've had a little experience with dentistry myself. If you come over to my house tomorrow I'll see what I can do to relieve you of those bad teeth of yours. Then, you can go to La Paz and buy yourself a pair of good dentures."

He paused the torture therapy for a moment and looked at me with one eyebrow raised, "How much will it cost me?"

"Oh, not much," I smiled. "It will cost you the price of a pain killer and a haircut."

He laid his clippers down and walked around to the front the chair and looked me square in the eye and said, "Pastor, I'll be at your house early tomorrow morning."

Sure enough, bright and early the next morning, Pepe knocked on our door.

"Good morning Pepe!" I said cheerfully. You're my very first patient in this town."

He grinned and shook my hand as he stepped inside. I took him out to the patio in the back of our house and sat him down on one of Faye's dining room chairs. My dental tools were all laid out on a small table ready to go. "Are you ready Pepe? This shouldn't take long," I said as I slipped a cartridge of Xylocaine into a syringe and walked over to where Pepe was seated. Then, he opened his mouth and I almost passed out. The stench was unbelievable! And, his teeth were much worse off than I'd originally thought. Some of them were rotten all the way down below the gum line. I began to think that the extensive training I'd received from my dental school buddies at Loma Linda was inadequate for this job.

You see, just before Faye and I left for Bolivia, we'd stopped by Loma Linda, California to visit family and several close friends who were in dental and medical school there. I knew that there was a great need for medical and dental care in South America, but the only real experience I'd had was pulling a few teeth as an assistant to a medical missionary when I was in my teens. Now, I was about to be *the* missionary and I knew that I would be a lot more helpful in the mission field if I had a bit more knowledge and experience in dentistry.

So, I called up Charles, one of my childhood friends. He came over to see me the evening before we were scheduled to leave for Bolivia. I told him about my plans and asked him if he could help me learn a few things about dentistry. After all, how hard could it be? The more we talked the more excited he became. Grabbing my arm he exclaimed, "Man if you are going to pull teeth, you'll need some equipment and some reference books. Lucky for you, you've come to the right place. I'll be back in just a bit."

In an hour or so, Charles was back. His arms were loaded with boxes and books. He proceeded to show me the techniques of pulling teeth and giving injections. He drew charts and demonstrated each instrument for me. His instructions lasted until early the next morning. Finally, rubbing his eyes and yawning, he said, "I've taught you all I know. All you lack now is the diploma!" Then, he added, "By the way, all these instruments are all yours. A bunch of my classmates and I wanted to give them to you to support your efforts in Bolivia."

It was all very exhilarating at the time. I remember how confident I'd been when Charles was done teaching me all there was to know about dentistry during that one evening. I was all ready and rearing to go out and be a dentist.

Of course, now that I had a real patient on my hands, things were just a bit different. As I looked into Pepe's mouth my heart rate increased and I began to sweat - profusely. Was it the hot sun? Maybe it was the smell coming out of Pepe's mouth? The palms of my hands were so wet with sweat that it was hard to get a good grip on my instruments. But, there was no turning back now. So, I injected the Xylocaine to deaden the nerves around what remained of his teeth. Then, I stepped back to get some air and looked up at the sky. As I wiped the sweat off my face with my sleeve I noticed something. The balconies that surrounded our patio were packed full. Dozens of our neighbors were watching me from every angle - like vultures anxious for a feast.

Now, the pressure was really getting to me. What if I failed? I'd never live it down. These thoughts were racing through my head in circles, but I shook them off and looked back down at Pepe. I checked to see if the Xylocaine had done its job. It had. Pepe couldn't feel a thing. It was now or never. So, I began by pulling the nubbins that were once his front teeth. They came out fairly easily. I began to feel a bit better. Perhaps this wasn't going to be so bad after all?! I began to relax and even joked with Pepe a little.

"When you get your new teeth you'll have so many women chasing you! In fact, you'll have to take your teeth out on occasion just to scare some of them away."

Pepe chuckled and nodded his head. I continued pulling out one tooth after another without a hitch – until I came to a big molar on the left side of his jaw. That tooth just wouldn't budge no matter what I did. I pulled and twisted on that tooth for what seemed like an eternity, but nothing happened. Then, all of a sudden, part of it cracked off in my forceps!

Pepe began to moan. I gave him another injection. Sweat started dripping down my face again. I began to chisel and dig for the rest of that tooth. Finally, I got a good hold of it with my forceps and pulled on it as hard as I could. Suddenly, the entire tooth broke free with such force that I almost went through the top of his mouth with my forceps. This particular tooth had huge twisted roots attached to it. I held it up for all to see as I smiled with triumph. The crowd on the balcony broke out in applause, yells and whistles. However, Pepe started spitting lots of blood all over our patio and Faye was trying desperately to wash it down the drain before the flies moved in.

I didn't know why Pepe would be bleeding so profusely? So, I looked around in his mouth to see if I could spot the problem. Right away I discovered that the large roots of the tooth I'd just pulled had split his gums wide open when they came through. Blood was just pouring out of the lacerated hole. I tried to suture it back together, but my hands were too big and clumsy. The blood and the smell finally got to me. I started to get nauseated and a bit lightheaded.

"Faye," I groaned, "Take over and see what you can do."

So, Faye stepped right in and took over. Being a professional nurse and all, she had absolutely no problem with blood or unpleasant odors. She washed out Pepe's mouth and, in just a few minutes, she had his lacerations sutured up as neat as and pretty a finely stitched quilt. She gave Pepe a shot of antibiotics and put some extra tablets in an envelope for him to take over the next several days. Then, she patted him on the back, told him he did just fine, and helped him find his way to his own house to recover for the rest of the day. As she turned to come back home she called back to him, "Now Pepe, remember to take one tablet three times a day."

I climbed the stairs to our bedroom, lay down on the bed, and prayed, "Please Lord, let this dear soul live!"

The next day, much like the king of Persia going to check on Daniel in the lion's den, I went to see my first patient. I knocked on his door and waited. About a minute later, he opened the door. Poor Pepe. He looked like he'd been beaten up by an entire gang in a street brawl. The left side of his face was very swollen and severely bruised. It looked like a party balloon with a mixture of black, green and various shades of blue colors. I just stood there in a daze for a minute. Finally, I regained my composure and tried to at least act as professional as I could.

"Well Pepe, let's see how things are coming along. You'll have some soreness for a few days. That's normal of course. Not to worry. Now sit down for me will you and let me take a look."

Pepe dutifully sat down in his own barber's chair and opened his mouth for me. As I looked around, I was pleasantly surprised. Things looked pretty good and the horrible smell was gone.

Within a few days, the swelling did actually go down dramatically and Pepe looked almost normal. After that, it didn't take long for Pepe to inform the entire town that I was the best dentist in Bolivia. Soon, I was flooded with patients. They made a long line outside of our house. After a while, we simply couldn't deal with the demand. So, we decided to limit dental day to Tuesday. After that, every week starting early each Tuesday, a line of people would arrive at our house. Once we had breakfast Faye would go out and usher them to the back patio have them sit down on a row of chair's we'd set up for the occasion. Then, I would inject them with Xylocaine, down the line, and we would pull teeth all day long. Pretty soon, I became pretty proficient at it. And many people in the town of Chulumani were so very grateful to us. It made a hugely positive impression.

As Jesus showed in His own ministry, the Gospel generally begins with an effort to address the physical needs and sufferings of people. Once these basic needs are met, people are far more open to hearing and appreciating the rest of the Gospel's message.

Mico

It was early in the morning. The sun was just coming up over the hills when they came and surrounded my back door. One of them called out to us, "Please, can you help my brother?"

We had just moved out of our apartment in downtown Chulumani into our mission house at the edge of town. I'm still not quite sure how these men found out where we lived or that we could help them. Perhaps news of our dental work with Pepe had spread farther than I thought? I was thinking at first that perhaps they needed some emergency dental care, but when I opened the door, I saw a group of farmers carrying a man who was covered from head to toe with blood. His face looked like it had been through a meat grinder. I stood there in shock for a moment before regaining my senses. As I invited them in, they quickly told me the story.

Earlier that night the injured man and his brother, now sober, had been drinking with friends when they got into a heated argument. The brothers began swearing at each other and trading insults and then they started shoving each other. Suddenly, one brother took the bottle he was drinking and slammed it against the edge of the table, breaking it in half. He then proceeded to repeatedly jab and grind the jagged end of the bottle into his brother's face and the neck, deeply cutting and lacerating much of his brother's face before their friends could break up the fight.

I had them lay the injured man on a cot in the dining room where Faye and I could examine him. The man's brother was deeply concerned and very sorry for what he had done. It was truly a gruesome sight. Large slabs of flesh lay opened on the sides of his brother's face. Part of his lip hung limply to one side. Luckily though, the bottle had missed all the major arteries. It took most of the morning for Faye and me to clean up his wounds and stitch everything back together. Then, we gave him a shot of penicillin and prayed that the infection that was sure to come would not be fatal. Somehow though, he never did get an infection. To this day I believe that God did something extra in addition to the penicillin. After about ten days, he came back to our house to get his stitches removed. I was very surprised at how well his wounds had healed in such a short time. He wasn't going to win any beauty contests to be sure. However, given what he'd been through, he looked remarkably good.

Soon after this, the young man's uncle asked us how much he owed for our medical services. I laughed and shook his hand as I told him that our services were free. But he wouldn't hear of it. He insisted that he give us something.

"I have no money," he said, "but I've brought something as a gift. Please Sir. I have it outside."

So, I walked outside with him to have a look. He took down a little cloth bundle that had been hanging in a tree and laid it down on the ground for my inspection. I walked over and knelt down next to it and started to examine it. In the middle of a pile of dirty rags was a little ball of fur. It looked like a kitten.

"What is it?" I asked.

"Un tigre," he responded. Then he told me that he had been hunting the week before and killed the mother and then found her two kittens. He thought maybe I'd want one. I looked at the little blue eyes and the pink nose and it was love at first sight. The little "tigre" was so cute I could not resist taking him.

I took the little tigre to Faye and said, "Look at this cute little guy."

"What kind of cat is it?" Faye asked.

"From the spots and the coloring, I think he's an Ocelot. Isn't he beautiful?"

I was hoping that Faye would like him too, but I could tell that Faye wasn't too excited about raising this orphan.

"Don't these cats get big?" she asked with a frown and a concerned look in her eyes.

"Yup," I smiled and nudged her playfully, "I hear they get as big as twenty-five to thirty-five pounds!"

She relented and we kept him. We called him Mico. I don't know exactly why we came up with that name but it sounded exotic. It didn't take Mico long to grow into a thirty-two-pound cat. He was sleek, powerful and beautiful. He had an angelic face and a champagne coat dappled with dark spots. When he was little he had the free run of the house, but it didn't take long for Faye to kick him out. Unfortunately, he'd picked up a very annoying habit of marking everything in the house as his territory - with his urine. The smell was absolutely awful. So, Faye declared the house off limits to him. Of course, I felt sorry for poor Mico, but he didn't seem to mind so much. He soon took up company with our German Shepherd, Chino. They quickly became fast friends and both slept together in Chino's dog house at night. And, during the day they were often seen together. The only time they had any real disagreement was at feeding time.

One day, we heard Chino yelping. We ran outside just in time to see Mico clamp his teeth firmly into Chino's neck. We had to forcefully rescue the dog. Chino had tried eating the Mico's food. After that, however, he never tried it again. In fact, when it came to eating, Chino always let Mico eat first from then on.

Sometimes it was hard to remember, but Mico was a wild cat and had wild instincts. And, as he grew older, he became more and more aggressive. At night he would leave our yard and go hunting. In the morning we would find whatever unfortunate animal he had killed on our front porch as a kind of gift to us. While this was thoughtful and all, it was also a problem because not all of Mico's kills were from the forest. He had trouble telling the difference between domestic animals and wild ones when it came to hunting.

One day, when Faye was in the kitchen fixing dinner, Sean, who was just three years old at the time, came running into the house yelling, "Mommy, mommy, mommy! Come quick! Come quick! The kitty is hurting the chickens!" We ran to the backyard. It looked like Custer's Last Stand. There were dead chickens everywhere. Mico has systematically butchered every one of our chickens and all of the little chicks except for the one that Sean had in his hands. Faye was especially furious because our chickens were just about the age when they were supposed to start laying eggs.

The last straw came late one afternoon when we heard a blood-curdling scream from the house above us. Mrs. Menes, the school teacher's mother, was yelling, "That cat is killing my chickens!"

Faye was in the middle of doing supper dishes. She dropped everything and flew out the back door and ran up the hill to help save our neighbor's chickens. Mrs. Menes had arrived at the chicken coup and had caught Mico methodically killing her chickens just like he'd killed ours. She had made a grab for Mico who had a chicken tightly clamped between his teeth. A terrible fight was in progress for control of a battered chicken when Faye arrived. There were feathers everywhere. Mrs. Menes was yelling, the cat was growling and the chickens were cackling. Faye grabbed Mico by the back of his neck. When the cat realized who had him, he instantly calmed down and dropped the chicken. Faye carried Mico out the door and gave him a toss. Then she went back to check on Mrs. Menes who stood in the corner of the hen house holding her arm and crying. Long jagged cuts ran down her arm where Mico's claws had deeply raked her.

"Come on down to our house, Señora, and we'll have you fixed up in no time." They walked into the house and Faye sat her down at the kitchen table. As I came into the kitchen, Faye's eyes shot daggers at me.

She smiled sweetly at Mrs. Menes as she said, "Tui will fix you up."

I looked at the poor lady's arms, but I didn't understand exactly what had happened to her at first. Then, in English Faye whispered in my ear, "It's your stupid cat again!"

Then I looked again at Mrs. Menes' wounds in horror.

"Mico did that?!"

I asked Faye to help me clean the wounds while I went to find something to use to suture up Mrs. Menes. It took dozens of stitches to put everything back together. I'm just grateful that there were no lawyers around.

That night I lay in bed doing some serious thinking. Mico's wild nature was getting him into too much trouble. Faye kept reminding me that one day he might go after our boys. He was already big enough to knock them down when he played with them. A couple of times he made them cry when he nipped them a little too hard. I had to admit that there were a lot of things about Mico that concerned me. But he was such a charmer. He would jump up into my lap and growl and nibble around gently on my hands and arms. It was his way of showing affection. He loved to follow us on walks. He was just an overgrown lovable tomcat as far as I was concerned. Not really all that bad. But Faye did not see it that way.

"You've got to get rid of that cat before he kills someone!"

So, one morning I got up early and went looking for Mico. I found him in the dog house munching on a chicken. I took the chicken away from him and he followed me to the jeep protesting. I put the chicken's carcass in a backpack and tossed it onto the passenger's seat of the jeep. Mico jumped in after it. He had ridden many times with me, so he didn't suspect that today was different. I slid into the seat next to him and cranked the engine to life. I studied him sitting in the seat beside me. The early morning sun bathed him in a warm glow. I couldn't help feeling that here sitting next to me was one of God's most beautiful creatures. We drove for miles down a winding dirt road. Mico made his way over to my side of the jeep and laid his head in my lap. I gently rubbed his head and ears. His growls informed me that he was enjoying my attention and the ride. I felt so depressed! I was struggling with the idea of setting him free in the jungle to be on his own. I know it's strange, but I was even thinking about how Abraham must have felt taking Isaac up the mountain to sacrifice him.

I finally found a wide spot along the road and pulled over and stopped. A little creek lapped over the road. I had not seen houses or people for quite a while. This would probably be a good place to set him free. I picked up the backpack and jump down from the jeep. Mico followed. We walked along the stream through thick woods until we came to a clearing. It was a beautiful area covered with deep grass and wildflowers. Butterflies floated from one flower to another drinking in the nectar. I sat down by the stream. The warm sun, the gurgling water, the lush carpet of flowers made it seem like the Garden of Eden. But I felt awful because I was going to abandon a friend and destroy a trusting relationship. As I was sitting there thinking about how I was going to implement my plan of escape, Mico stopped chasing butterflies and came over and sat beside me. I spoke to him softly.

"Well, Mico, I can't associate with you anymore. Why can't you stop killing chickens? I love you so much, but I've got to leave you here you know. You're just too dangerous to have around people."

I quickly stopped rubbing his head and jumped to my feet. It was now or never. I pulled my backpack off, reached in and pulled the dead chicken out. I threw it into the field as far as I could throw it. Mico chased after it. He immediately attacked the chicken and began devouring big chunks of meat. I eased myself slowly into the woods and ran as fast as I could for the jeep. As I drove away I was loaded with guilt.

For the next few days, I constantly thought of my cat. Finally, Faye said, "Why don't you go and see if you can find him and see how he's doing?" As soon as church was over I drove back to the wide spot in the road where I had left Mico. As I opened the door to get out of the jeep, I noticed a man and a woman walking out of the woods. They were crossing the road right in front of me. What the man was dragging by the tail behind him caused my heart to freeze. It was a dead animal. I slammed the door shut and ran to catch up with them. "What do you have?" I inquired.

The Campesino (country farmer) lifted the cat higher for my inspection. He broke into a large grin.

"Un tigre montes!"

I was in shock. It was Mico. "How did you kill him?" I asked, trying to stay calm.

The man could still see my concern, so he relaxed his hold on Mico's tail and let him slip to the ground as he explained, "This cat was attacking my wife while she was washing clothes in a stream not far from here. He was running toward her growling. I heard her screaming. She was running and the cat was chasing her. I killed him with my machete. I thought the cat was loco."

Unfortunately, Mico's love for human companionship got him into trouble. How was this couple to know that Mico's growls were a friendly greeting and that he was chasing after human companionship?

I still think of Mico every now and then and look forward to a time when friends will no longer have to be separated and when the stunning beauty of nature will no longer be marred by natural tendencies that are not so beautiful. Someday, it will all be beautiful.

The Funeral

I have been to a great many funerals in my life. Usually, they are very solemn and sedate affairs. However, there is one funeral that I will never forget. I was in Bolivia at the time.

Generally speaking, Bolivian funerals are not at all like the funerals I've experienced in the United States. They are much more interesting. There are all kinds of interesting funeral traditions in Bolivia. For example, there is often a separate funeral ceremony for the clothes of the deceased where the clothes are washed and then burned so that the dead in the spirit world will have something to wear in the afterlife.

Many Bolivians also believe that death is another dimension of life and that time spent in contact with the spirits is necessary to have peace and happiness in this life. Some of these spirits are thought to live in the skulls of the deceased. They have the power to visit people in their dreams, to heal, and to provide protection for the family. So, the skulls of family members and loved ones who have died are kept in the family home on special altars. Once a year the family crowns the skulls with fresh flowers and dresses it up. They make offerings of coca leaves, cigarettes, alcohol and various other items to thank the spirit for its protection during the year. Also, these skulls are sometimes taken to the cemetery for a special mass and blessing.

There is one day, in particular, the Day of the Dead, "El Dia de los Muertos," that is very important in Bolivian culture. On this day, a day observed toward the end of October, special food is prepared to take to the cemetery to feed the spirits. Bakeries make "dead man's bread" to sell. They are round loaves decorated with sugar skulls. The departed souls are remembered with fondness and good humor. Long before daybreak people stream into the cemetery laden with candles, flowers, incense and food that is decorated to resemble symbols of death. Many take blankets and picnic lunches and sit by the graveside and eat. Children eat little chocolate hearses, candy skulls and bread coffins. They believe the candles, loud music and strong incense will guide the spirits through the confusion of the tunnels of the underworld to the grave site and seat of honor on the blanket to share in the picnic and other festivities. During this time, many households also set up offering altars (ofrendas) to the departed. Some even claim that they have visits on this day, every year, from their departed friends and relatives who thank them for the food and drink that has been left on their graves and poured on the ground (It is a common practice to pour a little portion of one's drink on the ground to share with the dead and their gods).

Most of these celebrations of the dead originated as a form of ancestor worship when the Incas worshiped the Sun God on the day of the corn harvest. The Catholic Church incorporated these days of celebration into "All Saints Day" - mixing Catholic and pagan beliefs.

In any case, after having attended several of these funerals I had come to expect such things. However, I was completely unprepared for what I experienced when, one day, I was invited to officiate at yet another Bolivian funeral.

We had just moved from Cochabamba and been in Chulumani for about six months when a young man knocked on my door and asked if I would be willing to conduct a funeral for his uncle Chupa. Chupa had been a dedicated member of the local Adventist church and I had more than a passing connection with him because he had known my father. So, I was more than anxious to accept this invitation as a way to give honor to a man who had been a friend to the father I had lost as a little boy.

Also, I had been working on a funeral sermon for several weeks so that I could preach in Spanish at the funerals I was asked to attend. As I prepared this sermon, I was trying to think of a way to reach people with the Biblical view of death as a state of unconscious sleep until the Resurrection Day. I knew it would be very difficult to break through so many superstitions and long-held and long-treasured traditions. Yet, I felt that this funeral presented a perfect opportunity to share what really happens after death.

The day of the funeral came. I was to meet with the family at the home of the deceased that evening. According to Bolivian tradition, it would be a big event that began with an all-night viewing of the body where relatives and friends sit around the edges of the room with the casket in the middle. There was an unlimited supply of alcohol, coca and cigarettes. Bolivian funerals are very expensive and many times families feel required to take out loans in order to provide all the necessary amenities.

After the all-night vigil, tradition dictates that the casket be carried in a grand procession through the town to the cemetery at the edge of town. Then, there would be a graveside service. So, early that morning more and more relatives and friends started to show up. Soon, there was a very large crowd of people. Even though it was still relatively early in the morning, many in the crowd had already drunk too much chicha (local corn whiskey), and they were quite drunk. Some were so drunk they forgot all about the reason for the festivities. Still, with all the diplomatic skill I could muster and the help of several mourners I managed to keep things moving along. It did take quite some time, however, to extract the wooden coffin from a house packed with people drunk and bleary-eyed from a night of drinking and chewing coca. I could tell that tempers were on edge and heated arguments were breaking out here and there amongst the crowd of well-wishers. So, I eagerly encouraged some of the stockier and more sober members of the group to pick up the coffin and move it out of the middle of the crowd. I relaxed a little as we began to make our way through the winding streets of the town. However, as the procession continued more and more people began to join us. The chicha flowed freely and more and more people became more and more unruly and agitated.

Suddenly, fighting broke out near the casket and the pallbearers dropped their precious cargo and joined in the mêlée. I vainly tried to calm the crowd, but to no avail. Fists, legs, arms and people were flying everywhere. Then, after what seemed like an eternity, the fighting abruptly ceased for some strange reason. Some sort of an agreement had been reached by some mysterious means. I had no idea what had caused the fight or why it had suddenly stopped. I looked around and saw a man emerging from the crowd, walking toward me and the casket with a hammer held firmly in his right hand. He walked right passed me without seeming to notice me at all. Then, without any hesitation, he began pounding off the lid off of the casket. Another person appeared with a pair of pliers and, with the help of others, reached into the coffin and pried open the dead man's mouth. Now this was something new to me. I drew closer to get a better look. The man with the pliers began to extract the teeth, the gold teeth, from the dead man's mouth.

I suddenly realized what all the fighting was about. I'd heard the saying, "You can't take it with you," but this was taking things to the extreme!

"Poor man!" I thought to myself. "Good thing you don't know what's going on."

I'm sure that some of the family members were afraid that he would come back and haunt them - and that is why they hesitated to join in the extraction efforts and fought to prevent it in the first place. However, in a few minutes the task of recovering the gold teeth was done and the deceased could finally rest in peace. The pallbearers picked up the lid, slammed it back into place, and nailed it shut. The coffin was again lifted onto the pallbearers' shoulders and the procession continued its journey.

Finally, we arrived at the gates to the cemetery. To my dismay, we found that the gates were locked! But, this did not slow the procession one little bit. They simply proceeded to climb over the wall, coffin and all - and I joined them.

Once over the wall and in the cemetery, I expected to find a nice gravesite with a hole for the grave already dug. Of course, I shouldn't have been that surprised by this point that the gravesite had not yet been prepared, aside from a couple of shovels stuck in the ground.

Again, the coffin was rudely dropped several feet to the ground as a discussion commenced as to who was to dig the hole. Soon, several teenagers were recruited to take turns to do the digging. Meanwhile, the rest of the mourners sat down to observe and give pointers. I sat down with them to await my opportunity to begin my carefully crafted sermon. Others from the town continued to arrive. Many sat on the adobe wall surrounding the cemetery and chatted like a flock of crows. Jugs of chicha were continually passing around and around the group. They would each fill little glasses with chicha, splash a little offering on the ground and then down the rest of the contents like drinking from a shot glass.

The ground was hard clay, so the digging was slow going. And, after about half an hour or so, the teenagers gave up - having only managed to excavate a shallow rather narrow grave.

At this point, all eyes turned toward me. Finally, it was my turn. So, I rose to my feet and took my place beside the coffin - and began my sermon. By this time, of course, most of the congregation was stone drunk. Some had already passed out and were lying on the ground almost as dead the deceased. I was also not at the top of my game. The morning events had unnerved me, to say the least. All the zeal I had built up for my sermon, for preaching the gospel message of what happens to the dead, had left me. When I talked about the dead not knowing anything, that in death the dead are asleep and are unaware of the passage of time, it seemed to me like my definition of death described the majority of my congregation that day. Most were asleep and were completely unaware of anything that was going on around them. I began to think in terms of a temperance sermon rather than a funeral sermon. So, I cut my sermon short since the only people who were sober enough to hear me and could sing any of the hymns for the service were a dozen or so members from the local Seventh-day Adventist church.

Finally, as I made my closing remarks and as the last notes of the closing hymn echoed across the valley, the coffin was raised and dropped into the open grave. It fell about a foot into the hole and abruptly stopped. I knew the grave was shallow, but not that shallow. Part of the casket was still above ground after all. Turns out that the casket was wedged against a narrow spot and simply wouldn't budge. Again there were heated discussions among the group as to what should be done. They pushed and shoved on the casket for most of an hour, but to no avail. Finally, two half drunk and rather hefty cholitas (Indian ladies) clambered aboard and jumped up and down arm-in-arm in order to steady each other. Suddenly, in an instant, the earth released its grip and the coffin, along with the ladies, dropped to the bottom with a heavy thud. From the depths of the grave came grunts, squeals, and not a little swearing. Of course, the cholitas were too hefty to get out of the hole by themselves, and had to be rescued by the pallbearers - as the teenagers were pitching the dirt into the hole. Finally, a simple rough-hewn wooden cross, with the word "Chupa" written on it, was set to mark the grave.

It was late in the afternoon and starting to get dark as I left for home. "What a funeral!" I said to myself, shaking my head and laughing out loud.

As I think back on this funeral and smile as I review my memories of that day, it seems to me that the Lord must also have been smiling and shaking his head as he sent His guardian angels to stand by and mark the gravesite of His good friend, and the good friend of my father, Sr. Chupa.

An Illegitimate Son

We had been in Cochabamba a few months when one morning Faye announced, "I don't feel so good! It feels just like the time I was pregnant with Sean."

"You can't be!" I stammered. "Remember what the doctor said when we had Sean. He swore that the Pope would become a Seventh-day Adventist if we ever had another one that communist Russia would cease to exist. And, the last time I checked, the Pope is still Catholic!"

Faye laughed, "You have tough little soldiers. If there is a way to get there, they will find it." Then, looking down she added, "With the complications I had with Sean's pregnancy, I am not too excited about having a baby in Bolivia!"

I had to agree with her. From the experiences I had had with Bolivian doctors, I knew that most of them were inadequately trained - to put it politely. I even knew one "doctor" who missed his entire fourth year of medical school because of a local revolution, but was graduated with full honors anyway. When I assisted him in surgery for something as relatively simple as a hernia repair, I had to tell him how to do it, since he had very little hands-on experience actually doing surgery. He would usually prepare for such operations by reading about the surgery in his medical book the night before. As for my own experience, I had worked as a scrub tech during four summers while going through college. So, as far as practical knowledge was concerned, I really did know more about surgery than he did – which was very fortunate for the patients.

Unfortunately, however, this same doctor used the same tongue depressor on dozens of his patients throughout the day, without bothering to wash it, and used the same speculum for several pelvic exams on his female patients – again without bothering to wash much less sterilize anything. To be honest, he didn't seem to know much about germ theory, and likely hadn't ever heard of germs or something as specific as "bacteria".

So, obviously, I was quite concerned for Faye and who might help her during her pregnancy and delivery. Finally, however, after checking out several doctors in Cochabamba, we settled on Dr. Fritz, a German doctor who had moved to Bolivia after WWII. He had specialized in obstetrics in Hamburg. I had a suspicion that he might have been a former Nazi. However, I never told Faye about my suspicion, since he seemed to be our best option at the time.

His clinic was called Copacabana. The name sounded more like a casino than a small hospital to me, but it was spotlessly clean and by far the best place in town. So, we signed on with Dr. Fritz.

It was a good thing too because, as the due date drew near, Faye began to have breathing problems. She was so small that there was no room for the baby to expand. He was pushing up against her lungs. Since it was close to her due date Dr. Fritz advised immediate delivery. However, my birthday was on May 24th, two days away. "Can't we have the baby on my birthday," I asked Faye hopefully?

"No way!" she said quite emphatically through gritted teeth. "I am having this baby right now! I don't want to wait another day!" The doctor adamantly agreed with Faye's decision. So we packed her things and headed for the clinic.

As soon as we got to the clinic, Dr. Fritz wheeled her into the operating room and laid her out on the operating table. As Faye lay there looking around, she saw about twenty medical students who had been invited to observe the delivery. Suddenly, without warning, the nurse standing beside her pulled off her sheet, exposing her in all her glory to the entire room full of students. Then, without comment, the nurse rolled her on her side for the spinal. Unfortunately, as in her previous C-section with Sean, the spinal anesthetic did not work. She could still feel everything. Yet, Dr. Fritz decided that things were so urgent that the operation must continue regardless of Faye's discomfort. So, he proceeded to cut her open without putting her under general anesthesia for fear that the anesthetic might kill the baby. Of course, during this process, Faye screamed bloody murder because of the extreme pain of every cut into her abdomen. Mercifully, as soon as he reached the baby, they finally put her under general anesthesia and she started to go to sleep. However, just before she went under she asked, "What is it?"

"It's a boy!" they all shouted in unison.

"Oh, no," Faye moaned as she went to sleep, "all this for another boy!"

She had so hoped for a little girl – as did I at the time.

Four hours later the nurse and doctor rolled Faye by me on a gurney. She was draped from head to toe, head and all, with a white sheet - and she wasn't moving at all under the sheet. I got a wrenching feeling in the pit of my stomach.

"Doctor," I stammered, "is… is she dead?"

The doctor looked at me and smiled. "Everything is fine. There were a few complications but things are fine now. She'll be awake soon. We are taking her to her room now. You can stay there with her. We will bring the baby to you shortly.

Faye slept through the night, but early the next morning she pushed herself out bed and began to walk around the room and noticed the crib that had been brought in during the night. She walked over and picked Shannon up and held him close.

"He is so long and skinny," she said as she smiled at him and gently stroked his little nose and cheeks. Then she laughed as she added, "With his dark skin and dark hair he looks just like all the other Bolivian babies."

I laughed, "He looks a lot like me!"

From the doctor we found out that Faye had gone through quite a bit of surgery while she was knocked out. He had had a rough time trying to stop the bleeding during the surgery. And, since her uterus was in such terrible shape and had almost ruptured, he felt that having more children would be a tremendous risk. So, he decided to "pocket" her ovaries on either side of her uterus to keep her from ever getting pregnant again. He had also repaired a hernia on Faye's abdomen – at no extra charge! Our total fee for delivery, repairs and hospital stay was just four hundred dollars.

Of course, even though Shannon was not a girl we were so delighted and happy to have him. He was ours and he was healthy and he was beautiful and he looked like me! What could be better? However, when we went down to the courthouse to register his birth we were in for a shock. Somehow, Faye and I had misplaced our marriage license! And, since we could not prove we were

married, the city registered him as “un hijo natural” (an illegitimate child). To rectify this problem, we went to the American embassy a few days later and they gave us a birth certificate that read, “Shannon Lawrence Theron Pitman, son of Tui and Faye Pitman.”

So, to the Bolivians, Shannon is illegitimate. But, to the Americans, he is legally ours – something we all still laugh and rib Shannon about to this day.

Shannon’s graduation from Loma Linda University School of Medicine

The Adoption

While I was acting medical director of the clinic in Huancana, Bolivia, I was visited by a lady from the area of Chulumani who had a chronic cough. After performing a physical exam and listening to her lungs I diagnosed her with advanced tuberculosis. I gave her the prescribed treatment for the disease - forty injections of streptomycin (in forty separate syringes to take once a day for forty days) and a year's supply of isoniazid (INH) tablets. Yet, I was still very worried for her.

She lived in desperate poverty with her common law husband. They had produced eight children together in just seven years. This constant cycle of pregnancy, childbirth, and nursing had taken a serious toll on her body. Advanced tuberculosis was the last thing this woman needed. I desperately wanted to see her cured of the disease. So, I carefully and repeatedly showed her husband how to give the injections explaining, "Give your wife one of these shots every day for forty days. Also, give your wife one tablet every day for a whole year."

As an afterthought, I turned to the woman and added, "In your condition make sure you do not get pregnant. Another pregnancy is likely to kill you now that you are sick with tuberculosis. So, I am going to give you some tablets to keep you from getting pregnant until you are cured of tuberculosis."

I placed all the medicines in a little box and handed them to her.

"That will be fourteen bolivianos," (about a dollar) I said.

"But señior," she entreated, "I cannot pay for the medicine. I have no money."

I gave her a big smile and patted her on the back, "Don't worry Señora. This is not a problem. Please take the medicine. I will cover the cost for you."

She smiled back weakly, "Gracias Señor. Que Dios le bendiga" (Thank you and God bless you).

I forgot all about this lady until six or seven months later when she showed up at the clinic again. I was shocked to discover that the tuberculosis was worse than before! And, it was quite obvious that she was very pregnant, yet again. She was in a horrible state, coughing and spitting up blood.

"Did you take all the medicine I gave you?" I asked.

She looked at the floor as she spoke, "No señior, I began feeling better after a few days and we sold the medicine."

"What about the birth control pills," I asked in amazement?

"Oh," she smiled up at me hopefully, "My husband took them every day just like you said!" Then, she added as she looked down at her pregnant abdomen, "But, as you can see, they didn't help."

I patted her on the shoulder and tried to explain that she was the one who should take the tablets, not her husband. Then, I gave her another injection of streptomycin as well as additional doses of the injectable form and additional INH tablets.

"I hope we can stop this disease, but your pregnancy has complicated matters significantly. Please come back and see me in a few days."

Unfortunately, she never came back.

Several weeks later a young girl, about six or seven years old, came to our house on the hill and knocked on our door.

"Please come! Please come!" she said as she urgently motioned to us with her hand to come with her. "I will show you where we live," she said. "My mother just had the baby, and then she died. We did not think you and the señora would be needed since my mother has had so many other babies without any problem. The baby is also sick, but still alive. Please come and help us."

We followed the little girl into town up several winding streets to her house. As we entered the dark room we could just make out the body of the dead woman lying on a crude bed and a baby boy nestled next to her. He was so tiny - obviously quite premature. His hands and feet were blue. The little thing was so weak that he could not suck or cry. His umbilical cord has been cut with a rusty tin can lid and tied with a dirty string. Flies were everywhere.

Faye carefully cleaned the baby and wrapped him in a clean soft blanket. Fortunately, she had also brought several bottles and baby formula with her and began to feed the baby by dripping the formula into his mouth one drop at a time.

While I talked to the father and his plans for a funeral for his wife, Faye took the oldest girls and showed them how to prepare the formula and bottles for the baby. Then, we left for home.

After a couple of days without any news, we decided to go back and see how things were progressing. As we suspected, things had gone from bad to worse. The bottle was lying on the dirt floor with flies buzzing all over it. The baby was on a pile of old rags in the corner. The oldest girl came to us in tears. "The baby will not eat! He is dying!"

The father came over to me. His face was downcast. "I have too many children to take care of. This baby is dying. You take him. I give him to you. Maybe you can help him live."

I looked over at Faye in a state of shock at the sudden life-changing request. My eyes searched hers as I asked, "What do you think?"

To my surprise, Faye quickly responded without any apparent hesitation. "It's worth a try!" she said as smiled at me, and then over at the baby's father.

We picked up the tiny baby and took him home. Faye wrapped a hot water bottle in a towel and put it in an empty shoe box, and then padded the box with a soft cloth. The little baby was so very tiny - a little larger than the palm of my hand. He easily fit into the shoe box. I had no idea how we were going to keep him alive. But, we were going to give it our best effort.

For the first few hours and into the night Faye fed the baby with an eye dropper. Since he had no strength to suck, the milk just ran down his throat. Things did not look too promising the next day when his umbilicus became infected. We decided to give him an injection of penicillin. There wasn't any fat on this little body. We had to pull up the skin and slip the needle in just under the stretched skin.

"This is either going to kill him or cure him," Faye declared.

I prayed. Faye continued to use the eye dropper to feed him, hour by hour, through the day and night and the next day... and the next and the next. Soon, she started to feel very very tired and stressed. On top of everything, we had two little boys of our own to care for. Amazingly, however, in just a few days, the baby (whom we named Pedro by now) began to suck from the bottle all on his own - and his color began to improve! Then, one morning, Faye looked up at me with a smile and announced, "I think he is going to make it! But, I don't know about me!? I am not sure I'm going to make it! I'm so drop dead tired and completely exhausted."

However, just when things began to improve for Pedro, tragedy struck our entire region. A horrible epidemic of measles broke out in our town and in the surrounding areas. Since no one had been immunized, the disease spread quickly and many children began to die.

One father came to me and pleaded with me, "Three of my children have already died! Now, I only have one child left alive - and he is also very sick. Please señor, please come and help me!"

He had walked all night to get help for his son. I packed some medicines, put them on my motorcycle and we rode for two hours along a dirt road and then walked another three hours along a steep jungle trail to get to his home. I stayed in his home for three days trying to save his last child. Thankfully, with the Lord's help, his son pulled through.

Unfortunately, while I was gone, my youngest boy, Shannon, came down with the measles as well. We had been told that because of his young age he could not have the vaccine – that he needed to wait until he was a little older.

Now, Faye not only had tiny sick Pedro to deal with, she now had baby Shannon, only nine months old at the time, spiking a high fever. Soon, Shannon began to bleed from his ears as well and Faye just about lost it. She was desperate to save both Shannon and Pedro. Forgetting her exhaustion, she struggled to see both of our babies through their own individual crises. Thankfully, with excellent nursing care and God's never-ending help, she saved our family when so many around us were dying.

I was told some time later that about half the children in our own town died from this one outbreak of measles. I have read that before the Conquistadores came to the Americans that the population of the Americas was a little over two hundred million people – more people than lived in Europe at the time. However, those living in the Americas had no natural immunity to the diseases of Europe. It has been estimated that close to 90% of the population in the Americas was killed by diseases brought by in by the Spaniards and their pigs. When De Soto landed in Florida he brought with him six hundred soldiers, two hundred horses and over three hundred pigs. De Soto did a lot of bad things but the worst thing he did, in the estimate of some, was to bring pigs. Europeans had lived with these animals for hundreds of years and had built up resistance to the diseases these animals carried - diseases like smallpox and measles. Such diseases can be transmitted from animals to humans. The poor people of the Americas had no natural immunity. So, they had a very hard time surviving these new European diseases. Probably, this is the main reason why Cortez was able to conquer the Aztecs, who far outnumbered him - because a very large number of the Aztec population was killed by smallpox.

And yet, my boys Shannon, Sean, and Pedro were somehow spared. And, within a few months, Pedro had gained weight and was very healthy, robust, and strong. At first, we thought that we might try to adopt him. However, with all that we had gone through and the difficulty of raising our own two small boys, it was simply too much for us to handle yet another small baby. So, we started checking around with the families in the town. However, no one was interested in adopting Pedro. His own father didn't even want him back. We even went and checked with Señorita Rocha. She must have been in her late fifties and still a single "señorita."

"Are you kidding?!" she exclaimed! "There is no way I can adopt a baby! No one would want to marry me if I had a baby!" Then, after looking down at little Pedro, she smiled as she said, "He is very cute though. I do wish I could take him."

Fortunately, we found a young couple who worked in the mission office in La Paz who wanted to adopt a baby. So we informed them about Pedro and in a few days they came to Huancana and picked him up. We let him go with mix feelings of sadness and joy. Of course, his new family was so excited to have a new son.

Over the years we lost track of Pedro and we have often wondered what became of him. Several years ago we visited the Adventist school at Montemorelos, Mexico. We found a Bolivian lady who was working at the bakery and asked her if she knew Pedro. "Oh yes," she said, "He is quite a lively young man!"

Such experiences, though painful, exhausting, and even desperate at the time, are among some of my most fulfilling memories of our time in Bolivia. These experiences helped me to trust in God and His leading my family and me no matter what happens to be going on around us. I know that He cares for us and for our future – and that he even sympathizes with our current wants, needs, and desires.

Peep the Gladiator Chicken

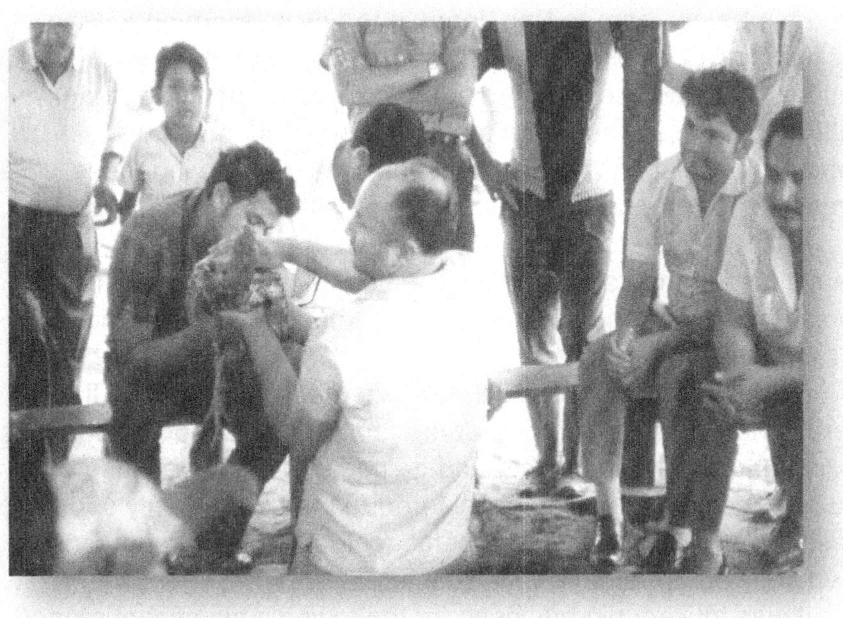

When I was there, San Joaquin was a small little Bolivian town that appeared unimpressive except for two things - cats and fighting cocks (roosters).

Hundreds of cats of every hue and variety occupied the town. Even so, it was a relatively neat and clean town by local standards. However, this had not always been the case. A few years before the town had been a very dirty disgusting place to live. The townsfolk had historically been rather careless about their garbage. They simply threw any garbage or left-over food out of their windows and into the streets where it collected in heaps and piles along the alleys and roadways. Rats multiplied by the thousands and scurried over the mounds of garbage in search of food. Of course, these rats carried fleas that bit the people. And, one day, the town was struck with a terrible outbreak of hemorrhagic fever. The population was decimated by the disease and a great many people died. Within a few months, the cemetery on the outskirts of town became the most popular place to be.

The Bolivian government asked the United States to send a send a medical team to San Joaquin to advise them on how to wipe out this plague before it began invading other towns in the Beni. Of course, these advisors recommended cleaning up the garbage, cutting the grass around the town, and bringing in a large population of cats. Within a very short time of following these directions, the rat population was wiped out; and so was the fever.

After that, the town became somewhat famous for its cleanliness – and its cats. Yet, San Joaquin had another more ancient claim to fame as well. It was famous for the best fighting cocks in the world.

Cockfights were no small matter in that region. These fights were serious events and not for the faint of heart. Much blood was spilled and much money lost and gained. Probably because of its brutality, cockfighting was considered to be a very manly sport. So, when the big cockfight tournaments took place, all the manly men in town showed up to bet on the roosters.

It was all very big business for the town as significant money changed hands on a regular basis. Some would wager homes, cattle and large sums of cash on the outcome of a single fight. Many owners treated their prize birds better than they treated members of their own family.

The fighting pit was located at the edge of town in the back yard of one of the wealthiest merchants in town. His spacious backyard was shaded by large avocado trees. In the middle of the yard was a very large gazebo. And, inside this gazebo was a circular smoothly raked dirt floor measuring about ten feet in diameter and enclosed by a short solid wooden fence. This was the fighting pit. The men sat on tiers of wooden benches that surrounded the pit.

Señor Guzman, the owner of the largest store in town, had invited me to come and observe. I've always had a soft spot for animals and didn't really want to watch chickens tear each other to ribbons. However, it would have been seen as very rude of me to refuse such an invitation. Also, I had never before been to a cock fight, so I finally decided to go.

I arrived a little late. The place was already packed with people. Señor Guzman graciously escorted me to a seat near the front and then excused himself in order to take care of some personal business. Several big ranchers in the Beni had flown in with their top contenders. Señor Martinez, a heavy-set man with a Poncho Villa mustache and half closed eyes, sat on the other side of the ring holding his most prized rooster. I watched as he handed the large rooster over to his peons who tethered the bird to a small stake on the outside of the building. Looking down from where I sat, I watched the bird strutting back and forth the length of his tether. His black and dark green feathers were glistening in the sun. He was a huge magnificent bird.

Just then a thin man sitting next to me interrupted my thoughts. "He is not only one of the biggest cocks around but very quick. In the last twenty fights, no bird has lasted more than two minutes with him. Señor Martinez has promised to give 100,000 bolivianos to anyone whose bird lasts longer than three minutes with him. The bird's name is Satanas – because he certainly is a devil. Señor Martinez brags that there is no bird alive that can beat his bird. Many of us have lost a lot of money on that fat man." Lowering his voice he continued, "I am told that Señor Martinez makes money on other things besides cockfighting and ranching. I am told he is also big in the drug business."

I had to admit that "Satanas" appeared overpowering. From my seat, I had a clear view of all of the roosters that were tethered near the arena. None of the birds matched the magnificence of Satanas. Off to one side, I saw a frail teenage boy kneeling by a scruffy looking bird. I had never seen a more pathetic looking creature.

"Surely," I thought to myself, "that boy is not planning on fighting him. He doesn't stand a chance against any of these other birds."

The little man next to me interrupted me again, "That little rooster belongs to Mario." Then he lowered his voice to a whisper and continued, "Some people say he is the illegitimate child of Señor Martinez." Then shrugging his shoulders he added, "Who knows? Maybe Señor Martinez has a soft spot for the orphan boy. Mario does odd jobs for him."

I questioned, "What is he doing with a fighting cock?"

The little man smiled. "That is a very interesting story. Señor Martinez has some of the best fighting cocks in the Beni. One of his best hens got involved with a small rooster of questionable reputation. The eggs the hen laid were destroyed, but Mario was able to rescue one of them. He incubated it in the shack where he slept and named the chick that hatched Peep. Peep is not much to look at but he is a fighter. He has been in three contests and each one was a brawl. Although he was pretty badly beaten up, he managed to win each one. In the last one, he was beaten so severely that everyone thought he was finished but Mario pulled him through. Mario doesn't want to fight him again but Señor Martinez talked him into fighting him because the crowd enjoys the show. This is going to be Peep's last fight because Mario is too attached to the bird."

After listening to the story of Mario and Peep, I'll have to admit that I also began to admire the bird, and secretly began rooting for the bird, despite myself. However, in looking over the crowd of contenders it became difficult to see how little Peep could handle any of them.

My attentions were brought back to the fighting ring by the voice of Señor Gomez calling the owners together for the selection of the opponents. After the selection process, Señor Gomez announced who would be fighting. A murmur went through the crowd as the strengths and weaknesses of each contestant were discussed. When the final fight was announced, the audience gasped and then began to laugh. The final combatants would be Peep vs. Satanas. It didn't seem very amusing to me. I wondered how Mario was feeling. I felt sorry for the boy – and for his rooster. Poor Peep was about to be slaughtered for the amusement of the crowd.

Then, everyone stopped laughing and silence fell over the arena as they watched the owners preparing their roosters for battle. Razor sharp metal spurs were attached to the rooster's legs. Cockfights are a deadly business. It is a life and death struggle. One thrust in a strategic place and life is over. I thought about the gladiator fights in the ancient arenas of Rome as I watched the men and their reaction to what was about to take place. They appeared intoxicated with excitement.

The first fight pitted two of the local favorites. The owners with their roosters stepped into the ring. Each man gulped water from long-necked bottles and spit water into the rooster's face. This action put the rooster on full alert. Then they turned the roosters so that they faced one another and moved the roosters back and forth toward each other until they became infuriated with each other. Then, the men released their birds. Immediately, the roosters viciously attacked each other. Each bird tried to gain a height advantage on the other so that they could thrust a well-aimed steel spike through the other's head. They repeatedly flapped their wings, circled, fretted, jumped, and thrust their spurs at each other. In a matter of minutes, both birds were covered in blood. The men yelled and screamed with each movement of the birds they supported. However, as the battle continued both birds began to tire from the loss of blood and became less and less aggressive. The fight was declared a draw and the birds were withdrawn from the ring. Boos and catcalls followed. The owners washed their birds in a big tub of water and treated their wounds. These two birds would live to fight another day.

Not all of the birds were so lucky. Several were instantly killed by a well-placed thrust to the head. Others won but were badly wounded and died shortly after the fight. Some were horribly crippled. The more bloody the fight the more the crowd enjoyed it and the more the money flowed.

I was getting sick watching all the gore but I stayed, strange as it may seem, because I wanted to know what was going to happen to Peep – even though I knew deep down that it too was going to be a bloodbath. Hopefully, it would be a quick merciful death for poor little Peep.

Finally, it was time for the final match of the day. Satanas, the Beni champion, was to fight Peep, the scrawny local who had barely won three fights. When the two birds got into the ring it was an obvious mismatch. Spectators laughed and joked about the fight. The betting was entirely over the time it would take Satanas to finish off Peep. Most bet that the fight would not last more than

30 seconds. This fight would wet everyone's appetite for the big fight the following week when several large cocks were to be flown in from outside the country.

In the ring, poor Mario talked to and petted his precious little Peep. You knew there was a real bond between the boy and his rooster – a pet that he had tenderly cared for and raised by hand since Peep was still inside his egg.

But, now the fight was on. The two roosters required little prompting to get worked up. The big rooster immediately went on the attack. A big blood spot appeared on Peep's side. Everyone anticipated the fight to end in seconds. Men yelled out bets. Still, Peep hung in there. He was a tough and quick little bird. After each flurry that appeared to be his last, he still stood up on his own two feet. The feeling in the crowd began to change. The men began to believe that Peep could actually last more than three minutes. Each time that Satanas charged and Peep stayed on his feet the crowd cheered. When Peep managed to stay alive more than the three minutes the crowd erupted in cheers. Their local bird was still on his feet. Satanas began to tire, but his repeated attacks on Peep had taken their toll. Peep was covered in blood. The crowd yelled for the fight to stop. The bird had proven his courage. But, before Mario could cross the ring to pick up his bird, Satanas launched a final attack on Peep. It was more than the little bird could handle. A spur sank deep into his body and in a moment Peep sank to the ground motionless. The boisterous crowd fell silent as the big rooster stood over his victim and began to crow. Mario was stunned. It all happened so quickly.

"Peep!" he screamed.

Señor Martinez smiled.

Then, before anyone could recover from the abrupt defeat and before Mario could reach his fallen friend, Peep made a sudden move. In a flash, he was in the air and with one swift slash he almost decapitated Satanas. The big bird fell over – dead!

Señor Martinez jumped to his feet. His half-opened eyes now wide with shock and rage! Not only had he lost hundreds of thousands of bolivianos in bets (including the100,000 bolivianos he owed Mario), but his prize bird lost his head to a little, scruffy, unknown bird named Peep!

The crowd went wild, throwing their hats high in the air and breaking open bottles of beer and wine. The town celebrated for days. And, even though the little rooster survived, he was badly injured and never fought again. Still, Peep enjoyed his retirement. He became the town legend and remained as proud and cocky as ever. Nobody could deny that Peep was a little bird that had great courage and heart. Mario was as proud of him as any boy ever was of a beloved pet. He carried him everywhere he went from that day onward.

As for me, I decided that I had seen my first and last cockfight. But, I will always remember little Peep defeating Satanas – like David and Goliath.

We too can be like little Peep. With God's help, we can stand against Satan himself in battle and withstand all of the fiery darts, thrusts, and jabs he throws our way – because there is someone who will fight for us. Jesus is someone strong and mighty who fights for us and who has already dealt Satan a deadly blow, and given us *His* victory.

There is a neat promise in the Bible found in Genesis 3:15 that I like to read whenever I think about Peep and his fight, and my fight, with Satanas.

"And I will put enmity between you and the woman, and between your offspring and hers; he will crush your head, and you will strike his heel."

Trinidad

Our old DC-3 swooped down from the clouds and flared out over the grass runway. It came bouncing and sliding to a stop, kicking up billows of dust as it taxied toward the terminal. As I made my way out the door of the plane a blast of hot air greeted me. A large crowd had gathered to inspect the incoming passengers. I searched through the crowd for a familiar face. Numerous young boys tugged at my pants determined to get my attention to earn a few bolivianos for carrying my luggage. Young girls leaned seductively against door frames adjusting their blouses to best reveal their physical assets. Young men eyed the women who passed by them. The hawkers who lined my path toward the terminal were enthusiastically promoting various colorful artifacts produced by local artisans.

Then I saw him. He was making his way toward me from the terminal. He was a huge man who moved effortlessly through the crowd. Everyone quickly moved out of his way and cleared a path in front of him as he quickly walked over to where I stood. Then, as he stood in front of me looking down into my face, he opened his arms wide and gave me a bear hug that nearly crushed the life out of me.

Then, he stood back, still holding me up by the shoulders, and said in a big booming voice that was full of sincere joy at my arrival, "I am Pastor Ernesto De La Tore."

Before I had the opportunity to react, he reached down, grabbed my luggage, and began cutting through the crowd like an icebreaker plowing toward the North Pole. I quickly followed in his wake.

He yelled at me over his shoulder, "Our taxi is waiting and so is our supper."

The taxi was an antique 1948 Ford. As we walked up to the car, Ernesto announced, "I paid Jose to wait for us. It's the best taxi in town (I found out later that it was the only functioning taxi in town).

Jose looked up at us and grunted as he pulled his short stocky body from behind the steering wheel. Large clouds of smoke floated around his enormous head. Rivulets of sweat cascaded down his bald head and over his puffy red cheeks and into the foliage of a large mustache. He threw down the stub of his cigar and pulled from his pocket a filthy handkerchief and mopped his face and head. Greeting us with little bows, he said, "Jose Antonio Luis Esperanza de los Padres, at your service."

I took a close look at the taxi and realized there wasn't any room. There were already three people sitting in the back and three in the front. A large part of the back seat was occupied by one of the largest ladies I had ever personally encountered. I estimated her weight to be well over three hundred pounds. The trunk was also crammed with luggage. I had no idea how Ernesto could possibly fit anywhere in Jose's taxi.

I let out a low whistle. "Maybe we'd better look for another taxi?" I questioned. "Nonsense!" Jose shot back. "We just need a little adjustment. I can put your luggage on the top of the trunk."

Jose waddled a few feet to the back door and barked out an order for everyone to move over. I could hear the chorus of complaints and oaths issuing forth from the passengers as they struggled to comply with his request. In a few moments, a little space began to develop on the left side and Jose motioned for me to get in. I pushed and squeezed myself in. It was a very tight squeeze. I was wedged in next to a small teenage boy. The large lady, Señora Gutierrez, had pinned the slightly-built man to her right against the door. He was wedged under her right arm. Most of him had disappeared. His protests had become muffled and soon he resigned himself to his fate.

Then, Ernesto began to push his large frame through the door. Jose grunted and pushed from the outside in assistance. Señora Gutierrez began to swear and complain loudly. The small man who was buried somewhere inside Señora Gutierrez started making muffled sounds again. I too was beginning to disappear under Señora Gutierrez's other armpit. I didn't know where the teenage boy had disappeared to. The smell of sweat mixed with Señora Gutierrez's pungent perfume almost made me pass out. Still, no amount of pushing or maneuvering could get Ernesto into that taxi.

Mercifully, Jose decided to give up and pulled Ernesto out. Jose's large red face protruded through the door. His breathing was heavy. Vainly he searched the back seat.

"Juanito!" he barked. "Get out! Get out!"

I got out and gulped in mouthfuls of fresh air. Juanito crawled out from under the folds of Señora Gutierrez. You could tell that he was more than happy to comply with Jose's request. He seemed happy to be alive. Jose motioned for me to get back in.

"We have room for you now," he declared in a loud voice.

I took several gulps of fresh air and climbed back in. I was now sitting next to Señora Gutierrez. Ernesto shoved his large frame through the door. He was half in and half out. Jose started his shoving from the outside again. With one final shove, Ernesto was in and Jose slammed the door triumphantly.

"Ah," he beamed as he struggled to get behind the steering wheel. "I told you that we had plenty of room."

I was sitting partly up Señor Gutierrez's lap. My head was bent onto my chest, forcefully pressed downward by the ceiling of the car. Juanito sat dejected on the front right fender. "Comfy?" questioned Jose as he leaned over to start the engine. I felt like a sardine packed in rancid perfume. And, each time we would hit a rut I would sink deeper into Señora Gutierrez's ample bosom.

On the way into town, Jose seemed drawn to every pothole in the road. There were no shocks on his car. They had worn out years before. Every hit rattled my teeth. Señora Gutierrez really had a way with words. I learned quite a few new ones on our way to town. Ernesto kept repeating, "Lord, forgive her!" Mercifully, it did not take long to reach our destination.

We were greeted by barking dogs and cackling chickens as they scurried out of the way. Ernesto threw open the door and launched himself into the street. Fresh air mingled with dust rushed in. I slowly unwound myself from Señora Gutierrez. To this day, I don't know what happened to the little old man on her right. He may have suffocated on the trip from the airport. For days I was reminded of Señora Gutierrez because her perfume lingered on in my clothes and skin. It took quite some time before it eventually dissipated and I no longer thought of her on a daily basis.

Ernesto slapped me on the back. "Welcome to my humble home!"

It was a large two-story wooden building. I could tell that, at some time in the past, it had once been a pretty fancy house. However, it had since fallen out of repair and there were only traces of paint left on the building. It had been built many years before by a Señor Garcia. He was the wealthy local padrino (the godfather) of that area of the Beni and he had a lot of power in that area. No one could do anything without his permission. He also had the pick of any of the women of the town – and he had taken full advantage of this particular privilege. He had fathered more than fifty children over forty years or so. And, as a result, half the town of Trinidad was related. There were Garcias everywhere. Of course, morals in the town were almost non-existent. It was common to see very large families where each child had a different last name.

Of course, I had visions that my church had become established in this town to serve as a beacon for morality. The bottom of the building functioned as a church and the second floor served as living quarters for the pastor.

Putting his massive arm around my shoulder, Ernesto pointed me toward the stairs and back patio. "My wife has prepared us a wonderful supper. I know you must be starved."

We made our way up a long flight of creaky stairs. Ernesto opened the screen door and ushered me into the kitchen. I was greeted by Juanita. She was tall, fair skinned and pretty. She ushered us to the plain wooden table. Already seated around this table were three lively children – including two boys who were carbon copies of their father and a girl who looked like her mother in miniature. The little girl was in the process of hitting her older brother over the head with her spoon.

"Children, children," Juanita pleaded. "You need to behave. What will our company think of you?"

"Go out and play now!" Ernesto commanded, and they quickly obeyed him without another word.

Juanita repeatedly motioned for me to sit down. "You must be very hungry after that long trip," she said.

Before I could respond, Ernesto pushed me forward toward my chair. "Let's eat!"

Juanita placed large bowls of steaming soup in front of us. Piles of hard crusted bread were in the center of the table and a tall glass of lemonade stood by each plate. Ernesto bowed his head and quickly said grace. Then he began to spoon soup into his mouth enthusiastically. He would reach across the table and break off large chunks of bread and stuff them into his mouth as he continued to talk. He talked while waving his spoon in the air with one hand and shaking a piece of bread in the other to emphasize various points in the conversation. And, on occasion, a shower of bread crumbs would shoot out of his mouth and spray the table when he got a bit too excited. I watched transfixed as he would drop his bread and reach into a small bowl filled with tiny red peppers. He'd take one or two in his hand, and in mid-sentence, he would pop them into his mouth.

Then, quite suddenly, he stopped eating. He picked up one of the little red peppers and held it in front of my face for inspection.

"It's called picante," he said as he thrust it closer to my nose. "Try it. It adds a lot of flavor to good soup."

I prided myself on having a cast iron stomach. I'd eaten some pretty hot stuff in my life without difficulty. So, I casually reached up and took the little picante from Ernesto's hand and, without a moment's hesitation, popped it into my mouth. For a few moments things went fine. I smiled at Ernesto as I settled back into my chair, munching on my little picante as I took another spoonful of soup. Then, out of nowhere, my whole head erupted with fire. Drops of sweat popped out on the top of my head and tears began to roll down my cheeks. Instantly, soup and pieces of pepper flew out of my mouth. I tried to talk but the words would not come. I just looked at Ernesto and pointed at my mouth in desperation. I gasped, sputtered, coughed and finally got out the words, "More lemonade! More lemonade!" This stuff was lethal! I could just imagine the newspaper headlines the next morning, "Missionary eats picante and dies!"

Ernesto leaned back in his chair and let out a roar of laughter. "A bit hot aren't they?"

Juanita stood watching us with her hands on her hips and fire in her eyes. "You're a naughty boy! Why did you do such a thing to our new guest?"

Then she turned to me and patted me on the shoulder as she handed me a piece of bread with a big splash of butter on it. "Here, try this. It may help a little with the burning. And here's another glass of lemonade."

I had no taste buds left for supper that night.

There is a text in the Bible that goes like this, "It's the little foxes that spoil the grapes." Sometimes we have a tendency to feel that little sins in our lives are not all that important. They are so tiny they can't possibly hurt us. When I am tempted to feel this way, I am reminded of the little picante. A small thing can sometimes cause a lot of damage.

After supper, I was ushered into the living room. It was a large room with mahogany floors. It was simply furnished. Several wooden chairs were scattered throughout the room. An old couch dominated the middle of the room. Ernesto dropped his large frame onto the couch. With his foot he pulled a wooden chair over and propped both feet on it. I found a comfortable looking chair and pulled it across from him and sat down. Ernesto leaned back and cupped his hands behind his head. I stared at him for a moment and said. "I am curious. You have been a pastor for nine years and you still aren't ordained. Why?"

He stared back at me with a broad smile. "It is a long story but what else are you going to do this evening?"

As Ernesto started telling me his story he got a faraway look in his eyes as he explained how he had grown up in an Italian family who had immigrated to Argentina during the Second World War.

"My parents were devout Catholics, Italians," he said. "It seems to me that any good family should have several children - enough so that one can be a lawyer, one a doctor, and one a priest. That way all the family problems will be covered". He was to be the priest. However, his family's conversion to Adventism changed his plans for the priesthood. Instead of becoming a priest, he decided to become an Adventist pastor. He studied theology at the Adventist college in Argentina. Then, after college, he received a call to begin his ministry in Bolivia.

His first assignment was in Sucre. He was full of enthusiasm. Sucre was a city of culture and history. The city held the distinction of being the constitutional capital of Bolivia. There were beautiful Catholic churches everywhere. The University of St. Francis Xavier, the oldest university in the Americas, dominated the city. The whitewashed red-tiled houses further enhanced the atmosphere of the city. Ernesto was very eager and determined to convert the entire city to Adventism. One of the first things he did was to hold a series of evangelistic meetings in a large rented hall. He went around town putting up posters and passing out invitations. He ran advertisements on the radio and in the newspaper. However, he did not directly identify himself as an Adventist pastor. On opening night the auditorium was only half filled with people. Rather than be discouraged, Ernesto preached with great emotion and enthusiasm. He paced back and forth and moved in and out of the audience to answer questions. His enthusiasm was contagious. Each night more and more people came to hear him. After one week of meetings, the crowd was so large that some had to stand outside and look through the windows. His series was so popular that the Catholic bishop and city fathers became concerned. They took counsel together and decided to send their brightest theologian to the meetings to check it out. After all, their young theologian had just returned from doctoral studies at the Vatican in New Testament theology and was teaching at St. Francis Xavier University. This should be a piece of cake for him.

Unfortunately, the theme of Ernesto's sermon that night was on the change of the Sabbath to Sunday. The special music had just ended and Ernesto had just started to speak when in walked the young Catholic theologian and several prominent Catholic Church leaders. They made their way down the aisle, and, after haggling with several on the front row, sat down in the vacated chairs. Ernesto continued with his presentation. Toward the end of the sermon, the Catholic theologian stood up and loudly proclaimed, "You are confusing the people with rubbish and lies! Everyone knows the Catholic Church was given authority by Christ to change the day of worship from Saturday to Sunday. What more do you need them to know?"

The debate between the two young men became heated. Ernesto descended from the platform and the priest went forward to meet him. The crowd rose to get a closer look. The two men stood eyeball to eyeball. The discussion became more and more heated. When the priest yelled an insult and stuck his finger into Ernesto's chest, Ernesto lost control and unleashed a roundhouse with his right fist that hit the priest flush against the jaw. The priest staggered a few steps and fell like a large tree being hit by a bolt of lightning, scattering chairs in every direction. The priest's associates rush to the body of their fallen champion and tried to revive him. Ernesto stood in the aisle in shock.

"What have I done? I am so sorry!" he kept repeating.

In a few minutes, the police arrived and arrested Ernesto and took him to the city jail.

When the Mission brethren found out what had happened, they immediately contacted their attorneys, who with much difficulty and with the promise that Ernesto would not return to Sucre, were able to free him from jail. After Ernesto made many tearful apologies to the brethren, it was decided to move him to the city of Oruro.

Oruro was not a city that was historical or Catholic like Sucre. On top of this, Ernesto decided that public meetings were too dangerous. He opted instead for personal Bible studies as his new approach to soul winning. Once again, he embarked with enthusiasm on this new endeavor. In no time he had a large group of Bible studies all over town. There was a problem with such success, however. In those days, it was difficult to get around the town. It took a small fortune to ride the bus. It also took a lot of time. So, he decided that a motorcycle would save time and money – even though he had never ridden one before. Still, he had his mind made up and quickly found an affordable old Czech motorcycle. Fortunately, he was a quick learner and soon he was speeding all over town. In fact, he loved the speed of the motorcycle and went everywhere as fast as it would go. He ignored all traffic signs: stop, one way and speed limits. He was constantly in hot water with the traffic police.

Then, one day he got into a particular hurry. After all, he was late for a Bible study. As he was flying along on his trusty motorcycle, he came toward one of the busiest intersections in the city. As he approached, he noticed that a large bus was also nearing the intersection at a high rate of speed. Yet, Ernesto calculated that he could beat the bus through the intersection. So, he poured on the gas. The motorcycle surged forward. Unfortunately, Ernesto's calculations were wrong. He and the bus arrived at the intersection at precisely the same time. There was a tremendous crash. The motorcycle smashed into the side of the bus and lay in the street like a crumpled piece of paper. Observers explained that Ernesto flew over the top of the bus and hit a fruit stand on the other side of the street. He lay on the sidewalk amid pieces of wood and fruit. An ambulance was called. When it arrived, Ernesto was pronounced dead by the attendants and loaded into the ambulance and taken to the morgue.

Papers on his body indicated that he was a pastor for the Seventh-day Adventist Church. So, the Mission officials were notified of the pastor's death. The Mission president and secretary contacted Mrs. De La Tore and made plans for the funeral, but before they could claim the body, a janitor who was cleaning the morgue noticed that the corpse on the gurney had a toe that was twitching. A physician from the hospital was sent to check on the body and discovered that Ernesto was still alive. He was transferred to the intensive care unit. Although he had suffered numerous fractures and a brain concussion, he was alive and began to improve.

After several months Ernesto was released from the hospital. And, after listening to his tearful pleas and promises of reform, the Mission brethren decided to move him to La Paz, where they could keep a close eye on him until he was fully recovered. They also restricted him to bus use only and things settled down to a normal routine of pastoral duties.

Then, several months later, Ernesto went to the Mission office to get supplies. There were only two secretaries in the office when a phone call came in from the airport. It was the South American Union president on the line. He was on a stop-over on his way to Lima and he had a few hours to spare and wanted to know if someone from the Mission could pick him up. The secretary responded that no one was at the office because all the men had gone to lunch. However, Ernesto was listening to the conversation and decided that this was an emergency.

"I'll take care of it," he yelled as he headed out the door. "Tell the Union president I'll be there in about half an hour."

Ernesto walked down the street to the Mission parking lot. There were several old cars there but nothing he could use. However in the back of the lot sat an old jeep. He went to the gatekeeper for the key. "Hey," responded the gatekeeper. "They haven't used that jeep for months. They have been having trouble with the brakes and the engine."

"I need it anyway! It's an emergency!" countered Ernesto.

He grabbed the key from the gatekeeper and ran across the lot to the jeep. He jumped in and cranked the engine. The battery began to groan. Finally, the engine coughed and came to life. It backfired badly and a cloud of smoke poured out the back end. Ernesto put it into gear and the jeep jerked onto the street.

The airport was located on a plain called the Altiplano. It is surrounded by mountains. One of the most majestic is Illimani. The city of La Paz itself is situated in a huge depression, like a giant bowl, that drops steeply down from the Altiplano. In order to get to the airport, one has to take a road that rises sharply out of the city. At the top, the airport is at over 13,000 feet in elevation - the highest commercial airport in the world. Many tourists visiting Bolivia for the first time get their first taste of altitude sickness at this airport. All most visitors have to do to get light-headed and nauseous is walk from the plane to the terminal. The locals advise that visitors sip a little coca tea to help ease the nausea, which usually helps.

In any case, as Ernesto pulled onto the airport road he gunned the jeep and flew down the straightaway. He came squealing around the corner into the parking lot, barely missing an army truck that was parked at the entrance to the terminal. Soldiers scattered in all directions. The jeep bounced off a curb and came to a sudden stop. Ernesto spied a parking space and yanked the jeep into reverse. He saw a light pole too late and backed right into it.

"I guess the gatekeeper was right about these brakes," He muttered to himself as he jumped out of the jeep to take a look at the damage. Fortunately, the jeep already had so any dents in it that it was hard to tell if the pole had caused any additional damage. So, Ernesto briskly walked to the terminal and waved cheerily at the soldiers, who by now had sheepishly returned to their places. He took the steps two at a time and hurried through the entrance. As he carefully studied the people seated in the lobby, his eyes came to rest on a distinguished grey-haired gentleman who was looking through papers he had pulled out of his briefcase.

"Ah ha!" Ernesto thought to himself. "It's the Union president," as he made a bee-line for the older gentleman.

"Let me introduce myself," he said, interrupting the man's concentration. The gentleman looked up in surprise. "I am Ernesto De La Tore and I am here from the Mission office to pick you up," he smiled as he held out his hand.

"It's about time!" Shot back the older gentleman, with a slight European accent. Ernesto helped the man put his papers back together. Then, he reached down and picked up his briefcase in one hand and, with the other, he escorted the gentleman out the door toward his jeep.

As they passed the soldiers all of them suddenly snapped to attention and saluted the two men as they walked passed. Ernesto paid no attention, but the older gentleman returned the salute.

When they arrived at the jeep, the distinguished gentleman balked at getting into such a beat up vehicle. In a solemn tone, he exclaimed, "This vehicle is a pile of junk! I can't believe the Mission would send you to pick me up with this! They must be in worse financial shape than I thought." Looking around he noticed the soldiers and the truck. Then a smile broke out on his face. "At least they provided me with some security!"

Ernesto shook his head and commented to himself, "He's sure got a good sense of humor." Then, he turned the key and tried to start the jeep, but nothing happened!

"It must be a dead battery." He thought to himself.

So, he turned to the gentleman and announced, "We've got a little problem here, but I'll have it going in just a minute."

The old man shook his head as Ernesto jumped out of the jeep and ran up to the soldiers that were milling around the army truck. In a few minutes, half a dozen soldiers came over to the jeep. Ernesto got into the jeep as the soldiers pushed the jeep out of the parking space and down the road. After they built up a little speed, he popped the clutch and the jeep jerked to life. Billows of smoke engulfed the soldiers as they dropped behind. Ernesto waved his thanks as he slammed the accelerator down to the floorboard. His guest grabbed his seat to stabilize himself. Cold air whipped through the broken windshield and ruffled his snowy white hair. "What about the escort?" The old gentleman yelled above the roar of the engine.

In no time at all, the road began to wind its way down the three or four miles into La Paz. The grade was very steep and a long line of buses and trucks slowly groaned their way up the road toward the Altiplano. Ernesto fell behind a long string of trucks that were slowly grinding their way down the steep road into the city. He looked for a break in traffic so that he could pass. After a while, he noticed a small break, just big enough to pass four or five trucks. He slammed down the gas pedal and the jeep lurched forward as it flew out into the opposite lane. His passenger began to mumble something about Mary as he crossed himself several times. The space was shorter than he expected, so he pushed the gas pedal all the way to the floor. The engine screaming at top pitch as the jeep raced, head on, toward the large bus right in front of it. Then, just at the last moment when a head-on collision seemed absolutely certain, Ernesto swerved out of the way into a small opening in the line of trucks. The bus that he had almost hit drove slowly by as passengers leaned out of the doors and windows yelling curses at Ernesto. After a few minutes, Ernesto, unfazed by the first close call, saw another opening in the traffic and pressed hard on the gas to get around the truck in front of him. Just then, a large curve appeared. Ernesto slammed on the brakes, but the pedal went to the floor without any resistance at all. The brakes were completely gone! He desperately pumped the brake pedal again and again. His white-knuckled hands gripped the wheel as he tried desperately to keep the racing jeep on the road through the corner. The old man began to cross himself again and yelled out, "Holy Mother of God save us!" just as the jeep left the road at top speed. The jeep then went right through a billboard advertising Bolivian tires. Both men were taken to the hospital for observation where, after a few days, they were released, with relatively minor injuries.

Of course, the old gentleman didn't turn out to be the Union President after all, but was an ambassador for the German embassy.

Ernesto laughed as he saw the shock on my face.

"So, you understand why I'm here now? After many tears and pleadings, the Mission brethren moved me to the jungle where there are no roads. Just little dirt trails. They have also prohibited me from driving any motorized vehicles of any kind. I have been using a bicycle for the last two years and I haven't had any more wrecks and haven't been in any fights."

Then, he leaned forward and added in a loud conspiratorial whisper, "I have been told I have a good chance of being ordained this year."

I heard the other day that Pastor De La Tore has had a very outstanding career in the Lord's work. God never gave up on him and he never gives up on us either.

Tunari

I'd been to the school at Vinto, Bolivia several times to look at my father's grave. He was buried at the base of Tunari, the mountain that killed him. As I stood in front of his marker I could look across the valley at the majestic mountain of Tunari off in the distance. The story of his crash flashed into my mind and I began to imagine his decent into Cochabamba from over that mountain. I tried to imagine the panic that he and Antonio must have felt when they realized that they were going to crash (Thursday, November 11, 1946). When shepherds found the plane early the next day on Friday morning, they found Antonio some distance from the crash. He had evidently tried to bail out, but the plane was too close to the ground. His chute was partly opened. They found my dad still inside the plane. His head had been crushed by the top of the windshield. These shepherds had made their way down the mountain to inform the army about what they had found. The army sent soldiers up the mountain to recover the bodies. They placed the bodies of both men in their parachutes, loaded them on mules and brought them down the mountain to Cochabamba. At 11:00 o'clock on Sunday morning, they were buried with military honors at the general cemetery in Cochabamba. In the group who attended the funeral were members of the American and Czech colonies, the vice-counsel of the United States and Adventist Church officers. My mother, sister and I arrived too late for the funeral.

I had heard that parts of my dad's plane were still on the mountain. So, I decided that I would climb up there to see it for myself. There was a Mission youth leader, let's call him Peter, who was visiting the school at Vinto to conduct a week of prayer. I met him as I was walking across campus to my Jeep. "Hey, you going home?" he asked as he walked toward me. I waited until he caught up with me before I answered.

"I've just been thinking about climbing Tunari."

"Why would you want to do a thing like that?" he replied.

"Let's just say I am sentimental. My dad was killed on that mountain and I want to see if his plane is still there."

"When do you plan on going?"

"I plan to go this Sunday. I figure it will take a couple of days, so I'll have to take a sleeping bag and some food."

With a big grin he asked, "Can I come along? You may need some help when you get up into the mountain."

For the next couple of days, I was busy getting things organized for my trip. By that time I'd already built up a good tolerance for the high altitude. So, I felt that, physically, I could handle the climb without too much of a problem. Faye had gone to the market and spent most of the day on Friday baking so that we could take some goodies on our trip. That Saturday night I packed my gear. Faye convinced me to take our maid, Delfina.

"She's as strong as a mule," she told me. "Besides, Delfina would enjoy going."

So, there would be six of us on this "hike" – to include a few teenagers from the school who wanted to come along.

At the base of this mountain, we passed by the home of Simon Patino. Simon owned a palatial mansion with tile floors, marble staircases and pure gold faucets in the bathrooms. Delfina told us that Patino was a controversial figure, but was still one of the greatest success stories of the 20th century; and told us his story.

Simon was born in Cochabamba about 1868, the son of very poor and humble cholo (Indian) parents. Although unschooled, he had a brilliant mind. As a young man, Patino acquired a small mine in the 1890's and expanded his holdings until he became a millionaire. He moved to Europe, where he served for many years as a Bolivian diplomatic agent. He extended control over tin mines in British Malaya, built smelters in Germany and England, had homes in Paris, New York, and in a few other cities around the world. He married off his son and daughters to very wealthy French and Spanish families with long pedigrees. Then, in 1924, he returned to Bolivia and built three great homes, including an extravagant house in his native Cochabamba, at the cost of several million dollars. However, the white aristocracy of Cochabamba snubbed him and would not accept him as one of their own. So, he left Bolivia for the last time. Many of the tin miners gathered at the airport when he left to throw bottles of blood at him as they yelled that this represented the blood that he had sucked out of the Bolivian people. Obviously, he wasn't popular with the common worker. Amazingly, although he is not well known today, Patino was probably one of the wealthiest men in the world in his day. When France fell in 1940, he retired to New York and died in 1947.

Our trip progressed well the first day. By evening we were high up in the mountain. We had crossed and re-crossed an icy cold stream that tumbled down our pathway. The air was thin at 18,000 feet. We were all worn out. Even Delfina was tired and breathing hard. Still, we wanted to make it to a lake that was near the crash site before dark. By now, there was only an hour left of daylight and the lake was about three miles away. Still, it would be a tough climb to get there in our condition. So, after a little conference, we decided to set up camp where we were. We put up our tents and laid out our sleeping bags. Peter came over to where I was struggling to put the last strap on my tent pole.

"You've got a pretty small tent there."

I looked up. He was standing there like General Patton. Hands on his hips and feet spread apart.

I grunted, "I am not planning on putting an army in there, just me. Besides, the smaller the tent the less there is to carry."

"Really?" He shot back. "If you're interested in such things, you'd better put the food you're carrying in that backpack into the tent with you tonight. The kids that are with us have told me that there are wild dogs up in this area."

I saluted as a stood and said, "Yes Sir."

Then, I turned back to finish my work on the tent and he wandered over to the next tent to check on their progress.

I muttered to myself, "He invited himself on my trip and now is acting like the director of war operations. The next thing I know he'll be telling me how to tie my shoes. I haven't seen anything alive for the last four or five hours."

I rummaged through my backpack looking for food for supper. Faye had done a wonderful job getting food packaged and prepared for everyone. I found a couple of sandwiches and a bag of nuts. I pulled them out and walked over to the little fire where the others had gathered. I sat down by Delfina. The fire was casting ghostly shadows around us. The warmth of the fire felt good against the chill of the evening. It was going to feel good to get into my sleeping bag. I looked at Delfina and smiled.

"You and Faye did a wonderful job of packing our food."

There was a chorus of agreements. We told stories and sang songs, but it soon became too cold to keep sitting there. Finally, I stood up, said good night to everyone, and crawled into my tent and into my sleeping bag. Then, I remembered my backpack with my food. I jacked myself round until I could reach out and pull my pack in. But with the pack in the tent I had no room to lie down comfortably. So, I secured the flap on the pack and placed it just outside my tent door. I snuggled back down into my sleeping bag.

The next morning when I woke up and groggily stumbled out of my tent, I discover to my horror that something had attacked my backpack and made off with all of my food. The contents of my pack were scattered over a very large area. I just stood there scratching my head.

Of course, at that moment, Peter walked up and surveyed the scene. Then, in an all-knowing voice he said, “You are so stupid. Didn’t I tell you not to leave your bag outside?”

It was time for breakfast and he went over and pulled his bag out of his tent and shared his food with the others. I stood there feeling stupid, but was also quite hungry and was hoping for a hand out as well. Since I lost my food after being warned, he seemed to be wanting to teach me a lesson. Never mind that I had paid for all the food and Faye had made all of the food for everyone on this trip. But, he never offered me any of it. He just sat there taking great relish in slowly eating his food and licking his fingers very carefully, one by one. I could feel the anger boiling up inside of me. I sat there staring at him without saying a word.

Finally, breakfast was over and I was the first to put on my pack and head up the mountain. I didn’t want to get near anyone. I’d been such a fool to let the dogs eat my food and I was still upset that Peter wouldn’t share anything with me.

The higher altitude made walking even more difficult than the previous day. You could walk a few feet and then you’d start to get sick. We all had to stop every minute or two to catch our breath. It took a whole lot of time and energy to go what seemed like very short distances. It took us till 2:00 o’clock in the afternoon to make it to the lake – a lake which rested at a very high elevation of 20,000 feet! The lake has been created artificially by a dam that had been built by Simon Patino, which he used to produce electricity for his palatial estate at the bottom of the mountain.

As I sat on the dam overlooking the lake, I could feel deep hunger pains. I was very hungry by now. Again, it was time to eat and Peter pulled out his lunch and passed it around to the young people. He looked over at me and, with a big laugh, announced, "None for you, Tui."

It was all I could do to keep from jumping up and slugging him. Who in the world did he think he was? God? I sat down on a boulder and just stared at him through squinty eyes. I couldn't believe what was happening – yet again! I shook my head, tried to be calm and spoke to him as calmly as I could.

"I can't believe you are doing this to me."

He sat there and just grinned at me.

"You deserve it," he said as he laughed again at my plight.

A little later in the afternoon, not too far from the lake, I found pieces of fuselage that looked like they could have belonged to my father's plane. I was very happy to have found my father's plane and was really glad that I had made the effort. However, the entire trip was unfortunately tainted by what Peter had done to me.

On the way back down the mountain, Peter took the lead. He set what seemed to me to be a very fast pace. I lagged a little behind because I was getting sick. Delfina lagged a little behind too. She stopped until I caught up with her.

"Here," she said. "I've saved these cookies and sandwich for you. I know you must be starved." Stretching out her arm she handed me the plastic bag of smashed cookies and a sandwich.

I patted her on the shoulder. "Thank you so much Delfina! You've just saved my life!" I said as I quickly dove into the contents of the bag.

"That pastor is crazy for treating you like that," she blurted out suddenly.

"Yup," I mumble through a mouthful of food.

The trip down the mountain was much faster than the climb. By the next afternoon I was home. Faye had a fantastic meal waiting for me. The ache in my stomach had calmed down but my mind was a whirl of bad feelings.

"I'll get even with Peter if it's the last thing I do on this earth!" I said to myself through clenched teeth.

I know that everyone must at times get feelings like this. It's only human to get angry when people treat you unfairly.

Then, one day, I was reading my Bible and came across this verse.

"Be kind one to another, tender hearted, forgiving one another, even as God for Christ sake has forgiven you." – Ephesians 4:32

I sat there thinking. How had people treated Christ? People had not been too kind to Him. They beat and whipped Him. They spit in His face. They slapped Him around and yanked the beard off His face. They jammed thorns into His head and swore at Him. They threw Him down on some hard rough wooden cross and pounded iron spikes through His hands and feet. And what was His response to all of this? He loved and forgave them.

That got me thinking. I guess I've treated God pretty shabbily at times myself. Yet, he says that still loves me despite how badly I've treated Him.

So, I decided that I needed to follow the example of Christ. I needed the miracle of forgiveness in my life. I asked the Lord to remove the hatred I had in my heart for Peter, and He did. To Faye's amazement, this young man and I eventually became very good friends.

The day of the crash: November 11, 1946

Collana

We had been in Bolivia one year when we were invited to go to the fifty-year celebration at the church at Collana. Elder Bean and his wife, who were one of the first couples to pastor in the district, traveled with their son from Colorado to be present for the celebration. His son drove them all from Colorado through Mexico, down through Central America, and into South America in a Dodge van that had been set up as a rolling clinic. It was a tough trip for a couple in their eighties. But, they were there for the celebration. On Sabbath afternoon he showed us the little mud hut where his family had lived. At the side of the church were two tombstones. Under one lay the remains of their youngest son who had died there. I marveled at the dedication of these early missionaries.

In the middle of the afternoon, services were stopped for lunch. Blankets were spread on the ground. Indians ladies with their dark hair in braids scurried back and forth setting down pots of rice, chunos, soup, chicken and goat meat.

Chunos, in particular, are thought by the locals to be one of the greatest culinary delights of the world. It's hard to understand exactly how chunos taste without having actually tasted one. But, to get at least some idea as to the flavor of these delicacies, consider how chunos are prepared. The base substance of chunos is the potato. It is said that potatoes originated in Peru and Bolivia and there are a great many varieties of potatoes in this region, but chuno potatoes are unique to the Altiplano. They are small little potatoes that are grown at very high altitude. When they are harvested they are placed in water to soak and freeze. The water is then squeezed out by barefooted Indians who stomp on them for quite some time – and the process is then repeated several times. The final product is a black, smelly, freeze dried potato. The best way to eat them is not to chew them but swallow them while holding your nose. I don't know why but one little chola (Indian woman) thought it her duty to make sure my plate never stayed empty. As soon as I would finish choking down my chunos, she'd bring me some more – and I'd smile gratefully up at her as she grinned back at me with her toothless smile.

But, the conversation was good. I mostly just sat there listening to the stories of the old timers and the early days of establishing this local church.

Things had been very difficult in the early days. There had been a lot of prejudice against Adventists. One of the village chiefs, encouraged by the local priest, had repeatedly threatened to destroy the church. Wells were filled in with dirt and some of the buildings at the mission station were destroyed. One night he gathered a group of his friends together and they set out to attack members of the church who had gathered for prayer. To build up their courage, the gang of thugs first stopped by a tavern for some chicha (the local whiskey). After getting heavily intoxicated they staggered down the street yelling insults and oaths. Some of the townsfolk who heard them ran to the church to warn the members of what was about to happened. The doors were locked and the small group gathered closer together and prayed fervently for Divine help.

In a few minutes, storm clouds gathered, lightning flashed and thunder boomed so loudly it shook the ground. Suddenly large hail stones began to fall. The old chief and his companions were caught in the open ground between the town and the church. They quickly abandoned their attack and beat a retreat back to the tavern. They arrived bruised and bleeding. After a hasty conference, they decided to abandon their destruction of the church until a later date.

Several weeks later, the chief decided to strike again. This time the Bolivian cavalry, who just happened to be on maneuvers, rushed in and rescued the church members – and ended up staying for several weeks to protect the mission. Eventually, after multiple foiled attempts, the chief simply gave up trying to destroy the church. However, the Catholic priest didn't give up so easily.

The nearly toothless old man who was sitting next to me told me about the repeated efforts of the Catholic priest, Father Miguel, to destroy the church. One time, he had several of members kidnapped and taken to the Catholic Church. Pastor Ferdinand Stahl, who had just begun medical work among the Indians of the area, heard about this and got rather upset. Evidently, Pastor Stahl was not one to back down from a fight of any kind – and this was one of those times. So, he strapped on a big six gun with a belt of large bullets, mounted his big white mule, and rode over to the Catholic Church to meet with the priest. When he got in front of the church he dismounted, dropped the mules reigns on the ground, walked straight through the front door of the church, down the aisle, and up to the alter in the front of the church where Father Miguel was sitting.

"Stand up Padre. I've come for my members. I do not plan to leave without them."

The shocked priest sheepishly led Pastor Stahl to the back room where he found his missing members. They had been badly beaten to within an inch of their lives. It seemed as though he had arrived just in time or none of them would have survived the ordeal.

Of course, this event put Pastor Stahl on Father Miguel's radar screen and he tried, several times, to have Pastor Stahl killed. Then, one day, as fate would have it, Father Miguel came down sick. When Pastor Stahl heard about Father Miguel's illness, he decided to go to the priest's home and see if he could help him get better. So, he packed his medicines, kissed his wife goodbye and climbed up on his trusty white mule, and headed off on his two-day journey to where Father Miguel was lying sick on his deathbed.

Pastor Stahl stayed with the priest for two weeks. He bathed him, feed him and gave him his life-saving medicines. At the end of two weeks the priest had recovered enough to walk around the house and do a little housework. Ferdinand decided that the crisis had passed and he packed his things and loaded up his mule for the trip home. However, before he left, Father Miguel brought out a gift. He was insistent that Pastor Stahl take it - even though Pastor Stahl made it very clear, over and over again, that his services were free.

"I am not paying you," Father Miguel explained. "This is a little something that will show my appreciation for your kind service to me. I insist that you take it!"

So, finally, to be courteous, Pastor Stahl accepted the gift and tied the bag on the back of his saddle. It was a hot afternoon and he was glad when the sun went down and the dark shadows cooled the trail. He arrived home early in the morning. As he was unloading his things, the bag fell to the ground. So, he walked over, picked it up, and peeked inside. It was a large round ball of goat cheese – a local delicacy. However, on the long hot trip home, it had turned a bit rancid in a few spots on the outside.

"No matter," he thought to himself, "I'll simply trim off the outside of the cheese and it will still be just fine for supper."

Just then, however, his pet dog came bouncing up to greet him. So, he set the cheese down to give his dog a little pat on the head. Then, as he leaned down to pick up the saddle, his dog made a quick lunge for the cheese and made his escape around the back of the house. Pastor Stahl gave chase to try to retrieve his cheese. As he rounded the corner of the house, he saw that his dog had already eaten a bite off of the ball of cheese.

"That's Ok," he thought, "The rest will still be good."

He quickly walked toward his dog, commanding that he stop eating his cheese. The dog obeyed, dropped the ball of cheese, looked over at Pastor Stahl, and then, suddenly, fell over – dead!

Pastor Stahl was shocked! He took the ball of cheese over to a chemist friend to have it examined and found that it had been filled with arsenic. Luckily for Pastor Stahl and his family, only his dog had been harmed by Father Miguel's treachery.

Several weeks later Father Miguel was fully recovered and was visiting the Catholic Church in Collana. Later in the evening, following an afternoon of heavy drinking, the disheveled priest materialized from the side of an adobe tavern and swayed down the sidewalk toward the Adventist church. The sweet odor of chicha encircled him. In his drunken state, he never noticed the truck that was speeding down the street toward him. Then, just as the truck drew near he decided to cross the street. As he staggered out in front of the speeding truck, there was a loud screeching of brakes and then a sickening thud. When the driver realized what had happened, he quickly stepped on the gas and sped off in a swirl of dust, leaving the body of Father Miguel dead in the middle of the road – just a few paces from the little church there in Collana that he had tried so hard to destroy.

Traveling on Two Wheels

When we first arrived in Bolivia I was told that the job that I had been called to run no longer existed. After spending several months getting acquainted with the country, I was assigned to run rolling clinics and pastor several churches. Unfortunately, they informed me that there was no money to purchase a rolling clinic. They said that I would have to raise the money to buy one.

I always felt that these mission requests were like asking a doctor to come and run a hospital in the jungle only to be told, "By the way, we don't have a hospital, you'll have to raise the funds and build one!"

Eventually, I did raise just enough money to buy my own used Scout International – which proved to be a disaster. I never was able to get more than twenty miles down the road before something would break on the Scout and bring my journey for the service of humanity to a screeching halt.

Very quickly I was fully persuaded that I would spend a small fortune and my future inheritance on trying to fix that pile of bolts. So, I decided to sell the Scout and buy a more reliable, and therefore cheaper, method of transportation. With the money I received from the sale of the Scout, I went looking for a motorcycle. I soon found one at a motorcycle import business in Cochabamba. It was a Honda 350. It was brand new and the biggest bike they imported into the country.

My first big trip on my new Honda was down into the jungles of Chapare. I had received word from the mission office that there were several groups that needed a visit. So, I loaded up my bags with medicines and packed a few clothes for a one week trip. I would spend the Sabbath with a group of Adventists who lived where the road ended at the river. River boats unloaded cargo and empty gasoline drums and picked up supplies to take to the Beni. Dozens of trucks were parked by the river, all waiting to unload and load their cargos.

The road into Chapare was dangerous. It was so narrow that they only let traffic enter the region on Mondays, Wednesdays and Fridays. On the other days, traffic would be allowed to exit. So, I left early Monday morning before the sun had come up to head into Chapare. It is a beautiful trip. For several hours the road wound its way up the mountains and I rode above the clouds. It was a heady experience. Everything was so beautiful. Even the road down from the mountain into the jungle was quite spectacular. As I came down from the mountain tops into the jungle of Chapare, I crossed several streams that flowed from cascading waterfalls which spilled over the road and into the dark canyon below in a spray of mist on a background of lush green and beautiful colored flowers, exotic orchids, and millions of butterflies.

The thick brush and huge trees were beginning to envelop the road when I rounded a curve and suddenly met a large wild boar that came crashing through the underbrush and charged down the road right toward me. It happened so suddenly that I had very little time to think. I was moving along at a pretty good clip. The hog had razor sharp tusks that protruded from either side of his large bony head. I knew that if I put the brakes on too fast I might lose control of the bike in the loose gravel and it would slide out from under me. If that happened, the old tusker could inflict plenty of damage on me. So, in a split second, I decided to gun the bike and see if I could get by him. But, that old porker evidently had the very same idea. At the moment I swerved, he swerved too, in the same direction, directly into my path. I hit him head on. Suddenly, I felt myself levitating above the road with the bike under me. I must have cleared the ground by at least four feet - or more. As I was airborne, the hog was rolling down the road squealing loudly in protest. Time seemed to slow down and I saw and heard everything in slow motion. It seemed like quite some time before I came down and hit the road with a heavy jolt that nearly threw me over the handlebars. Somehow, miraculously, I managed to stay astride my Honda and maintained control. As time returned to a more normal speed, I looked behind me and saw the old hog stagger to his feet, shake himself vigorously, and charge angrily into the undergrowth beside the road – completely unharmed.

Late in the afternoon, I pulled up to the home of one of our leaders. Eduardo was butchering a goat in his front yard. His wife was at the side of the house cooking supper. He laid down his knife, wiped his hands on his pants and walked over to the motorcycle.

"Bienvenido!" (Welcome) he said with a grin.

As I dismounted he embraced me with a big hug. His smile was as bright as the late afternoon sun that was just touching the tops of the trees behind his house. He invited me to sit on their porch and introduced me to several members of his family. He waved to his wife.

"Maria, get Pastor Pitman something to drink."

Maria quickly disappeared into the house and soon returned with a large glass of lemonade. It was sweet and tart at the same time, quite good and very refreshing. She had squeezed the juice from several large lemons taken from a tree in her backyard.

After a few minutes of small talk, Eduardo rose from his chair and announced, "Let me show you around my place." Some distance from the back of his house ran a small stream from which a channel had been dug to bring water to the house. Conveniently, the water pooled in a rock-lined receptacle right next to the house.

Then, the overflow from this basin ran back to the stream down another channel.

"I made this for Maria." Eduardo smiled with pride. "It saves her having to walk down to the stream to get water for washing clothes and for cooking and drinking. It's also large enough to take our baths in."

I noticed a short distance upstream a little boy was urinating into the stream and further up pigs were wallowing in the muddy edge.

I suddenly remembered the lemonade. "This water looks so murky. How do you get such clear drinking water?" I asked, trying to hide the worried look on my face.

"Oh, that's easy. We just pour it into these big jugs and let it sit overnight. By morning all the junk has settled to the bottom and we have pure clear water for drinking."

I began to think about all the bugs that I just drank in that glass of lemonade - from amoebas to tapeworms.

"Oh Lord!" I silently pleaded. "Please save me."

I anxiously awaited the explosion of my bowels, but as the days went by nothing developed. I am certain that God performed a miracle for me that day. And, after that experience, I decided to give my first lecture on water hygiene. I spent the next few evenings giving Bible studies and health lectures with different groups throughout the area. And, during the daylight hours, I would hold clinics.

On Sunday morning that following week I awoke early. I had to get an early start to make it home before it got too dark. It would be about a ten-hour trip. So, I packed my things, said my goodbyes and promised to return soon.

The trip was uneventful until I started climbing into the mountains. I had been traveling about two hours when I came to a stream that was flowing over the road. The week before, I had crossed this stream with little difficulty. Now, I noticed that the road was rather wet, but I had no idea how much it had rained since I'd last been this way. So, I gunned the bike and entered the stream. In a matter of seconds, I was in serious trouble. The fast moving stream completely engulfed my bike and was quickly pushing me toward the edge of the road where the stream fell as a waterfall several hundred feet to the rocks below. I don't know why, but the bike kept running under water and the momentum got me across to the safety of the other side a few meters before I would have gone over the edge. However, as soon as I pulled out of the stream the bike backfired and died – and wouldn't start. I was soaked and it was getting very cold. So, I started walking, pushing my heavy Honda along the dusty road. Fortunately, not too far from the stream, I found several thatch-roofed huts. I was very glad to see that wisps of smoke were filtering out through the thatch. So, I pushed the bike up to the cluster of huts and announced my presence, but no one responded. Undaunted, I poked my head into the darkened doorway of one of the huts and saw a little old lady cooking in one corner of the room and an old man lying on a cot at the other end. I asked if I could use the heat of her fire to dry some clothes. She nodded, but said nothing. I pulled my soaked sweater and a pair of jeans out of my bag and wrung the water out of them as best as I could and placed them on poles near the fire. As soon as I had warmed myself a little I went outside to work on my motorcycle.

I removed the spark plug and dried it out by the fire. However, the bike still wouldn't start. So, I removed the air filters and dried them – and then dried the carburetor too, and several other parts. I dried everything I could possibly dry. Between my clothes and motorcycle parts the little hut looked like a Chinese laundry. After several hours my clothes and my motorcycle were pretty dry and warm. I changed clothes outside behind a rock fence and then proceeded to reassemble my bike.

I prayed a little prayer and after the third kick on the starter, it roared to life. I let the bike run a few minutes while I went back to the hut and handed the little lady some money and said "Gracias Señora".

She smiled with two or three of her teeth remaining as she said, "Gracias Señor."

It was late in the afternoon and the sun was beginning to set when I finally started on my journey again. I knew that the road would still be open until midnight, so I still had a few hours remaining to finish my trip. As darkness settled down and I began to gain altitude on the twisting mountain road I became aware that the temperature was also dropping precipitously and I started to get very cold again. I stopped the bike and put on my sweater and rain breaker and felt much better. By now I had reached the top of the mountain and was driving through intermittent cloud banks. Suddenly, as I rounded a corner, a bright light pierced through the dense fog. It was a large wide truck. And, it was bearing down at me at a very fast clip. What was that truck doing there at this hour?! No trucks were supposed to be on this road going this direction until after midnight! But, there it was and I had to react quickly or I would be crushed like a bug! Instinctively and pulled hard to the right and headed for the edge of the road, hoping that there would be enough room for the truck to pass without clipping into me and knocking me over the cliff. Fortunately, the truck missed me, but the road was wet and muddy and the brakes on my motorcycle did not slow me down at all when I applied them. So, I went right on over the edge of the cliff anyway down toward the rocks hundreds of feet below. Fortunately, angels must have been with me or I wouldn't be here today writing this story. Somehow, I landed, still sitting upright on my bike, on a small ledge just a few yards down the face of the cliff. If I'd come down just a few feet in any other direction, I would have missed that small ledge entirely and fallen to my death. I just sat there in stunned silence in the deep darkness trying to adjust to what had just happened. My pants were ripped and I was bleeding from a small wound on the side of my head. Although I was in some pain, I didn't think anything was broken. I was able to stand up and, with great effort, I managed to drag the heavy bike up to the road. And, miraculously, it started. However, as I started to drive down the road again, I noticed that I was having difficulty seeing out of my left eye.

Several hours later I arrived at a small truck stop at the bottom of the mountain. I was cold and hungry. So, I decided to stop and get something warm to eat and drink and also fill up my gas tank. Several trucks were parked there waiting for midnight so that they could continue their trip to the jungle. As I entered the restaurant one grizzly truck driver looked up at me from his table and inquired, "Who did you get into a fight with?"

"No one! Why do you ask?" I grinned.

He smiled as he shook his head, "Señor, you look terrible!"

The sun was just coming up when I drove my bike into the driveway of our house in Cochabamba. Faye came running out of the house to greet me.

"What in the world happened to you?" she said with concern in her voice and fear in her eyes. "Your left eye is completely filled with blood and your clothes are all ripped up and torn."

"Well," I explained, "God has been especially good to me on this trip. Remember the text in the Bible where God says that, "The angel of the Lord encamps round about those who fear him and He delivers them" (Psalms 34:7)? Well, my angel sure worked overtime on this trip! I'm just glad to be alive! Come into the house and I'll tell you all about it..."

Puerto Adventista

Puerto Adventista was a thousand-acre ranch located on the Mamori River – one of many tributaries of the giant Amazon River. The Adventist mission had tried for many years to make the Puerto Adventista Ranch profitable, in order to support a boarding school in the Beni. The ranch was supposed to provide work opportunities for the students to pay for their own education.

At that time, the most promising industries in the region were cattle and lumber. Several North American families had donated cattle and equipment for the project. However, because of poor management and greed, the school never materialized. In fact, several of the "caretakers" hired to work at the ranch had actually sold off most of the cattle and pocketed the money. When the mission inquired about the losses, they were told that disease, thieves, and even attacks from wild cats had decimated the mission's large herd of cattle.

Finally, the mission decided to fly Dr. Louis Navallo, the general farm manager who usually worked at the boarding school in Cochabamba, over to the ranch in order to make an assessment of what to do with the remaining cattle. I was chosen, for some reason, to be his assistant.

A few days later, Jerry, the mission pilot, met Louis and me at the San Joaquin airport to fly us into Puerto Adventista. The mission plane was an old Cessna 150. Since parts were hard to come by, it was rather bedraggled looking and seemed like it was held together with bailing wire. We were lucky the plane flew at all and prayed for a miracle that it would make it to the ranch. A motorcycle battery substituted for the original, the tail wheel was cut from an old truck tire and bolted together - and there was a constant miss in the engine. For most of the trip, we flew just a few feet over the tops of the trees and could easily see many details not usually seen in a flight over the jungle. At one point we flew over a very large tree that was growing along the bank of a river. It was a beautiful tree. However, as I was admiring its beauty, I noticed a massive snake lying on one of its branches. My eyes were as wide as saucers. I'd never seen a snake remotely close to the size of this one – as big around as one of the main branches of the tree!

"Hey Louis!" I yelled over my shoulder, "You'll never believe what I saw dangling in that large tree we just flew over!"

"What?!" he yelled back as he quickly looked out the window.

"A snake that was big enough to eat me as an *hors d'oeuvre*! It was absolutely huge!"

"Well, they do get pretty big in the Beni," Jerry said as he turned and grinned at me. "Just a few weeks ago they had a baptism at Magdelena. Well, sort of. You see, there is a big old anaconda that lives somewhere along the river near Magdelena. People have been trying to catch him for years. He is probably one of the biggest snakes in the world. They swear he is over thirty feet long! Anyway, it was Sabbath afternoon at the time and a large crowd had already gathered on the banks of the San Miguel River. The pastor preached a stimulating sermon before he finally led the candidates out into the water for the baptism service. The choir was singing hymns and the pastor had just raised his hand toward heaven to pray when the choir suddenly stopped singing and the crowd fell perfectly silent. Then, a couple seconds later, several ladies began to scream and frantically point toward the water behind the pastor. The candidates and the pastor turned to look behind them where, to their shock, they saw El Viejo, the giant anaconda! His large head was raised above the water and he was swimming directly toward the pastor. Witnesses said that the terrified pastor forgot all about his flock and shot out of the water like a Polaris missile leaving a nuclear sub and collapsed on the shore - with the baptismal candidates not far behind. At this point, the anaconda slipped soundlessly under the dark water and disappeared.

Several weeks passed before anyone had the nerve to try to reschedule the baptism. This time, however, the pastor held the baptism in a quiet little pond where they only had a few piranha to worry about.

Of course, El Viejo remains at large and his legend grows as people continue to try to catch him."

Surprisingly, Jerry's story had calmed me down a bit and I mentioned that when I was a little boy my dad happened to be walking down a trail one day near Guajara Mirim when he stepped on a large log that had fallen across his path. When he put his whole weight on it, the log began to coil. It turned out to be a huge boa constrictor! However, he didn't stick around long enough to measure it.

"I don't know about these stories," laughed Louis, "Are you sure they're true?"

"Oh yes, I'm sure they're real!' I protested. "After all, I just saw one in that tree back there with my own eyes!"

"There's Puerto," interrupted Jerry as he swung the plane around on its final approach. He put what remained of the flap down, and flared the plane gently over the runway. Finally, we had arrived safe and sound and I was glad to be stepping out of that death trap.

This was my first visit to Puerto. The ranch house was located on the edge of the river. It had a thatched roof, mud brick walls, and a concrete floor. The airstrip lay at the front of the house and served two purposes - as both a landing strip and a cow pasture. The mission had sent a radio message to Puerto to inform the caretaker there that we were coming and to clear the cows off of the airstrip. Also, the word of our arrival had spread far and near and a large crowd had gathered to meet us. I set up a medical/dental clinic at a little house nearby and Louis crossed the river to enlist the help of ranchers to help check on the mission's cattle. I checked the people who lined up to see me for TB, worms, bad teeth and general illnesses that commonly affected people in the Beni.

In about an hour, Louis returned with an assortment of cowboys. He announced, "They tell me that the cattle across the river have contracted hoof and mouth disease. If we are going to save the mission's few remaining cattle, we will need to vaccinate them."

Then, like a general taking command of his troops, Louis issued orders.

"Tui, you'll have to stop what you are doing and help me with these cows if we are going to finish before sundown. Sabbath starts about seven this evening and we have a lot to do before then. However, you can keep on seeing patients until we get the cattle rounded up and into the corrals."

Then, pointing a finger at Jerry he commanded, "Jerry, you fly into Trinidad and get the vaccine for the cows. We should have everything ready in a couple of hours."

The people in the Beni travel long distances by one of two ways: by air or on the river. Obviously, however, river travel took a lot longer than traveling by air. One could travel distances in minutes by air that it would literally take days to travel in a boat on the river. So, however beat-up our plane may have been, we were still very glad to have it.

We rolled a drum of gasoline from the shed out near the plane and poured the gasoline into buckets through a chamois. After filling the gas tanks on the plane, Jerry went around to the front to prop the plane while I climbed in to apply the brakes. After a few flips of the prop, the engine came to life. As smoke billowed from the plane, Jerry climbed in and I climbed out. He yelled above the noise, "Don't worry! I'll check on some new plugs for this engine when I get to Trinidad." Then, he turned the plane into the wind and gunned the engine. The plane struggled a bit to leave the runway and then slowly climbed skyward. He circled over the ranch, waggled his wings at us a couple times, and head toward Trinidad.

Meanwhile, back at the ranch, Louis was busy with the hunt for the cattle. I spent most of the morning pulling rotten teeth and getting rid of worms. The worms would come out like piles of spaghetti.

Shortly after lunch, I saw Louis and the cowboys driving the cattle in front of them. They arrived amid yells, bellowing, and whistles. They herded the cattle into large corrals on the other side of the airstrip. There were also a couple large sheds near these corrals, which contained the farm equipment. So, I walked over to the corrals to take a look.

The cows were the wildest looking animals I had ever seen. They had enraged blood-shot eyes and huge horns ready for use on anything that got in their way. They sharpened their horns on the posts and railings of the corral and looked for anyone to impale like a shish kebab. Finally, the cowboys managed to coax the last of these beasts into the corral.

Then, in the midst of all the excitement, Jerry flew in with the vaccine. I noticed that the plane's engine sounded a bit better.

"He found some new plugs," I said to myself.

Jerry had also picked up a passenger. His name was Juan Gomez. Juan had a ranch about fifteen miles from Puerto and wanted a lift. I met Jerry and Juan at the edge of the runway and picked up the vaccines.

"It will not take me too long to get Juan to his ranch and then I'll be right back to help," he shouted as he and Juan headed back across the strip to the plane. "Don't worry about helping me crank the plane, Juan can do it."

I began to walk toward the sheds with the package that held the vaccines. When I reached the sheds I turned to watch Juan and Jerry start the plane. Jerry leaned into the plane and gave instructions to Juan. "Push on the pedals with your toes. Crack the throttle open a little and flip the switch to 'on' when I yell contact.

"Got it," Juan said with a nod of his head.

Jerry made his way to the front of the plane, gave the prop a couple of turns to prime the engine, and then grabbed the prop with both hands and yelled, “Contacto!” as he gave a strong yank on the prop.

There was a pop and a cloud of smoke and the engine roared to life. At this point, however, Juan became so excited that he forgot about keeping his foot on the break. And, before Jerry could make it around and jump into the plane, the plane began to taxi down the runway. Jerry froze for a minute in disbelief. Then, after a few seconds, he began to wildly chase after the plane yelling at the top of his voice “Kill it, kill it!”

If something did not stop that plane it would soon be airborne! Jerry told me later that he was praying over and over again for God to stop the plane as he chased after it. The situation appeared to be hopeless. Then, all of a sudden, the plane swerved to the left, hit a large ant pile on the side of the runway, spun around a couple of times, and stalled. Jerry reached the plane and yanked open the door and killed the engine. Everyone ran up to assess the damage, which didn’t appear to be much. Juan, however, was quite shaken as he staggered out of the plane. His face was pale, his hands were trembling, and his knees were quite wobbly. When Jerry suggested that he get back into the plane, Juan flatly refused. He insisted that the much longer trip by boat would be preferable to certain death in that plane.

After we pushed the plane back to the front of the ranch house, Jerry walked over with us to the corrals. We told Jerry that maybe he should have taken up running rather than flying.

“You’re pretty quick on your feet there buddy,” I laughed as I slapped him on the back.

“It wasn’t half as bad as it looked,” Jerry grinned. “You should have been here when Elder Wilcox came into Puerto from the South American Division Headquarters for a visit. After his visit, as they were taxing to take off, the planes’ left wheel hit a hole that some animal had dug in the runway during the night. In an instant, the front of the plane went down and the prop hit the ground and almost bent in half!. Fortunately, no one was hurt. The pilot took the prop off the plane and beat it with a sledgehammer to straighten it out. Of course, after that, the prop had a lot of dents in it, but otherwise, it looked pretty good. So, he put the prop back on the plane and started it off. Of course, it vibrated the whole plane something fierce! It was so bad that it looked like the engine was going to be shaken right off the plane! Understandably, Elder Wilcox refused to get into the plane. So, they had to call for a military plane to fly him out of Puerto. Then, ironically, the military plane actually crashed during a landing at a fuel station and was totaled. Again, God's hand was with Elder Wilcox so that he was unhurt. Yet another plane had to be sent in to fly him out. Anyway, I'm just glad we don't have to get another prop. It took several months to get a prop to replace the one Elder Wilcox broke!"

As soon as Jerry finished his story about Elder Wilcox, Señor Louis, the vet, came over to the shed and announced that the cows were ready to be vaccinated. Louis was a short, middle-aged, slightly bald man with eyelids that were just a bit droopy. He didn't look as intelligent nor as energetic and enthusiastic as he really was. No matter what he did, he did it with all of his might. As a young man at the university, he had become an ardent communist. So, he was thrilled when he won a scholarship to study veterinary medicine in Moscow. However, after a few years of watching communism in practice, up close and personal, he was completely disillusioned with communism. After his training, he left Russia and returned to Bolivia to start a new life in his own native country. Soon after he arrived back home, he began to date the sister of a friend. As fate would have it, she turned out to be a Seventh-day Adventist. He really liked her and wanted to marry her as soon as possible. So, she had little trouble persuaded him to attend church with her. At first, he attended just to please her. But, despite himself, he started listening to the sermons and liked what he heard. It wasn't too long before he decided to be baptized and join the church. By the time I met him, he was a very committed Christian.

"Tui," he once told me, "I am convinced that all the 'isms' of this world will never solve a man's problems. Only Jesus can do that."

Louis stood outside the shed yelling above the noise of the corrals. "Tui, I am going to teach you how to shoot cows without a gun." He held up a big syringe in his right hand.

"We need to work fast if we are going to vaccinate them all before dark," He said as he smiled and pointed at the large syringe with a needle the size of a ten penny nail. "This is your weapon against disease. We've got plenty of vaccine. The bottles are in boxes next to the large corral." He looked in the direction of a young stocky teenage boy. "He will be your ayudante (helper)." Then, turning back to me Louis shouted, "Tui, have you ever done this before?"

The sun was gleaming off his sweaty bald head. "Not on cows like those," I stammered, trying to hide the fact that I'd really never done this sort of thing at all.

The cows continued to bellow, kick up dust, and swing their massive horns around from side to side. "Now, watch me carefully Tui! I'll demonstrate the proper technique on the first few cows. Then, you can do it on your own. It is simple! You'll have no problems at all."

Now, I had experienced a few cows in my time, but nothing like these cows. As a teenager, I worked on a dairy farm in Tennessee. I went to work at 4 a.m. and milked 52 sweet, gentle Jerseys. My buddies and I thought we were having a wild time when we went to the back lot and rode the heifers and were thrown into the manure pile. These wild cows made me feel like a matador with two left feet and they looked at me like I had a big red bull's eye painted on my chest.

"Let one in," yelled Louis to a cowboy standing near one of the gates.

The gate swung open and a big bull rushed in. The bull stopped for a moment and surveyed the scene before him, lowered his head, and charged straight for Louis. I turned my head and tried not to look, but I just couldn't help myself. Out of the corner of one eye I saw the huge bull charging right at Louis and I knew this was the end of my poor friend. Then, just before he reached Louis, he suddenly fell to his knees as if shot by a bullet. Two cowboys had thrown their rawhide ropes around the bull's neck and legs and secured the ends of their rope to a large dead tree in the middle of the corral. Before the bull knew what hit him, Louis rushed in and gave him a jab in the neck with a syringe full of vaccine. Another cowboy neatly applied a brush full of red paint to the head of the stunned bull. Then, the cowboys ran over and loosened their ropes. The old bull struggled to his feet and shook his large horns defiantly at them. However, he actually heeded the yelling and whistling as the cowboys directed him out of the corral. The whole thing went down like a beautiful ballet. I was very impressed. It looked so easy.

"See," laughed Louis, "There is nothing to it."

I was convinced. So, I eagerly climbed into the corral to get started. And, at first, things did in fact go rather smoothly.

"Perhaps Louis was right?" I said to myself. "This is as easy as falling off a log! These cows aren't so smart after all! – not much different than the milk cows I knew as a kid."

As I gained more and more confidence, I worked faster and faster and became more and more bold, and careless. Soon, the cows were coming in so fast that it was hard to keep track of them all. Then, one of the cowboys forgot to choke down a cow after tying her down. Without noticing this, Louis yelled over to me, "I'll get her!" as he ran up to her and gave her a jab with his syringe. A split second later, like a flash of lightening, she whirled around and, with her back hoof, kicked Louis right on his backside with all of her might and Louis went flying. He landed head first into in a pile of manure that the cowboys had raked up.

"I am alright. I am alright," he kept repeating as we ran over to him. Still, he didn't get up. His pants were ripped and a large and very deep red gash on his buttocks indicated that he wasn't alright. We helped him to his feet and steadied him on both sides as we helped him hobble to the shed where we dressed his wounds. The pain finally hit him.

"I am out of commission," he moaned. "Tui, you and Jerry will have to take over."

I looked at my hands, which were already blistered and bleeding from jabbing my syringe into tough hides for several hours. Now, I was going to have to work even harder, but the job had to be done. And, so far, I was doing quite well. Things were going so well in fact that I hardly even looked up anymore when the gate opened for the next victim.

Then, I saw him. At first, I did a double take because I couldn't quite believe my eyes. This time, when the gate opened, I saw the largest bull that I had ever seen in my entire life enter the corral. His horns spread out from his head like two branches of a large oak tree and huge muscles rippled on his back. He trotted out like he was the king of this domain before stopping at the opposite end of the corral to look things over. Evidently, he didn't like was he saw. His eyes glared at me. As soon as he saw me he lowered his massive head in my direction and started snorting and pawing the ground. Dust went high into the air and partially obscured the great beast. I began to feel a bit strange, just a bit queasy. Then, I lost all nerve and gave way to absolute terror as he bellowed and charged out of the dust cloud. He looked like a freight train coming right at me - and I froze to the ground, unable to scream or wiggle even my little finger. At this moment, one of the cowboys did actually manage to throw his rope over the big bull's horns, but the bull was too quick and far too strong. He pulled the cowboy along behind him like he was waterskiing. The cowboy had no time to wrap the rope around the dead tree. However, it did allow me a fraction of a second to gain my wits and make a leap for it. I literally jumped clean over the fence beside me as the bull's horns missed me by a fraction of an inch. Then, the bull whirled around to charge at the cowboys who were at the opposite end of the corral. As the bull began his second charge, another cowboy ran up and threw his rope, which caught the bull's front legs. In an instant, this mighty beast fell as though he were nothing more than a sack of potatoes tossed to the ground. Quickly, another cowboy ran up and threw his rope around the bull's head and slung the other end around the old tree. The bull staggered to his feet and began to pull and throw his head around, but this only caused the rope to tighten more and more around his neck, cutting off his air supply. Moments later, the bull fell to the ground - unconscious.

Now, I was suddenly brave again. I climbed back over the fence, quickly ran to the side of the fallen bull, and plunged the needle into his huge neck. Then, the cowboys ran up and released their ropes. I felt a little cocky about our subjection of this monster, who was still unconscious. So, I turned my back on him as I casually walked toward the opposite end of the corral. Suddenly, my daydreaming was shattered. All of the cowboys were jumping up and down yelling at me. It was hard to understand what they were saying given all the noise they were making. So, I turned around just in time to see the bull coming at me like a hurricane. He was only a few yards away, giving me only enough time to notice that his head was lowered and his horns were bobbing back and forth as he tried to decide which horn to kill me with. There was no chance to escape. So, just before impact, I closed my eyes and went limp. In an instant I was spinning in all directions before landing in a heap on the ground. I felt a searing pain shoot through my left knee. Miraculously, I'd only been hit by one of the horns, and was somewhat surprised to still be alive. But, I still kept my eyes tightly closed. I just knew that in a couple of seconds those razor-sharp horns would be sticking into some vital part of my anatomy or that his massive head would smash me like a little bug.

However, in a flash those cowboys were all over that bull, beating him with ropes and sticks to divert the bull's attention long enough so that someone could drag me out of the corral. Their quick reaction had saved my life! However, they still didn't have him entirely under control and he literally tore up part of the fencing of the corral and several cows escaped through the hole.

Jerry came running up to me as I lay moaning there on the ground.

"Are you badly hurt?" he asked.

"I think my knee has problems," I said through clenched teeth. Help me get over to the shed so that Louis can have a look at it."

Jerry called over one of the cowboys and together they carried me over to the shed. My head was beginning to spin. Louis was also still in significant pain, but he stood up, groaned, and hobbled over to take a look at me.

"Well Tui, let's see what that crazy bull did to you."

With a wince, he lowered himself to the ground and carefully pulled aside my torn pants. The area around my knee was turning black and blue and was beginning to swell. Fortunately, the bull had not gored me, but his horn had hit my knee with such force that one of the larger blood vessels in my leg had ruptured. In a few minutes my left leg was twice the size of my right leg.

Louis wiped the sweat off his head and looked at the cattle in the corrals. "This place is a disaster," he declared. Pieces and parts of fencing were scattered all over. The cowboys were able to repair the fencing and soon rounded up the cattle that had escaped. However, Jerry was looking a bit worried. In a solemn voice he said, "I guess I'll have to get in there and finish the job."

Louis and I both responded at the same time.

"No way!"

Louis added, "We only have a few cows left to vaccinate. Better that a few cows perish than we all end up dead. In this situation we need a pilot healthy enough to fly out the wounded!"

I looked over at the corrals where the cows that were yet to be vaccinated were bellowing. The cowboys were cursing at them and trying to get them set up for another round. I noticed that most of the cowboys had been injured that day - in one way or another.

So, I yelled over at them, "Let the cattle go! We're done for the day!"

The battle was finally over and the cows had won. Well, perhaps it was a stalemate. With the help of the cowboys, we made our way to the plane. Louis paid the cowboys for their work and Jerry put our luggage on the plane. With a lot of groans and moans, Louis and I situated ourselves in our seats. We said our goodbyes and promised to be back soon. Then, with tremendous effort, I worked the brakes as Jerry flipped the prop. The plane roared to life and Jerry climbed aboard. In a few minutes, we were in the air. As the plane banked over Puerto Adventista we could see the cows, now the size of ants, streaming across the scrubland. From our perch high in the air the cows didn't seem nearly as intimidating as they had moments before. The sun was beginning to sink as the Sabbath hours approached.

From time to time I've thought about this experience and reminded myself that the struggles and trials of this life that seem like huge insurmountable mountains are, from God's perspective, nothing more than little ants to be solved with a flick of His finger. I then remind myself that someday the problems, struggles, and pain that we've faced in this old world will seem insignificant, maybe even trivial, when viewed from the light of heaven. For me, this helps me look beyond the trials of this life that seem to overwhelm me at times, knowing that nothing is too hard for God.

Tarija

In the middle of February of 1972, the mission received a letter from "Alfredo de Palmyra." Alfredo was asking if it would be possible for the mission to send a pastor to Palmyra to study and baptize a fairly large group people who had become interested in the Adventist faith. Alfredo went on to explain that on a trip to Santa Cruz to pick up supplies for his business he had come across some Adventist literature. After reading it, he enthusiastically started sharing what he had learned with his friends and neighbors.

The Mission decided to send Peter, the Mission youth director. I was to tag along to hold clinics and help with the Bible studies. This was exciting news! It seemed to me like it would be a grand adventure. However, the trip would not be easy. Palmyra is a very isolated valley high in the Andean Mountains located near the Argentinean border. Getting there requires riding a mule for several days along treacherous trails that wind through magnificent mountains and steep valleys. The closest town of any size was Tarija.

Tarija was a good-sized town at that time, with a road, an airstrip, and a rail line. Peter contacted me by radio and we made plans to meet in Tarija. We would spend a couple of days purchasing supplies there in Tarija before taking a truck some forty miles to meet Alfredo and his mules for our trek through the mountains to Palmyra.

I decided to take the train from Cochabamba to Tarija. I enjoyed riding on the old trains. They were pulled by wheezy old steam engines and had a very rustic feel about them as they moved through some of the most beautifully rugged country in the world. I would look out of my unwashed window and soak it all in as the track bent itself around mountains and crossed deep chasms that contained gurgling brooks playing leap frog over moss-covered boulders. Occasionally our train would vanish into the mountain side and darkness would engulf us. There seemed to be something mysterious about these mountains. The Indians worshiped them.

"Excuse me Señor," my Indian seat mate interrupted my thoughts when he saw me staring in amazement out of my window, "You can never trust the mountains! You have to be careful of the mountain gods. You have to stay on the good side of them. They can get angry. That is why I always make a peace offering to them of chicha (corn liquor). When things get really bad we offer them llamas (an animal related to camel) to calm them down."

As I sat there looking at these enormous mountains, I sympathized with the fear and even superstition of my Indian friend. In my own travels around in and through these mountains, I'd seen many very strange things happen. The mountains could definitely turn on a man. It was difficult to even scratch out a living among them and I could see how someone who didn't know any better could come away with a sense that these mountains were alive and vengeful beings who demanded sacrifices to be appeased. In fact, in years past, many humans had been sacrificed to these mountains. Their mummified remains are still being discovered to this day. Occasional stories would still come around every now and again of human sacrifices still taking place among these mountains. And, even I would occasional feel that the devil was using these mountains to try to murder me and my family. My father had been killed in a plane crash on the peaks of Tunari when an unexpected storm had trapped him and his pilot in a blind-end canyon, causing them to fly into the mountain side. I had seen huge boulders tumbling down the mountain in an apparent attempt to crush the life out of my family while we traveled the narrow mountain roads. Mountain streams had snatched away my little boy Sean as we swam, and only with the grace of God had I been able to save him. I hated to admit it, but I was a little nervous when it came to those mountains... and I gave my Indian friend a knowing and sympathetic nod as I added, “But, God is good to us”.

Our train frequently stopped at small mountain villages. Peddlers would board the train with trays piled high with food, cooked pork, goat and chicken, kettles of rice, chunos (potatoes), small loaves of bread, coffee and chicha. I bought a small loaf of bread and quickly washed it down with some chicha fresca (the unfermented form of the corn drink). I was starving and that bread and chicha fresca really hit the spot. The pleasant chatter of Indian sales women, clad in bright hand-woven dresses and bowler hats, brought all the sleepy passengers to life. Some of the passengers made their way down the aisle, stepped off the train, and nonchalantly relieved themselves alongside the track. After about twenty minutes or so, the engineer blew the whistle and passengers made last-minute purchases before hurriedly maneuvering their way back to their seats. As the connectors banged together, huge clouds of smoke billowed from the old steam engine and the train slowly began to move down the track. I watched once more as Bolivia swept by outside my window. The train seemed to sway and lurch, like a local drunk heading home after a long night at the bar.

We traveled all night. Then, just as the sun was rising over the tops of the mountains, we pulled into Tarija Station. The porter made his way down the aisle announcing loudly, “Estamos en Tarija!” I rubbed the sleep out of my eyes, put on my backpack, reached down to pick up the rest of my luggage. I moved along with the others toward the doorway and stepped down onto the platform. The station appeared almost deserted. I wandered outside and spied a vintage taxi parked on the empty street. At first, there didn’t seem to be anyone inside. It was all rather strange. Where was everyone? I walked over and circled the car slowly. There was an old man, with his head thrown back against a folded coat, asleep in the back seat. Small snorts punctuated his breathing. I gently knocked on the window. No response. Then I yelled at him through the window.

“Is this taxi available?!”

The old man shot up like a jack-in-the-box. “Si Señor. Where do you want to go?”

“I want to go to the Seventh-day Adventist church,” I replied.

“Yes, I know where it is. It is close. But, this early in the morning I will charge you extra and you pay in advance,” he added rubbing his eyes with one hand.

I handed him some bills and threw my luggage into the back seat and slammed the door several times to get it to shut. A couple blocks later we arrived at the church. I would have walked if I had known it was just down the street. I laughed to myself and shook my head as I got out of the taxi and unloaded my things.

“Smart taxi driver to charge me before I found out...”

There was a little old lady sweeping the street in front of the church. The taxi left and I turned to talk the woman. “Do you know anyone who can let me into the church?”

She smiled and answered, “I live in the church and I have been waiting for you. Your room is waiting for you.” Looking at me with questioning eyes she continued, “I was told there were two of you coming. Where is your friend?”

“Oh,” I responded, “My friend is coming later today on the plane.” She smiled again. “I’ll have his room ready too.”

I followed her through the front door of the church across a patio toward a set of rooms. She stopped in front of one of the doors and fumbled in the pocket of her apron for the right key. I noticed her calloused hands and her stooped shoulders. She did have an angelic smile, but was missing most of her teeth. Life had been hard for her, but she still radiated such a sweetness of character. She opened the door and step back for my approval. The room was small but clean.

“It’s wonderful,” I smiled down at her. “With all the stops, the noise and hard wooden seats on the train, I’ve slept very little and would like to take a nap.”

“I’ll be around the church if you need anything,” she smiled back at me as she turned and walked across the patio. I closed the door and, still fully clothed, threw myself onto the bed.

In what seemed like a few moments later, loud pounding on the door jolted me to consciousness.

“Who is it?” I mumbled.

"It's me, Peter!" he called out joyfully as he swung the door open and walked into my room. I rolled over to the side of the bed and sat up.

"What time is it?"

"According to the little old lady outside, you have been sleeping all morning. Siesta time is over my friend!" Slapping me on the back he continued, "Up and at it! We've got a lot to do before we leave on our trip tomorrow."

Peter was big, tall, and blonde, and stuck out like a sore thumb among all the dark-skinned dark-haired Indian natives. Everyone could see us coming from a mile away and it seemed as though everyone wanted to sell us something. The town had gone from what seemed like a ghost town to a bustling metropolis.

Somehow we made our way through the crowd to the large central market. Coca vendors spread piles of leaves in front of them on the ground. Carcasses of butchered cattle hung in the open air, gathering swarms of flies. Rows of lifeless heads of cattle lined the street, staring into space. It was enough to make anyone want to be a vegetarian. In fact, I had actually been a vegetarian when I first arrived in Bolivia. However, I found that being a vegetarian had some tremendous problems. When I told the Indians that I was a vegetarian, they served me rice with fried eggs piled on top. Eggs were very expensive for them. I didn't want to throw the eggs away, especially when the cook sat there and watched me eat. That would have been most rude of me. So, I ended up eating a great many eggs. I remember that during a particular two-week trip visiting various towns and villages I ate fifty-two eggs! That was enough to start a small egg business. I was sure that eating that many eggs was going to give me a heart attack sooner than later. So, I asked myself, which was worse? - The chicken or the egg? I decided to go for the chicken. However, as I pondered the hanging meat in the market turning black with flies, I began to have second thoughts about the wisdom of my decision to turn carnivorous.

Peter was moving fast. If he hadn't been so tall and blonde, it would have been hard to keep track of him. He quickly moved from place to place bargaining excitedly for items that we were going to need for our trip. The smells of the food and the conversations of the people distracted me. Soon, I was so busy bargaining for something that I actually I lost track of Peter. But, in about an hour I came across him dragging several large bags behind him.

"Hey," he grinned, "I've got a few more bags back there. See if you can find us a taxi."

Although taxis were at a premium, I managed to find one. It was my old friend from the train station. I promised to pay him well if he would wait for us as we drug the bags with our purchases and piled them in the trunk and the back seat. At the last moment, Peter decided to run back to the market to buy a few items he'd somehow forgotten.

"I won't be long," he yelled as he disappeared into the crowd. After a few minutes, the impatient driver began to honk his horn and Peter reappeared loaded with more large bags. As he ran toward us at top speed he suddenly tripped over a pothole in the road and fell spread eagle onto the street. His bags flew in every direction. I rushed to where he was trying to pick himself up.

"Hey buddy, you all right," I asked as I tried to help him up?

"Oh, I don't think so," he moaned. "I think I have messed up something pretty good!"

"Let's see if you can stand up," I said, trying to sound encouraging.

Peter was heavy! I strained with all my might, but couldn't budge him. I motioned to the driver for help.

"Hey you, cab driver, please come over here and help me get my friend to the cab."

"My name is Raúl," he said as he came to my rescue.

Together Raúl and I were able to help slowly inch Peter to his feet and maneuvered him to the car.

Peter continued to complain, "There is something wrong with my neck. I can't turn my head." Putting his hand to his neck he moaned, "I must have messed up a disc. It hurts like crazy!"

The cab driver and I worked very hard trying to get Peter into the cab. We pleaded, threatened, yelled, and coaxed and finally, after much groaning and yelling, on the part of Peter as well, we were finally able to get Peter into the back seat of the taxi.

"Where to now?" Raúl ask me as we caught our breath.

"Oh, please drive us to the church Raúl. I've got some medicine for pain that I can give Peter. I hope that will help him feel a little better."

But nothing happened. Raúl didn't start the taxi. Instead, he looked over his shoulder at me and whispered, "I know a cura that does wonders with sickness."

"What did he say?" moaned Peter.

Raúl raised his voice, "I know a doctor who uses natural remedies to heal the sick. He is very good at what he does!"

"He's a witch doctor," I explained to Peter.

Raúl shot back, "No, no! He really is a terrific healer! People from all around here go to see him. He has had some miraculous healings. You should try him."

Peter only grunted in response.

"Well, Peter," I smiled. "We've got to try something. Our truck leaves tomorrow and we have people waiting for us. This cura is the only 'doctor' in town. Maybe it is worth a try. Raúl seems to think he is terrific."

I looked back at Peter with a hopeful smile. Peter groaned, rolled his eyes and said, "I think I am going to throw up!" Raúl jumped out of the front seat of the car and threw open the back door.

"Get out!" he exclaimed as he pointed toward the street. Peter managed to climb out of the cab and, in a few moments, the contents of Peter's dinner hit the pavement.

"Please take me to the cura," Peter moaned, "I've got to have some relief!"

In a few minutes, the taxi was headed toward the outskirts of town. Though he tried, Peter found it difficult to sit up. As the neighborhood became more and more dilapidated the road followed suit. Real concern crossed Peter's face as we hit larger and larger potholes. Between clenched teeth he muttered, "What are you getting me into?"

"Don't worry," Raúl replied as he maneuvered around large piles of garbage. Dogs and cats were playing hide and seek in the holes and mounds that littered the street.

Suddenly Raúl slammed on the brakes as he spun the steering wheel. The taxi jerked to the left and we were all thrown to the right. Peter yelled out in pain as he slammed against the back door.

"I am going to have to fix those brakes," Raúl muttered to himself. Then, clearing his throat, he cheerily announced, "We're here!"

Peter cocked one eye opened and looked out the window. "Am I dead?" he moaned.

I slowly opened the door and got out to inspect the doctor's clinic. A broken adobe wall surrounded a medium size mud brick building. A gate dangled precariously on one hinge. Just beyond was a small yard that was strewn with garbage. Amongst the garbage a line of six or seven people sat, or lay on the ground, waiting to see the "doctor".

I excused myself as I picked my way through the yard, stepping over several people, until I made it to the front door. As I opened the door, I saw a small waiting room, which was also full of more people. I was impressed.

"At least he must have a good reputation," I thought to myself.

I asked one rather plump cholita (Indian woman) how one makes an appointment to see the doctor? "My friend needs to see him quickly. It's an emergency!" I explained as I pointed out the door toward the taxi.

"The cura is in his consultorio with a patient. He will be through shortly," she responded. "Then, he will see you."

So, I paced back and forth impatiently until, after just a few minutes, the curtains parted and the cura appeared. I was in shock. He was a big man in every sense of the word. He was tall and very heavy set. His large stomach protruded through a gap in his shirt where several buttons were missing. He certainly wasn't like any doctor I had ever seen before and he didn't seem to think much about maintaining sanitary conditions. His clothes were absolutely filthy. His shirt, in particular, was stained with everything imaginable and fragments of food from several past meals that had missed his mouth and greasy mustache were stuck to it. His eyes were crossed and he had to turn his head slightly to one side in order to focus one of his eyes on me. Down the stubble on his chin dripped the juice from a wad of coca leaves that was bulging in his left cheek. As I took a step toward him, the smell coming in my direction about knocked me over. At that point, I hesitated. Maybe this wasn't such a good idea after all. But, right about then, he smiled at me.

"What's the trouble my friend? What can I do for you?"

He really did have a very friendly smile and demeanor about him. So, I coughed, took a couple of deep breaths, and explained Peter's problem to him.

"I'll see him right away," he said as he turned to the side and spat a stream of coca juice on the floor.

"Thank you so much!" I said as I turned to make my way back to the taxi where Peter sat anxiously waiting.

"What does it look like?" Peter groaned as he tried to sit up.

I tried to keep a straight face. I didn't want to alarm him as I explained, "It looks great. I think we've found someone who can really help you. He'll see you right away."

At this, Raúl and I helped Peter out of the taxi and got him into the house. As the cura pulled the curtain aside and stepped toward Peter with one of his crossed eyes peering down at him, both of Peter's eyes bugged out and he started yelling out hysterically, "I'm a dead man!"

"Your friend seems to be a little disoriented," the cura commented as he turned and motioned to us. "Here, bring him into my consultorio and have him sit down on the blanket by that wall."

Of course, the blanket was just as filthy as everything else and Peter had seen just about all he wanted to see.

"Let's get out of here!" Peter hollered at us.

But, the cura was too quick. He quickly grabbed Peter's wrists with his large hands.

"What are you doing?!" Peter exclaimed with panic in his eyes.

"I am checking the pressure of your body to see where the damage is located," the cura calmly explained.

I leaned over and whispered into Peter's ear, "He must be doing something like an EKG."

"This is no time to make jokes!" Peter whispered back through clenched teeth. "Get me outta here!"

The cura slowly dropped Peter's wrists and solemnly declared, "The injury is on the left side of his neck. The pressure is down at that location."

Then, before any of us could do anything, he quickly walked behind Peter and cradled his small head in his two large, calloused, and very dirty hands. Peter started to scream, "Let go of..."

The cura suddenly moved his hands very very quickly for someone so large... and Peter's head too! There was a snap and a pop . . . and then silence. Peter didn't make a sound or move a muscle.

"Oh man!" I thought to myself as my own eyes grew as big as saucers. "The cura just broke Peter's neck like a little chicken!" I thought that Peter was either dead or paralyzed for life. Yet, as I stood there in stunned disbelief, not knowing what to do or say, I noticed that the corners of Peter's mouth began to form into a smile!

"Wow, I don't feel any more pain! I'm healed! I'm healed!" he said as he began to roll his head around and around. "It's a miracle! It is a miracle! How can I ever thank you?!" he said as he jumped up to shake the cura's hand.

Raúl leaned against the wall beaming. "What did I tell you? The cura is fantastico!"

Peter paid the cura's "consultation fee" of seventy-five cents and walked out to the taxi laughing and joking. "Did you hear the bones in my neck crack? Did you hear that? I thought he had jerked my head right off!"

Raúl laughed. "If you have just a little time I can take and show you some real big neck bones. Since you are in Tarija, you need to know what this town is famous for.

"What's that?" I asked.

"Dinosaurs! You've got to see the dinosaurs! Anyway, you gringos have used up most of my taxi time for today. But, since you've paid me so well already, I can afford to take a few hours off and show you what we're famous for here in Tarija."

Raúl turned out to be an amateur paleontologist extraordinaire. He drove us outside of the city where he showed us thousands of very large fossilized bones - mostly huge turtle shells the size of a Volkswagen beetle! It was incredible. We wandered around looking at fossils for over an hour.

It wasn't until late afternoon when we arrived back at the church. The little old lady at the church had hot soup waiting for us. As she banged around in the small kitchen we told her of our various adventures that day. However, when we told her about our trip to visit the cura, her eyes narrowed.

"It is true he does some marvelous things. But, he is also known to receive advice from the spirits. You must be careful of him."

I wasn't really aware of such things until then. I really had no idea that we were putting ourselves in any kind of danger with the spirit world (something I learned later was very serious business in those parts). However, I now realize that God was with us the whole time and knew of our ignorance and always sends his angels to be with those who love and serve Him – especially when we do foolish things on occasion.

Peter was much better though, and for that we were grateful, and thanked God for the miracle. There was still just a little bit of soreness remaining. So, the little old lady applied some hot fomentations that evening which seemed to do the trick. Peter was as good as new for our trip to Palmyra the next morning.

Palmyra

Very early in the morning an old Ford truck was sent to take us and our supplies from Tarija to the place where we would have to use mules and local guides to get us the rest of the way to Palmyra. Of course, the old Ford truck wasn't just old, it was on its last leg. Clearly, it had experienced one too many trips on the terrible Bolivian roads and had obviously experienced its share of road hazards - such as cows, rocks and other trucks. I laughed when I first saw her and decided to call her "Rosa" - because there were still some red splotches just visible among her innumerable dents, scrapes, and scratches. It was only a miracle of Bolivian engineering (twine and duct tape) that kept this old monster on the road and I was not at all sure that we would even make it to our mules in this bag of bolts.

Then, of course, there was the little problem that by the time we arrived at the loading area Rosa had already exceeded her load capacity. No matter. The driver assured us, quite fervently, that there was plenty of room!

So, reluctantly, we unloaded our cargo from the taxi and climbed the stake boards into the back of the truck. We were greeted by huge piles of produce mixed among numerous chickens, goats, pigs and dozens of people. I counted twenty-seven people total – besides us! I was sure that the Tower of Babel would pale into insignificance compared to the mass confusion and noise on that truck! Tony and I found bags of potatoes stacked in one corner. A bunch of chickens had already made their home there. But, we moved them aside and sat down among them. We soon situated ourselves amongst the chaos and were ready to be on our way.

It was a little after 1:00 o'clock in the morning when Rosa finally started grinding her way through the streets of Tarija. Her one working headlight pierced through the darkness as she swayed back and forth like she was on a drunken binge.

About an hour or so later, the driver suddenly slammed on the brakes to avoid hitting another truck. A rather plump lady tumbled down from her high perch above us and rolled right over several people before coming to a stop on the floor of the truck – relatively unhurt. However, those that broke her fall were quite irritated. One man, in particular, started swearing at her, introducing me to many new colorful Spanish words that I'd never heard before. The animals also took notice of all the yelling and swearing and soon joined in on the chorus. The round little lady, picked herself up, dusted off her blouse, hoisted up her skirt, picked up a stock of bananas, and waded through the baggage toward the man who was swearing at her. She then proceeded to beat him over the head with the bananas. At this point, several of the passengers jumped up to restrain the hefty little banana-wielding women. Still, every time she managed to get lose, she'd head back over to attack the man with the bananas again and again. This little drama took place at intervals throughout the night. It was impossible to sleep.

At daybreak our truck rounded a curve and there, on the side of the road, was a small group of mules and our two guides, Alfredo and Saul, huddled around a fire. The driver slammed on the brakes and big Rosa came to a stop in billows of smoke and dust. The fat little lady fell off her perch again and came rolling down among the piles of produce. We threw our luggage down, jumped off Rosa, paid the driver, and walked over to introduce ourselves to our waiting guides. As we did so, the driver revved up Rosa a couple of times, threw her into gear, and disappeared down the road in a swirl of dust and noise. The last person we could make out was the fat little lady who was, once again, perched high on the back of the truck - waving at us.

We were exhausted, but relieved to have finally made it in one piece. Alfredo and Saul were also just as exhausted. They had been waiting for us all night in the cold by the side of the road. But, our guides seemed very happy to see us. They grinned from ear-to-ear as they vigorously shook our hands and slapped us on the back and told us again and again how thankful they were that we had agreed to come.

You see, Alfredo was the main reason we were on this trip, and Saul was Alfredo's good friend. Alfredo had heard about Adventists on a visit to Santa Cruz. He had walked by an Adventist church one evening and had heard some singing inside. He liked what he heard and went in to listen – and then stayed to hear the sermon. He liked what he heard very much and asked for some books to read. As he journeyed home to Palmyra he read all of the books that he had been given by the church members. He was so excited by what he had just read that as soon as he arrived at his home, he told all of his friends and everyone else in his community all about what he had learned from his books. In just a few months he had a large group of people meeting together who wanted to join the Seventh-day Adventist Church. So, he sent a letter to the mission and asked them to send someone to baptize them all and organize a church. So, the mission sent Tony and me to do the job.

It did not take long to load the mules with our baggage and climb on their backs. My mule had a bent ear so I named him Flop.

Behind each one of our mules was a second pack mule. There were six mules in all. The people in the area preferred mules to horses because they felt that mules were more sure-footed and tougher. In this wilderness country, one had to pay a very good price for a mule.

At first, I wondered about this. When I was growing up in Tennessee I had horses. I thought mules were for hillbillies. Horses were for refined folks. However, over the next few weeks, I gained great respect for mules. Only mules could have survived the trails we traveled on that trip.

Our guides jerked their mules into a trot. I did the same, but was not used to a trotting mule, which was quite uncomfortable and difficult to get used to. For the first few miles, we saw nothing but walls of trees broken by an occasional little shack of a house with goats and chickens browsing around the small dirt yards outside. Faces peered out of doorways into the sunlight as we passed. At a clearing, a little boy of four or five ran naked after our mules laughing and smiling at us.

It was a beautiful, but very rugged, country. Palmyra is situated on the border between Argentina and Bolivia in a very secluded valley nestled in the Andes Mountains. The only way to get there involved a mule trip of several days – which, by now, I wasn't looking forward to since my backside was already starting to feel rather sore. Still, a long mule ride was the only option. There were no roads, only trails that wound around and around innumerable dangerous and very steep mountain gorges. Every once in a while, the trail would dip into a valley where it would halt at the edge of a rushing stream. On the other side, the

trail would pick itself up and run into the next series of mountains. In some places the trail was so narrow and so precipitous that looking off the side of the mule into the valley below made me feel a bit dizzy - like I was walking on air. During these times, I was especially thankful for Flop, my sure-footed mule!

On the second day of our trip we came to a wide river. We scouted the area looking for a place to ford, but there simply wasn't any good place to cross.

Saul smiled back at us as he said, "We will have to swim for it."

I was really hoping that old Flop knew how to swim, because the water looked very fast and rough. The guides led the way into the river. And, for some strange reason, Flop seemed especially anxious to follow. Obviously, he knew we were heading for home. I couldn't hold him back or even slow him down. He ran toward the river and plunged in right behind Saul and Alfredo - and suddenly disappeared beneath me under the water! It all happened so fast that I went completely under the water with him! I was in shock! Instinctively I let go of Flop and swam against the strong current for the opposite shore as fast as my flailing arms could carry me. I do remember gasping for breath at one point and looking back over my shoulder. I saw Flop's head pop up through the water and then he started to swim after me. After what seemed like an eternity in that water (probably just a few minutes) Flop and I were both standing on the opposite shore – alive!

"You and Flop don't seem to be very good at this," Tony said with a laughed as he rode up behind us.

"Hey, we get across any way we can," I smiled as I turned around. Everything, including my sleeping bag, was absolutely soaked. Luckily, Saul and Alfredo decided that we should camp right there on the river bank for the night. So, I had a chance to hang my things out to dry.

The next few days we passed through some very rough country. Flop began to shake his head as he walked along the trail. Evidently, he still had water in his ears. Several times he stumbled - badly. Once he even fell down onto his knees – and I almost fell off. Late in the afternoon of the fourth day, we neared the top of a steep ridge. The trail narrowed and twisted abruptly to the left. There were some sharp rocks protruding up through the path. Flop stumbled over them and went down on his knees again. He struggled to right himself. Then, in an instant, he lost his balance and lunged toward the edge of the cliff. I leaped off his back and grabbed a tree limb as Floppy went crashing down the side of the mountain. He must have fallen two or three *hundred* feet down the side of the gorge. He broke off small trees as he fell. I knew there was no way he could have survived such a fall. We hurriedly found a wide place on the trail and tied the other mules there and carefully made our way down the mountain to where Flop lay. He certainly looked dead. He was on his back with his four legs sticking up in the air. He wasn't moving at all, not even a muscle twitch, and he wasn't breathing as far as we could tell. I felt awful. I had grown attached to that mule over the past several days of harrowing adventures. But there was nothing I could do for poor Flop. So, we salvaged parts and pieces of my luggage. We took the saddle and put it on the pack mule that had been behind us and paid our final respects to Flop.

After five days on the trail, we finally saw, just up ahead of us, the hut of one of the families who had been studying the Bible with

Alfredo. It was dark. The glow of a kerosene lamp cast long shadows across the trail in front of us. A radio was playing softly inside the hut and a group of men sat on the porch talking in low voices. Alfredo waved and called out to the men before dismounting. He started talking very fast as he walked up to them, shook their hands, and walked inside the hut. I also dismounted and walked toward the hut just behind Alfredo and introduced myself to the men. They invited me to sit down. I hesitated. By that point I was so sore that I didn't know if I could sit down ever again. Finally, however, I did just manage to sit down on the side of the porch and tried to massage some life back into my aching legs. In a few moments Tony and our other guide, Saul, joined us. I could tell by the way that Tony was walking he too was feeling the pain of the trip as well. Moments later, Alfredo emerged from inside the hut followed by a little lady and her daughter. The little girl introduced herself as Sarita and told us that our soup was on the table as she pointed our way toward the door. Tony staggered to the table and carefully lowered himself onto a chair.

"The soup smells great!" he said as he adjusted himself painfully on the wooden chair and tried to smile up at our hosts through gritted teeth.

"It must be good," I said to Tony, in English so that our hosts could not understand me. As I tried to gingerly sit down in my own chair I added, "Thousands of flies seem to love it!"

I laughed as I remembered a joke I'd been told when I first arrived in Bolivia.

"Have you heard the one about how to determine if you've been in Bolivia too long?"

"No, but I'm sure you're about to tell me," Tony said with a half-smile.

"The first year you're in Bolivia and someone brings you a bowl of soup and a fly lands in it, you say, 'Take it away! I can't eat this soup! A fly fell into it!' The second year when you're eating your soup and a fly falls into it, you simply remove the fly with your spoon and keep eating the soup. However, once you've been in Bolivia too long you'll be eating your soup and, before you know what you've done, you'll see a fly buzzing around your head, grab it out of mid-air, and throw it *into* your soup!"

At that, Tony laughed out loud, and so did I, and both of us forgot about our aches and pains - for a little while at least.

After our soup, Tony and I were invited to spend the night. I slept near an open window in a bed consisting of a course blanket thrown over rough cut planks. At that time, it felt like a feather bed. When you're as tired and sour as I was, any kind of bed seems like a gift from heaven. As I crawled in, I placed my sleeping bag on one end of the bed to use as a pillow. Before closing my eyes for the night, I looked out across the room. I remember that the kerosene lamp lighted the room with a soft glow. Smoke from the kitchen fire floated around the room and filtered out through the cracks in the thatching of the roof. Right about then, various animals started coming into the hut to settle down for the night. Dogs and goats had found their favorite places on the floor and several chickens roosted in the rafters. I laid there on my back staring back up at the smoke drifting through the thatched roof for a couple minutes more before shutting my eyes and drifting off to sleep.

Then, in the middle of the night, I suddenly awoke. There was a heavy pressure on my chest! Aware that large snakes lived in the area, I was afraid to open my eyes. In my mind, I imagined a large boa constrictor lying on my chest ready to crush the life out of me. "This is it," I said to myself as I mustered up just enough courage to crack open one eye. To my relief and surprise, I saw that it was not a boa on my chest, but a large rooster who had made himself at home right in the middle of my chest! So, I slowly raised my hands and grabbed him. In spite of his loud protests I threw him out the window and settled back into my bed. Soon, I was fast asleep yet again. However, it wasn't too long before I felt the same heavy weight on my chest. Sure enough, the rooster was back. So, once again I threw him out the window. And, once again, he was back – even before I could go to sleep again! After a couple more rounds of this, I figured that rooster simply wasn't going to take no for an answer. So, I gave up and let him sleep on my chest for the rest of the night.

Early in the morning, before the sun rose, I awoke again. This time, I was itching all over. Millions of fleas covered my entire body from head to toe. They were hungrily eating me alive! So, I threw my rooster friend out the window again and made my way to a nearby creek. I remembered stories from childhood about how raccoons got rid of flees by picking up a stick, go into the water, and immersing himself, leaving only his nose, and the stick, exposed above water. The fleas would collect on the stick and the raccoon would release the stick, full of fleas, to float down the river. I figured that if raccoons could do it, why not me? So, I lay down in the shallow creek and the fleas stopped biting me. The water was cool and so relaxing that I soon fell fast asleep right there in the creek. Before I knew it, the loud crowing of my favorite rooster woke me up. The Sun had just started to come up. I tried to get up out of the creek, but by now I was very cold and stiff. It took some effort, but I finally managed to get out of the creek and walk over to the hut. I changed my clothes and the farmer's wife brought me a scalding hot cup of cereal coffee to warm me up. That did the trick. In about an hour or so I was feeling a bit better, but I still felt rather exhausted after my adventures with the fleas and the rooster that night.

After breakfast, Alfredo softly sang as he loaded the mules for our trip to the valley of Palmyra, only a few hours away.

"Why are you singing this early in the morning?" I grumbled.

"This is the best part of the day," he replied. "Come on

now. We must ride before the heat comes."

Even with the pain of remounting, the ride in the cool morning air revived my spirits. When our group finally arrived in Palmyra, a large delegation greeted us. Alfredo, Tony and I spent the next few days visiting many different families in the valley. I also spent several days conducting medical clinics. Alfredo had done a wonderful job teaching the people from his books and most were well prepared to join the Adventist Church.

So, a large baptism was scheduled for the next Sabbath afternoon. There was only one problem. Many of the couples who wanted to get baptized had been living together without formally being married. Not a problem.

"Why not kill two birds with one stone?" I said to Tony.

Tony agreed and, just before the baptism that Sabbath afternoon, we performed a mass wedding for sixteen couples - and their children who all lined up for the ceremony. Right after that, we all went over and gathered by a large stream for the baptism ceremony. Tony and I baptized over sixty people that day who had made their decision to follow Jesus and to join the Seventh-day Adventist Church.

That baptism proved to be the high point in the lives of the citizens of Palmyra valley. Tony and I were excited that we were able to help form a new church in an area where Christianity had been nonexistent. We departed for home full of courage and enthusiasm. And, to our amazement, Flop, my old mule who had fallen off the cliff, met us on the trail! He was slowly trudging his way home. Evidently, the fall had knocked him out, but hadn't quite killed him!

I'll never forget this trip. It was quite an adventure for me in so many ways. However, what I most remember about it is how God was able to work in the lives of so many people in so many simple yet amazing ways. Look how He led a little Indian man to walk down a darkened street to hear beautiful music and the gospel message - and then used that one little man to establish a large church in one of the most remote corners of the world.

The Road of Death

The road from Chulumani to La Paz snakes its way through mountain passes and down into low-lying valleys before it rises again over the Cumbre into the city of La Paz. It was always a beautiful trip. Cascading waterfalls fell freely from above the clouds that hugged the mountaintops before crashing into the fern-covered rocks below. In many places, the water spilled onto the roads and formed pools where gorgeous iridescent butterflies congregated to drink. Large multicolored parrots called to one another from among the tree branches and families of monkeys scampered here and there as we drove by. Among the walls of the wet canyon grew banks of wild orchids along with innumerable flowers of every hue and pattern.

The roads, however, were always treacherous. During the rainy seasons the road turned into knee-deep mud. And, during the dry spells the road turned into slippery ankle-deep talcum powder. This powder got into every nook and cranny. It was everywhere. Huge clouds of dust followed large trucks and settled over the countryside. The dust served to signal the approach of an onrushing truck. But, this didn't always help. Most of the time the roads were so narrow that only one vehicle could pass safely. So, there was no room to maneuver if someone was coming the other direction and didn't stop in time. Those who traveled this road were in constant danger of slamming into someone head on - Kamikaze style. Often such a crash would be so violent that the victims would be thrown well clear of the colliding vehicles and would go tumbling hundreds or even over a thousand feet down the mountainside. In the aftermath of such collisions, humans and cargo would be scattered over large areas of the countryside. On previous trips, I had seen the remains of trucks that had fallen off into the river far below. In fact, this road was so treacherous that hundreds of people died here each year.

There were also, of course, the occasional near misses. Two big monster trucks would come roaring down the road, stirring up huge clouds of dust like giant knights at a medieval joust. They would careen around a corner without a thought before suddenly realizing their precarious situation and slam on their brakes to rein in their steeds. Sometimes they would stop within a foot or two of one another. The drivers would dismount, neither one willing to give ground and throw verbal insults at one another. This confrontation would be joined by the passengers of both trucks. Eventually, one side would back down and the vanquished knight would crawl back into his truck and back it along the road until a place was found that was wide enough to let both trucks pass.

Some of the passes on this road were notorious for other reasons as well. It was at one particular place on this road that members of a victorious political party that had recently taken over the government vented their rage on some of the ranking officials of the losing party. These ex-politicians were loaded into a truck and driven into the Yungas until they arrived at a steep precipice that fell seven hundred feet to the valley below. They hung the tail end of the truck over the edge of the road and threw the human cargo out like sacks of potatoes. Fortune smiled on one man. As he fell he bounced off of several rocks and then landed in a small tree that had attached itself to the side of the mountain. Although he had several broken bones, cuts and bruises, he managed to survive for several days hanging there in the tree. Someone heard his cries for help and he was rescued. He hid in the Yungas until yet another coup brought him back into the good graces of the new government.

This, of course, was the new and improved version of the road to La Paz. Years before my arrival this road was even more dangerous to travel because it was infested with bandits (much like the people in Christ's day who had to travel from Jerusalem to Jericho). One famous outlaw lived in caves near the Cumbre (the highest point on the road to La Paz). He was notoriously brutal. It was said that his mother started him out on his criminal career. She first introduced him at the tender age of five to the art of picking pockets in the streets of La Paz. From there he graduated into more difficult subjects like armed robbery and murder. When things got too hot for him in La Paz he escaped with his gang of cutthroats into the surrounding mountains where he declared himself to be a revolutionary. His bloody tactics were legendary. As a kind of signature of his work, he would usually decapitate his victims. The government finally decided they had had enough of this thieving bandit. So, they sent the army after him. He was finally cornered in the mountains and, after a furious gunfight, was captured. He was riddled with bullets, but still alive. There was a quick trial and he was sentenced to hang in the main square of the city. Before his sentence was executed, he was asked if he had any last words.

"Sí" he responded. "Era totalmente la culpa de mi madre!"

Which means, "It was entirely my mother's fault!"

With the bandits gone, the road became much safer to travel – relatively speaking. It still remained, of course, one of the most dangerous roads in the world – as I'm sure it is to this day.

Even so, there were times, of course, when one was forced to travel this road - regardless of the risks. For example, when I was a boy of four, I came down with both whooping cough and malaria at the same time. My mother decided to take me to La Paz. My father would be flying in to La Paz from the Beni and she thought my chances of survival were better at a higher climate – but perhaps not quite as high as the Cumbre. When we got to the Cumbre, which was over 20,000 feet high, I stopped breathing. As she frantically tried to resuscitate me, she was praying over and over again for God to save me. The driver stopped the truck at a wide place in the road and my mother pulled me out of the truck and laid me at the side of the road still trying to resuscitate me. I was turning blue. Suddenly a car pulled up and a lady jumped out and ran over to my mother. "Here," she said. "Try this!" She handed my mother a capsule of something that smelled like ammonia. My mother broke it under my nose and suddenly I started breathing again. When my mom turned to thank the lady, she and the car simply weren't there. They had simply disappeared. I've always believed that this lady was my guardian angel who was sent to rescue me in answer to my mother's prayers.

Now, as an adult, I was back. And, after a few months in Chulumani, our supplies were running low. We had to buy the basics like cooking oil and wheat, and some gas for our stove. I also had to buy medicines for the clinic and give a report to the mission office. So, we decided to take the harrowing trip to La Paz. Faye was excited because we would be spending several days in La Paz with American missionaries.

"I will be able to talk to someone in English!" she smiled at me as we got ready for the trip.

I didn't have the heart to tell her how dangerous the trip would be.

Fortunately, however, we made it all the way to La Paz without incident and had a great time while we were there. Soon though, it was time to return to Chulumani. Our Land Cruiser was packed to the gills with our new supplies and we took our time as we maneuvered the twists and turns of the narrow road. Again, our return trip was quite uneventful - until we came to Undawvi.

Undawvi was more like a large truck stop than a town and was located about an hour and a half from La Paz. Truckers would stop there to eat and buy fuel. We stopped there as well to stretch our legs and get some food and fuel as well. It was good to get out and walk around for a bit. Barring problems, the trip usually took about six or seven hours, and it was good to break it up a bit with little stops like this along the way. The first slivers of dawn were just showing on the horizon. The chilly air washed over me. As I made my way to the roadside shacks that serve as restaurants offering cheap food I smiled at groups of children who were just starting to gather their goats. There were also small groups of truckers quietly sipping their morning coffee. Freshly slaughtered chickens and goats were hanging outside of the shops, waiting to be cut up and cooked for the hungry travelers. Dust from passing trucks hung heavy in the air. The town boasted a public restroom, which was quite unusual for the area, but I could not stand to use it. Most people used the floors and sinks instead of the commodes, and many preferred to simply relieve themselves along the back side of buildings. Beyond this, it is hard to describe Undawvi and all its sights and smells. One really has to visit Undawvi to truly appreciate the place.

The road at Undawvi split at this point with one road going south and one going north. The southern route was a longer but somewhat safer road through Caranavi. The northern route was shorter, but not as safe. I was thinking that we should take the safer southern route when one of the truckers told me that rains had made the road to Caranavi difficult if not impossible to pass. So, after talking it over with Faye, we decided to go north. After all, our journey had been uneventful so far. “We’ll be fine,” I thought to myself.

Things did go smoothly for a while. However, not too long after we left Undawvi we came around a corner and found a large boulder lying in the middle of the road. It had rained the day before, but the road was dry and dusty now. Bellows of dust floated around me as I stopped the Land Cruiser. There just was no way to get around that large bolder. So, I left the motor running and jumped out.

“Don’t let the boys out,” I called back at Faye. “It will only take a minute for me to move it out of the way.”

However, the boulder was larger than I had originally thought and it was quite a struggle to move it at all. Gradually, however, I shifted it back and forth, inch-by-inch toward the side of the road. After about five or ten minutes of this, I finally sent it crashing down the mountain side. I stood up and took a minute to catch my breath. I had just pulled a rag out of my back pocket and was wiping the mud from the boulder off of my hands when out of nowhere Faye started to scream at the top of her lungs.

“Tui Tui!!!!! Tui Tui!!!! Tui Tui!!!!!!!!”

Instinctively, I knew what was happening. I frantically ran to the Land Cruiser, threw open the door, jammed it in gear, and slammed the gas pedal to the floor. The Cruiser shot forward as huge rocks began to hit the road behind us – right where we had just been moments before. Within a few seconds, it seemed like the whole mountainside was crashing down on the road behind us before continuing its journey into the valley below. The road itself simply disappeared under the landslide.

We drove a little further and then I stopped and looked over at Faye.

"Wow! that was close!" I said in a horse whisper, still gripping the steering wheel so tightly my knuckles were white. "How did you know what was happening?"

"Well," Faye responded. "I saw that the road was dry and dusty but that bolder was wet. So, I looked up to see where it had come from. When I did, I saw small pieces of rock tumbling down toward us from high up on the mountainside. Then, I saw larger rocks breaking loose and starting to fall. That's when I started screaming!"

She looked at me and gave me a little smile as she gently rubbed my arm.

I gathered my little family together and hugged them as I repeatedly thanked God for His protection and care.

Every now and then life leads us to places like Undawvi where there is a fork in the road and we have to make a decision about which way to go. And, at such moments, we usually choose what seems to us to be the easiest or shortest way forward. Of course, what may seem like the best way at the time may actually be the worst or most dangerous way. Still, God is there and sends His angels to protect those who love and serve Him regardless of which fork in the road of life we happen to be on at any given moment.

Landslide in Chulumani

The Revolution

When we moved to Cochabamba we were able to find a nice house to rent in a very fashionable place. The owner was living in New York and only wanted Americans to rent his home. The cost was very reasonable at $75 per month, so we rented the house. Unfortunately, living in such a nice house caused us no end of grief because everyone thought that we were rich, including the Union president. It had two stories, a big yard surrounded by thick stucco walls, mahogany floors, tiled bathrooms and living quarters for a maid in the back. It certainly was a beautiful house. However, in hindsight, we probably shouldn't have chosen to live there.

One night, not long after we moved in, Faye was awakened in the middle of the night by a loud crash on our upstairs porch. She shook me awake, told me what she heard, and we both went to investigate. Just outside the upstairs door (a very nice glass door), we found a rock the size of a chicken egg. Just a few inches from the door there was a dent in the stucco of the wall. The rock had just missed its intended target.

It was dark, so it was pointless to try to see who did it. So, we went back to bed.

Early the next morning Faye was working in the kitchen when Delfina, our maid, came running in from buying milk. Excitedly, she told Faye that someone had painted a message on the stucco walls that surrounded our house. It said, "Yankees Go Home!"

Bolivian politics blew hot and cold and seemed to change at the drop of a hat. At the moment it was blowing hot, and Americans were not popular with a certain portion of the population. The slogans were usually generic and seemed fairly harmless, but the rocks crashing into our house at night made it a bit more personal.

For several weeks the American businessmen in our neighborhood had been bringing home anything of value from their offices. People gathered in little clusters in the streets and in the restaurants to discuss the latest rumors. On a Tuesday afternoon, Leonard stopped by our house. He was the science teacher at the Adventist school in the small town of Vinto and had been in Cochabamba picking up supplies. He had decided to stop by and see us on his way back to the school and was unusually excited about something and he half ran up to me.

"Yesterday an army helicopter landed on our soccer field! They just came in without an invitation or anything!" He said as he waved his arms over his head. "They walked around the campus looking into buildings and writing and asking questions - like who owned the vehicles on campus and where they were generally parked?" Leonard's face wrinkled and his eyes squinted as he added, "There is something strange going on!"

"I believe it!" I responded, quite concerned by the news.

Leonard continued. "I've heard rumors from the students that President Torres plans to nationalize everything and turn Bolivia into a completely Communist state. They are even saying that our school will be nationalized and made into a military academy."

I put my arm around Leonard's shoulder and said, "Things do look serious. Let's pray that the Lord will intervene to protect us and His school."

We had prayer together and then I walked with him back to his truck. As he got into his truck, he hesitated for a moment, and then looked at me through the open window.

"If the rumors are true, then the missionaries in this country are in a heap of trouble Tui. In this country, revolutions are a national sport. I hope we're not the football they plan to kick around."

As he drove off I yelled, "Take care of yourself, and be careful!"

The next week I was so involved in preparing for my trip to Chapare that I forgot all about the rumors. After all, there were always rumors floating around. My worry at the moment was my ten-year-old Scout International jeep.

I had priced a VW bus in La Paz. The owner wanted $12,000.00 for it! On my salary of a little over $150 a month, with half it going toward rent, such a price was impossibly high. Buying a new car was simply out of the question for us. So, I began to look for other forms of transportation. Then, one day when I as in Cochabamba I spied an International jeep sitting outside a grocery store. It had a "For Sale" sign on it. So, I stopped and checked it out. It had a new paint job and new tires. It didn't look half bad. So, I decided to go into the store and ask about it. The portly man behind the counter smiled over at me and said, "How can I help you today?"

"How much are you asking for that jeep out front?"

His face lit up. “Oh, Señor! It is a wonderful jeep! Everything has been reconditioned and it is in excellent shape. I am only asking $2,000 for it! - an excellent price for what I have in it. It would be a great buy for you! Come, take a look at it.”

It did look very nice, so I rashly bought it without a test drive.

Of course, my troubles with the jeep began almost as soon as I got it home. I had decided to drive out to the school at Vinto to show it off to Wilfred (another American teacher) the next day. I was feeling great and was very proud of my little jeep as I headed off that next morning. The little jeep ran just fine until I came to the turn off at the little village of Vinto for the Adventist boarding school. I slowed down before the turn and applied the brakes, but nothing happened. Fortunately, no traffic was coming and I managed to make it through the intersection and around the corner without hitting anything. After I finally coasted to a stop at the side of the road, I got out and crawled under it to see what had happened. I quickly discovered the problem. One of the brake lines had been punctured and a nail was stuck into it to plug up the hole. However, the hole was a bit too large for the nail and the brake fluid had leaked out around the nail. I was beginning to understand how mechanics worked in this country and why repairs were so cheap. For now, I’d have to walk the rest of the way to the school and get some help. Soon I found Leonard and Wilfred, and they helped me to fix the brakes on my new jeep.

I was feeling a little better about things until the next morning when I went out to start up my jeep. As I walked toward it, I saw a large puddle of oil oozing out from under it. It seemed to be leaking out from under the transmission. After I got that fixed, something else went wrong, and then something else and something else. It was never ending! Within a couple of weeks I was acquainted with every mechanic in town.

Finally, after having replaced what seemed like most everything that could be replaced on my jeep, Faye asked me to drive her into town to do some grocery shopping. I pulled up a couple of feet from the curb to let her out to do her shopping. She leaned over and gave me a kiss and then opened the door to get out. An instant later there was a tremendous thud. A man on a bicycle who was in a hurry to by-pass traffic had decided to come around the passenger side of our jeep and had impaled himself on our door. The front wheel of his bicycle was crumpled and he was lying on the sidewalk groaning in pain. He was extremely upset at us for having opened the door on him and demanded that we pay him for the damages to his bike. Of course, the door to our jeep was a complete wreck as well.

"What else could go wrong with this jeep?!" I thought to myself.

It didn't take me long to find out. I was planning a trip to Chapare, which was sure to test the mechanical ingenuity of the Bolivian mechanics that had been working on my jeep for the past several weeks. I awoke early Sunday morning and loaded the jeep with supplies and medicines, checked the water, tires, and oil, and asked the Lord to especially bless this bucket of bolts. Faye followed me out to the jeep. I leaned out the window and kissed her goodbye.

"Be careful." She said. And, patting my arm, she added, "I hear the roads to Chapare are terrible."

I smiled back as I said, "I don't really know if I'll need to be careful about those roads. I have never managed to get this jeep further than ten miles from home."

Then, I blew her a kiss, put the jeep in reverse and backed out into the street. Faye shut the gate and waved goodbye.

Several blocks later the predictable happened. Smoke started pouring out of the transmission.

I thought to myself, "You can say one thing about this stupid jeep. It's very dependable - dependable at breaking down every time I get in it!"

So, I made a U-turn and headed back home. However, very quickly the smoke became so thick inside the jeep that I could hardly see to drive. I had to stick my head out of the window to drive. When I pulled up to the house smoke was pouring out of the windows of the jeep and I was coughing and gasping for air. I threw the door open and staggered onto the sidewalk. Faye was in the yard working and came over to assess the damage.

"My my" she said as she smiled sweetly up at me, trying not to laugh as I stood there gasping for breath, "You're back so early!"

"It's not funny." I coughed. "I am selling this pile of junk as soon as I can!"

The mission had left a Toyota Land Cruiser at our house so that Dr. Barrientos, the new medical director of the Bolivian Mission, could use it on one of his trips. Since he was not due to pick it up for two weeks, I decided to use it.

"I should have taken this thing in the first place," I said to Faye as she helped me transfer the equipment. "I've got to hurry. I'll be late picking up Pastor Aguilar."

Pastor Aguilar was the director of the Cochabamba district. The jungle area of Chapare was also one of his responsibilities and for several months now we had been given repeated assurances that he would visit the area. Now he was finally ready, and I was supposed to drive him there. Ironically, however, he was not a man who tolerated lateness. He was a short well-manicured Chilean, almost oriental in his appearance, and was very precise in his speech and actions and was always very well-dressed - without a hair out of place. So, of course, he was impatiently standing on his front porch when I arrived, waiting for me. Yet, he didn't say anything as he carefully began to maneuver his packages and suitcase to the back of the Land Cruiser.

I jumped out and gave him a swat on the back, "I hope you haven't been waiting long!"

I could tell by the weak smile on his face that he was not too happy with me. I had arrived a bit late. He was probably the only Latin in the world that counted being exactly on time as something important. There was already a bit of tension built up between us, and my late arrival hadn't helped matters. When I had first arrived in Cochabamba I was more than willing to help him pastor some of the churches in his district. But he refused my offer for help. He felt I was after his job. The only thing he wanted me to do was to drive him around his district. I was rather upset with this arrangement because I had advanced degrees in theology and education and here I was chauffeuring another pastor around without doing any teaching or preaching.

"I didn't come here to be a Chauffeur," I thought to myself. But, I had a lot to learn.

Finally, we were on our way. On the outskirts of town, we turned onto the road that would take us to Chapare. Just in front of us, we encountered a huge traffic jam. Trucks loaded with produce were parked on the side of the road. Buses were blocking the road and no one was moving. Seated on the road were hundreds of school children. A handsome young man holding an Uzi machine gun stood in the center of the road among the seated children. Other men with guns stood at the edges of the road. For some strange reason, I decided at that moment that a good offense would be the best defense.

"Come on Pastor, let's go talk to the young man and see what's going on."

"I am not getting out of this car!" he glared back at me. His eyes showed real fear.

"Why not?"

"The Bolivians hate the Chileans. If they are having a revolution and they find out I am a Chilean they will kill me!"

"Well then, you stay in the Land Cruiser and I'll go and talk to the man."

I walked up to the young man with the Uzi and asked, "Are you the man in charge?"

He paid me no attention as he yelled out another command, "There's another bus load of kids coming. Put them on the road. We don't want any traffic coming in or going out of this city.

Then he turned to me and snarled, "What do you want?"

I smiled at him as I explained, "I am working with the Seventh-day Adventist Church doing medical work for people in this country who cannot afford to see a doctor. We plan to go to Chapare for several weeks and we are on our way with our rolling clinic." I pointed to our Land Cruiser with lettering on the side that said Clinica Rodante Adventista (Adventist Rolling Clinic).

The young man stared in the direction I was pointing. Then he looked back at me. "So!" He blurted out.

I continued. "There will be people who have walked many miles that will be waiting for us. I know you want what is best for this country. We don't want to let them down do we?"

He continued to stare blankly at me for several seconds. Then, suddenly, he barked out an order.

"Move the children and let the ambulance pass!"

Then, turning to look at me again he said, in a low voice that only I could hear, "I know the Adventists."

I thanked him, shook his hand, and ran back to the Land Cruiser. Pastor Aguilar held out his hands and urgently whispered, "Well, what did he say?"

"We are going to Chapare!" I smiled.

His eyes were filled with questions. "How did you do it?"

"I didn't do it. God did it!"

We were the *only* vehicle they let pass that day.

When we arrived in Chapare there were large groups of people waiting for us at the homes and churches of our members. Pastor Aguilar held nightly evangelistic meetings and, during the day, I held medical clinics. After we had been in Chapre for three days, we heard on the radio that the country was under the control of the Communists - although fighting continued in the larger cities of the country. Throughout the day we heard many threatening broadcasts against foreigners living in the country.

After the meeting that evening, Pastor Aguilar sat down with me near the front of the chapel and asked, "What should we do?"

I was beginning to think we made an awful mistake in leaving Cochabamba. I had left Faye and our two little boys alone in the middle of this big mess.

"Well Pastor, we need to get back to our families and see if we can get them out of the city or at least to some safe place."

Pastor Aguilar slowly nodded his head in agreement. As soon as we had packed the Land Cruiser and said our goodbyes we headed for Cochabamba to be with our families.

When we arrived at the outskirts of city the next afternoon we saw that soldiers were checking traffic. We stopped and they asked us for identification.

They checked our papers and then, inexplicably, without another word, we were both allowed to continue to our homes. Unbeknownst to us the revolution was over and the communists had been defeated.

As soon as I left Pastor Aguilar at his home, I rushed to my own house. On the way, I went by numerous overturned and burned-out trucks, cars and buses cluttering the street.

"There must have been quite a fight here!" I thought to myself. "I hope Faye and the boys are safe. Please God. Please God..." I prayed over and over again.

I pulled the Land Cruiser in front of the house, jumped out, ran to the gate and rang the buzzer. The curtains pulled back and I saw Faye's face looking back at me. The door opened and Faye and the boys came running out. It felt so good to hug them and kiss them and know that God had kept my family for me.

"I am so glad you made it home!" Faye exclaimed as she brushed back the tears and tried to stop her chin and lips from quivering.

When we were all seated on the couch I asked, "What happened while I was gone?"

"The second day after you left I heard these planes flying low over our house. I took the boys out into the yard to look at them. We were waving at them as they flew over. While we were waving at the planes, one of our friends from the church stopped by the house and told me that fighting was going on in the city. He told me that the airplanes were from the Bolivian Air Force and they were strafing the university down the street! He explained that the Bolivian Air Force had joined the counter-revolution against the Communists and they were attacking the university which had been taken over by the Communist students. Then, he urged me to go into our house, lock all the doors, and stay there until things calmed down. We've been locked in the house waiting for things to blow over ever since."

For the next few days we heard sporadic gunfire in the city. One of the houses down the street from our home was occupied by rebels. It was surrounded and, after an intense gunfight, they were captured and executed on the front lawn.

I was told by a Bolivian pilot that many of the Cuban students who were sent by Castro to help support the Communist revolution in Bolivia were captured, loaded on meat planes, flown over the jungle, and thrown out from several hundred feet in the air. There were so many killed in La Paz that the bodies of the dead overflowed the morgue. Piles of bodies were stacked in the backyard of the morgue, awaiting identification and burial.

Later, we learned the true extent of our danger and how we had been saved by the intervention of the United States government. All Americans had been put on a list to be imprisoned and then executed by the Communists after they had complete control of the government.

At the height of the fighting in La Paz, one of our missionary families was huddled together on the bedroom floor of their fourth-floor apartment. Bullets were hitting the walls and windows of the apartment. Snipers were on the roof tops of the buildings all around them. They were firing on soldiers below who were, in turn, returning fire. The mother and the children were extremely frightened except for one little girl who exclaimed, “Don’t be afraid momma! God will send His biggest angels to protect us.”

And, He did.

Return Missionaries

Return Missionaries

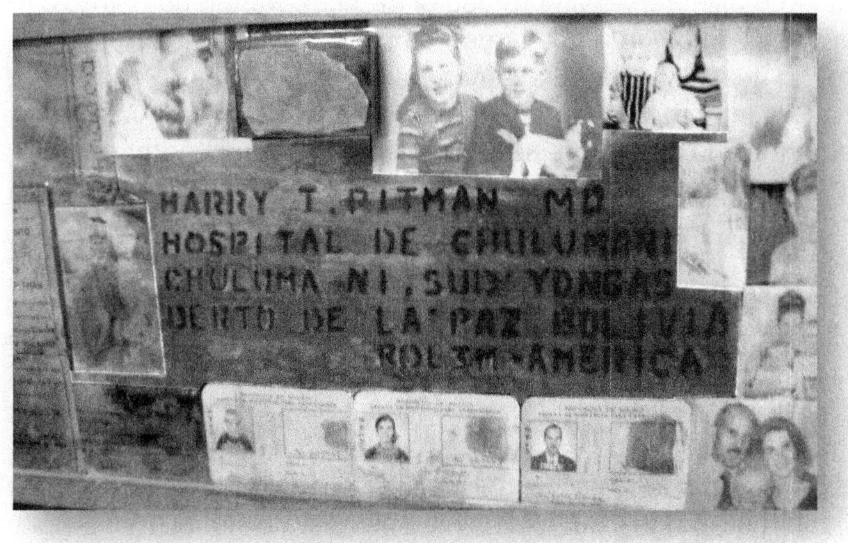

When we made a decision to leave Bolivia we only had a few weeks to get ready. It was a real struggle. Faye and I had grown to love Bolivia and the people there very much. We had also worked very hard to fix up the Bolivian pastor's house in Chulumani. It had been the house I had lived in as a little boy, so I was a bit nostalgic about that particular place.

When we first moved to Chulumani we rented an apartment in the middle of town. Then, the mission decided to move the previous pastor to a new district, which left the house on the little hill at the edge of town empty; and gave us the opportunity to move out of our little apartment into a real house and a good bit more room. However, the house wasn't what we expected when we first walked in to take a look at it. It was a huge mess. The kitchen and ceilings were covered with soot. The bottom of the kitchen sink had holes from rust. The floors were smeared with thick layers of dirt and wet slime. I couldn't believe my eyes, or my nose! But that wasn't all. I walked over to the kitchen window to look at the view and, as a looked down, saw that the former inhabitants had thrown all of their garbage over the years out of that particular window. The odor from that large pile of decaying refuse of all kinds wafted up to me, a pile which was also home to a large number of rats milling happily through their own little heaven on Earth. As we wandered in amazement through the rest of the house, we noticed that the majority of the window panes were broken. In one bedroom the floor was completely rotten and hung loosely from one side where it was still attached to the walls, exposing part of the basement below. The bathroom had greenish-brown slime sliding down the walls below leaking pipes. There were no light switches on the walls. Rather, the lights were turned on by connecting two exposed wires that protruded from the walls in the various rooms. There were happy healthy fleas everywhere and bats flew out of the attic in the evenings. The grass was knee-deep and the adobe walls around the house were crumbling and the broken gate hung loosely on one rusty hinge. But, we saw some potential in the place.

So, although we had limited financial reserves, we took some money out of savings and began to remodel the house. It took us several months of hard work to make the place livable. We started with the basics and replaced all the broken windows, fixed the plumbing, put in light switches, redid the adobe walls, fixed the floors and painted the house inside and out. Then, Faye made curtains for the windows and hung pictures on the walls. I hauled garbage out of the yard, cut the grass and put in a new gate. As I was removing the old gate, however, I found that my father's name had been stenciled on it. I felt even closer to the place just seeing his name there, and I still have that board with his name on it to remind me of him and our common experiences there in Chulumani.

When we finally finished our remodeling it was the best house in town. However, we didn't have very long to enjoy the fruits of our labor. We had only been in the house a few months when I received a letter from my mother telling me about an opening to go to medical school in Guadalajara, Mexico. If I wanted to attend, I would have to apply right away since classes were to begin in just a few weeks. Also, my oldest boy Sean came down with a mysterious illness about that same time. So, we quickly decided that it was time for us to leave Chulumani and our new home. Sean needed expert medical care at Loma Linda Hospital in California and I had to go to medical school in Mexico in just a few weeks. Things were suddenly happening very fast and it was a bit overwhelming at the time.

Of course, when the mayor of the town found out that we were leaving she came to our house and wanted to buy our toilet, the medicine cabinet, the wall switches and an assortment of other items. I tried to explain to Señora Alcalde (Mrs. Mayor) that these items stayed with the house.

"Oh pastor," she said, "That is not how we do it here! We sell everything but the walls when we move."

No wonder there was no toilet, medicine cabinet or light switches when we moved into the house! Señora Alcalde looked a bit disappointed in my decision when I told her that it was final. She was looking at the ground, with her eyebrows furrowed as if she was thinking hard about something. Then she looked up at me with a hopeful smile and asked if I might be willing to sell our stove or refrigerator?

"Those," I smiled back at her, "are for sale!"

"I'll buy them both!" she grinned as she shook my hand. "Don't sell them to anyone else! I'll be back to pick them up first thing in the morning!"

At the time I thought to myself that I wished some of the appliances in the States were made like they were made there in Bolivia. I thought it was a miracle that our refrigerator managed to function through all the electrical surges we had in the town without any apparent ill effects. For example, sometimes we had 110 volts coming into the house for a while when suddenly there would only be 70 volts coming in, which would then instantly surge to 180 volts. It was completely unpredictable. It all depended on how many people were using electricity in our town at the time. The refrigerator would respond to these sudden changes by running faster or slower. So, we always knew what voltage we had at any given moment by the sound the refrigerator was making at the time.

However, just before the mayor came back the next day to pick up the refrigerator, it suddenly stopped working. It just died and wouldn't turn on at all!

"Wow," I exclaimed as I showed Faye our dead refrigerator, "Maybe it was really God who kept it working this whole time?! I never could understand how it survived everything while we were here. Even though we can't sell it now, we can't really complain now, can we? I think we have gotten more than our money's worth since it worked like a horse for the past three and a half years without any issues at all."

Less than an hour later the mayor arrived to pick up her stove and refrigerator. Of course, I had to explain that the refrigerator had suddenly stopped working.

"Here in your money back," I said as I shrugged my shoulders.

"Oh, no," she shot back, "I'll take it just like it is. We have plenty of people here that can fix this little problem. It's very common here. You keep the money! I don't want you selling it to anyone else!"

"Ok... If that is what you really want," I stammered in disbelief as I shot up yet another prayer of thanks to God for looking out for us so often and so well.

Sometimes things just fall into place in such a way that it's hard not to see the hand of God behind it all. Within two weeks we managed to sell all of our things, settle accounts with the mission, get on the airplane, and arrive safely in Los Angeles. It all gave me confidence that God would work out all of the other pressing issues facing our family during that time.

Guadalajara

As I mentioned, one of the big reasons why we needed to leave Chulumani so soon after spending so much time and effort fixing up our new home there was that my son Sean, who was only about three years old at the time, became very sick. Chulumani was not the cleanest place to live. The streets and sidewalks were covered with human and animal excrement. Every morning people would throw their bedpans from the night before into the streets below. So, it was no surprise that the city was full of diseases of various kinds.

Sean had already come down with typhoid on top of being infested with roundworms and tapeworms. Then, rather suddenly, he became very sick again. He grew weaker and weaker to the point where he could hardly get out of bed. We were very concerned and took him to various physicians in La Paz and Lima, but no one could figure out exactly what was wrong with him. So, in desperation we made plans to go to Loma Linda Hospital in California on a vacation and see if their department of tropical medicine could give us some answers.

It was during this difficult time when we were praying for answers for our little boy that the letter arrived from my mother. She wrote that my sister had just been accepted into medical school at the Universidad Antonoma de Guadalajara in Mexico and added that there was one student who had recently dropped out. Since my sister was already going to be there she suggested that it would be nice to have us both there together. She warned me though that there were forty other students who were applying for that one spot.

Since I had been doing a lot of medical work in Bolivia, I thought it would be nice to know a little more about medicine. The idea of being a fully trained physician, like my parents, had a strong appeal for me. But, it was a longshot that I'd even be accepted – and I would have to spend so much time away from my family during my training. So, Faye and I earnestly prayed for guidance to make the right decision and talked it over, carefully weighing our options. We finally decided that if God wanted me to take medicine He would open the door. So, I sent in my application and left the rest in God's hands. A couple weeks later I got a call from the medical school saying that I had been accepted and that classes started in exactly two weeks! I was quite surprised that I had been the one chosen for that one spot out of so many applicants! Right then and there Fay and I knelt down and said a prayer of thanks to God for opening yet another door for us.

Even so, the decision for me to go to medical school was not an easy one for us. Sean would have to be evaluated and treated in Loma Linda for his illness. So, I would have to go to Mexico by myself. I certainly did not want to leave my family behind for so long. What should I do? Again we prayed and decided that God seemed to be leading us in this direction - that come what may, I really had to take advantage of this special opportunity I had been given. We simply had no other reasonable choice. Faye would stay in Loma Linda with Sean and Shannon as they were being evaluated and treated at the tropical medicine department. She would also work at the hospital and earn a little extra money to help pay my medical school expenses. And, her parents, who lived in the area at that time, could help take care of the boys.

The two weeks I had left with my family flew by in the blink of an eye. But now, it was time to say goodbye and head off to medical school. Still, it was good to be able to be with my sister and spend some time with her. It had been a long time since I had last seen her and we talked excitedly about how wonderful it would be to take medicine together!

When we arrived in Guadalajara we made our way to the campus and took our places in a long line of students who were trying to register for classes. However, the line wasn't moving very fast. The problem was that all documents had to have an "official seal" on them before anyone could be registered for classes – to include all grade school diplomas! All of our excitement vanished as we realized that neither one of us had any "official seal" on our *grade school* certificates – of all things! And, the registrar was very insistent that all documents come with an official seal or we could not register for classes – end of discussion. Our medical school careers were about to end before they even started! Linda and I were at our wit's end! We had no idea what to do. Then, a little miracle happened. A student from New York, who was standing next to us, opened an expensive-looking briefcase and pulled out a New York Tennis Club sealer.

"Here", he said with a devilish grin, "Let me have your grade school transcripts."

So, we handed them to him. Quickly, he impressed upon them the crisp seal of the "New York Tennis Club"! It did look impressive with two crossed tennis rackets and everything, but I doubted it would work. However, to my surprise, the registrar accepted them without batting an eye!

"What a relief!" I said as I shook the hand of our new friend from New York. "What is your name?"

"You can call me Alex," he smiled with the same grin and laughing twinkle in his eyes.

"Hey Alex," I said as I swatted him on the back, "Why don't you come with my sister Linda and me and have some breakfast with us."

"Sure thing! I'm starving!"

After finding the cafeteria and going through line, Alex noticed that neither Linda nor I took any of the breakfast bacon that was being served.

"Hey, is something wrong with the bacon here?" he asked.

"Ah, well, we just don't eat bacon," I explained.

"Why not?! You guys Jewish or something?"

"No, we're Seventh-day Adventists!"

"Well, you're better than I am. I am Jewish and I know I shouldn't eat the stuff, but I still do." Then he laughed, "You're better Jews than I am!"

I knew right away that Alex and I were going to hit it off. And, sure enough, we quickly became very good friends. However, there wasn't much time during those first few days to spend in idle conversation. Classes started the very next day.

Fortunately, I had the advantage of already knowing Spanish quite well because all of the classes were given in Spanish. Those who didn't know Spanish as well, to include my sister Linda who had become a bit rusty since we were kids, had to take Spanish classes in addition to the regular medical school classes - and pass a conversational Spanish exam. I didn't have to take those classes because I went to the Spanish teacher's office first thing and talked with her for about ten minutes in Spanish. After that, she signed a waiver for me so that I was excluded from having to take the Spanish classes. Of course, this gave more time to study for my medical class – an early advantage for me that didn't sit too well with Linda.

Unfortunately, that wasn't the only problem Linda had early on in medical school. One day, after only a few weeks of school, I found a note taped to the door of our apartment that said, "Your sister has been in an accident and is in jail. If you need a good attorney contact me."

I couldn't believe it! Right away I rushed over to the jail to try to get my sister out. I found her sitting with a dozen dirty men in a very dirty holding cell that had access to a toilet that didn't look like it had ever been cleaned. The whole place smelled to high heaven. While I was relieved to find that she wasn't hurt, I was still very curious as to why she was in jail?

"What in the world had happened?!" I asked from the other side of the bars.

"Well," she smiled up at me, "I was innocently driving home from class when a taxi pulled out from a side street and hit me! In fact, the cab hit me so hard that the impact threw an old man in the back seat out of the cab and into the street! The taxi cab driver took one look at his passenger lying unconscious there in the street and ran away. So, I got out of my car and started trying to help this poor man recover when the police arrived – and arrested me! They told me that since my car had been involved in an accident that it was their policy to arrest all those involved and hold everyone for trial! So, that's why I'm here in jail."

Her story and situation were so unbelievable to me that I found it quite amusing and started shaking a bit as I tried to suppress open laughter as she was telling me of her plight.

"What are you laughing at?!" she said as she broke into a grin and laughed a bit with me as she recounted her tale.

However, I soon regained my composure and went to work to try to get her out of there. The first thing I did was to call our mother and tell her what had happened. Right away she called the director of the University, whom she knew quite well. And, as it turned out, the director just happened to have a brother who was the governor of the state of Jalisco. His brother then made a call to the chief of police in Guadalajara who, in turn, made a call to the local jail. Within an hour or so my sister was released. It was amazing!

As far as the attorney who left the note on my door, I don't know how he found out about the whole situation, but it seemed to me, as I observed him in town after this event, like he had a very cozy relationship with the local police department.

In any case, now that Linda was out of jail, I asked her where her car might be? She didn't know and suggested that we ask the police. Of course, the police had "no idea" where her car might be either - except to advise us to "check the local junk yards." So, after looking through about fourteen different junk yards we finally found her car and had it towed to the local mechanic. And, in a few more days her car was finally fixed - at our expense of course.

It was just a different world there in Guadalajara, and the medical school itself was not exempted from the peculiarities of this world. For example, as with all medical schools, there was an anatomy class during the first year where we had to dissect and study cadavers. A small group of students worked on each cadaver and the various groups usually gave names to the particular cadaver that their group was dissecting. It was a bit morbid I know, but such is the nature of medical school in general and dealing with all the various stresses involved. I still remember that we named our cadaver "Minerva". However, the really strange part was that we had to provide for our own cadavers and our own skeletons to study! Some of the students actually paid grave robbers to dig up bodies from common graves so they could use the bones to study for their classes! This is because doing it the conventional way was extremely expensive. An entire pre-assembled skeleton cost about three to four hundred dollars – a whole lot of money at the time. It was much cheaper to simply pay someone fifty dollars for a body and then do the construction of the skeleton yourself. So, this is what a lot of students did, despite the macabre process involved.

One evening, as I walked into a medical student's house, I notice a strange smell. He was in the kitchen actually boiling off the flesh from the bones of a human body that he had acquired so that he could build his own skeleton. It all struck me like something from a horror movie! At first, I was just in shock over such things. However, I soon realized that there simply were few other viable options in that world. It was just a completely different mentality from anything I had ever experienced before – or since.

Not even the classroom environment was immune from the differentness of this unique world. Of course, I knew that some students would always try to cheat the system and get away with cutting corners. However, I was unprepared for the *degree* of cheating that took place there in Guadalajara. Many students developed it into a real art form, to the point that they never seemed to study at all. They would spend every weekend partying at the beach and then come back to school on Monday with hangovers. They would just buy the answers for the quizzes and tests from other students or even from the teachers themselves. Many times I was offered money, sometimes quite a lot of money, to share information during a test. I would try and reason with these students asking them, "What kind of doctor will you make if you pass because of cheating? I sure wouldn't want you operating on me!" But it made very little difference. All they wanted was the diploma without any regard for the knowledge that supposedly went with it.

Of course, what really got to me was that the many of the professors were in on it as well. Many of these professors would accept bribes in exchange for higher grades. It was simply accepted as a matter of course, without even a raised eyebrow, as being part of the local culture. And, some of the bribes were pretty hefty. One of the students gave his teacher a brand new car in order to pass his final exams. Such activity was openly encouraged. In fact, some teachers would consistently fail a certain percentage of those in their classes, "on a curve," so that they could charge extra fees to those who wished to retake their failed exams.

I'm proud to say, however, that Linda and I did things the old fashioned way. We studied very hard and passed all of our exams without any need for cheating or bribery. We knew that becoming a physician was a serious responsibility before God and we wanted God, and our mother who was also a physician, to be proud of us. So, we studied very hard to actually learn what we knew we needed to know to be good doctors. And, it paid off. Linda, in particular, overcame all of the early handicaps that she experienced and ended up as the top student in her graduating class. She went on to follow in our mother's footsteps and became an excellent pediatrician.

As for me, I wasn't so fortunate. My path in medical school came to an abrupt end when I received an urgent telephone call one morning from Loma Linda informing me that my wife Faye was very sick. She had been admitted to the hospital with a massively enlarged liver and was very jaundiced – "as yellow as a canary" according to my mother-in-law. It's hard to say when, exactly, she was exposed to the hepatitis virus, or even what strain of hepatitis she had, but she probably contracted the virus from an infected needle stick while we were living in Bolivia. Regardless, she had rapidly deteriorated and become extremely sick and the doctor even had doubts about her survival. He suggested that I come to Loma Linda immediately if I wanted to see her alive.

In shock and disbelief, I immediately made plans to leave Guadalajara and my dreams of becoming a doctor behind. However, leaving the country would not be so easy. I was told that it would take a few weeks to get clearance to get out of Mexico – time that I just didn't have. So, I decided to fly to Tijuana and just walk across the border.

On the flight to Tijuana, I made friends with a "Mexican-American" going by the name of Juan. He had driven down to Mexico to sell a car and now he was flying back to Tijuana to cross the border just like I planned to do. This gave me hope since Juan assured me that he had done this dozens of times before without any difficulty. But, when we landed in Tijuana the airport immigration official asked us for our papers. Of course, I had no papers that gave me permission to leave Mexico and Juan had no papers that gave him permission to be in Mexico in the first place.

The immigration officer politely said, "Señores, please follow me," as he ushered us down the hall to a waiting room presided over by a rather rotund guard who was sitting in a chair with his eyes half closed and his feet propped up on his desk. I saw my chance. I had no intention of being bused back to Guadalajara.

"Juan," I whispered sideways as I jabbed him in the ribs with my elbow. "Do you have twenty dollars?"

"Yes, but why do you ask?" he whispered back to me.

"I have about twenty dollars in change myself. Combined with your twenty I think we can bribe this guard," I said out of the corner of my mouth.

"It's worth a shot!" he nodded as he handed me his twenty.

I reached into my pocket and carefully arranged the various ones and fives I pulled out along with Juan's $20 bill. Then, I went over to the guard and explained to him that my wife was dying and I needed to get home to see her – while conspicuously holding the cash in my left hand. I am sure he didn't believe a word I said, but his lazy eyes widened a bit as they slowing drifted toward the bills that dangled loosely from my hand. I leaned forward with both my hands on the desk as I talked to him before standing back up, leaving the pile of bills on the desk in front of him. Then, very slowly, he stretched his arms and sat upright in his chair and looked at me for a while. After a minute or so, he slowly and deliberately stood up and pushed a few papers around on the desk, some of which covered the pile of money, before he casually walked over to the door. He paused for a moment before walking through the doorway. After a second or two, he quickly stepped back into the room and said, “You can leave, but don’t tell anyone I let you go!”

I didn’t wait a second longer. “Let’s get out of here!” I called over my shoulder to Juan as we both rushed out the door and down the hall to the back door. We ran down the street and flagged a taxi.

“Take us to the border crossing!” I yelled through the window. Jumping in the back seat, I handed the driver a ten dollar bill.

“Si Señores,” he answered with a broad toothless grin as he stepped on the gas.

The border was only eight blocks away, so the taxi driver was more than happy to take my $10 to drive us less than half a mile, and we were more than happy to get there as fast as possible.

Then Juan looked at me and blurted out, “What about our luggage?!”

“Are you crazy?! Forget the luggage!” I shot back.

We walked through the Mexican side with a group of tourists. When we got to the American side, the guard asked us where we were born and I answered in perfect English, “Fresno, California.” They let me pass through without further questions. However, when they got to Juan he had a slight accent and seemed a little nervous. So, they decided to detain him and asked him further questions. I waited for him as they led him down the hall to another room. After about fifteen minutes, they let him go.

“What happened in there,” I asked?

“You wouldn’t believe it! They searched every nook and cranny of my body. They thought I was smuggling drugs because they found a wad of money in my pocket. I had a very hard time convincing them that the money came from selling a car.”

Then, we walked over to the bus station and boarded a bus headed for San Bernardino.

Soon I was with Faye, but she was very sick. I thought that I had made it just in time to see her before she died. However, she asked for an anointing service and put herself in God's hands, healing or no healing. And, miracles of miracles, she began to slowly improve. It took several years for her to completely recover, but she did recover. So many times I've thanked God for preserving her life and giving her back to me. Sean was also successfully treated for typhoid and began to recover and both Sean and Shannon were treated for tapeworms and other intestinal parasites.

As for me, I began to look for a job. I had to provide for my family somehow – and simply couldn't leave Faye again to go back to medical school while she was still so weak. Again, we prayed about what we should do and a few weeks after Faye was able to leave the hospital I received an invitation to pastor a church in Alabama.

Now that I look back on it all, all the stress and trauma of those difficult days for our family, I can see how God was there all along. He didn't remove all the pain and suffering that this world threw at us, but He didn't let it overwhelm us either. He was always there with a new plan to meet every new emergency. While I think I would have enjoyed being a physician, I've also enjoyed being a pastor and I think that being a pastor has probably worked out the best for my family and my children over time. Both of my boys are good Christian men today, both dedicated doctors, and both love God very much and are training their own boys to do the same. So, far from being upset about having to drop out of medical school, I am so very happy that I placed my life and dreams and goals in God's hands and let Him make everything, even the bad things, work together for good for those who love Him (Romans 8:28).

An Adventure in Moving

Five months after I returned from medical school in Mexico, Faye and I received a call to pastor a church district in northern Alabama. Because of Faye's illness with hepatitis and my need for a job we decided to accept the position. Faye would fly to Alabama with the boys and I would rent a U-Haul truck and carry our worldly processions to our new home. On the back of the U-Haul truck that I had rented were written the prophetic words, "An Adventure in Moving." Most of the afternoon of the first day of our new adventure was spent loading our things into the truck. After everything was finally packed, we attached our antique Opel car to the rear end of the truck so that I could tow it instead of hiring someone to drive it all the way from southern California to Alabama.

Of course, back in those days, these moving trucks did not have air conditioning and the heat was oppressive that summer – especially through New Mexico and Arizona. The wind blowing through the open windows gave limited relief. Still, the trip was progressing nicely until I got through Albuquerque. I finally made it up into the mountains on the other side of Albuquerque and I was enjoying the views and cooler air. I was beginning to relax a bit and let my mind wander as the cool breeze swept over my face. Then, just as I was heading down the other side of the mountain range, I happened to notice in my peripheral vision that something unusual was happening in my rear view mirror. The Opel that had been behind me the entire way simply wasn't there. As I snapped back to the reality of the situation I suddenly realized that the Opel had broken free from the hitch and was *passing* me on the left! Now in full terror mode the only I quickly pressed on the gas to try to get back in front of the Opel on a short straightaway before the next corner. I slammed the gas pedal to the floor and the truck lunged forward. After what seemed like an eternity we gained a little distance on the independent car and then swerved in front of it and pressed on the brake – and prayed. Miraculously, it worked! I finally brought the truck to a complete stop and ran to the back to assess the damage.

The flimsy bumper had torn off of the car and was hanging off the tow bar in a crumpled mess. Otherwise, the front of the car had a few dents, but didn't look too bad relatively speaking. So, I got into the car and pulled it off to the side of the road. Then ran to the truck and drove it to the first wide area where I could park it. Fortunately, no other cars came by during this time.

Faye had told me that her Uncle Webster lived in Albuquerque. However, he had not maintained close ties with the family so he did not really know Faye and certainly didn't know me from Adam. However, I decided to try to find him anyway. So, I went back and got in the Opel and headed back to Albuquerque. The phone book in the filling station listed one Webster Heath. His maid answered the phone and told me that Webster was at work and gave me directions. I found that the pre-stressed concrete company he ran was a few blocks off the main highway. It was about lunchtime and the office was empty except for a stocky man sitting behind a desk looking over plans.

"Are you Mr. Heath?" I asked with a grin.

"Yes, what do you want?" he grunted without looking up.

When I explained to him who I was and told him of my dilemma, his face lit up and he raised himself from behind his desk and walked over to where I stood. Putting his arm around my shoulder he announced, "Well son, I have a solution for your problem, but first we need to eat and talk. The meal is on me. There is a little Mexican restaurant right down the road where most of the folks that work around here go to eat. It serves great tamales and a good spicy chili."

I didn't argue. I was famished and more than glad for a free meal. At the restaurant he wanted to know all the newest gossip about Faye's family.

"I haven't seen a lot of the family for several years. How is my brother Lawrence doing and what about his boys Lynn and Glenn? I wish I could have seen Faye and your children."

We sat there and chatted like old friends for quite some time. And, the tamales and spicy chili were absolutely wonderful.

Afterward, we drove back to his company.

"Why don't you pull your car over to the shop?" He winked at me as he continued, "And, I will put on a bumper that will never come off!"

So, I pulled the car into the large garage and he proceeded to make some measurements - whistling a little tune as he worked. In short order he had a piece of angle iron welded to my car. It was so heavy and stout that it reminded me of a cow catcher on a steam locomotive. The car squatted down a bit in front from the weight of it.

"There," he announced proudly as he took off his gloves. "You'd probably demolish a semi if you hit it with this bumper!" And I believed him.

Then, Uncle Webster hopped up into his pickup and yelled out of the window, "I'll follow you out to your truck and help you attach it."

Once we found the truck it wasn't but a matter of minutes before the car was securely attached and I was back on the road headed for Alabama.

"Well, that wasn't so bad after all," I thought to myself as I drove on down the mountain and found a motel for the evening.

However, the next morning when I pulled out of the motel's parking lot, I noticed that the truck's steering wheel seemed just a little loose. But, I didn't give it much thought. After all, I was enjoying the clear beautiful Texas sky and I was making good time. The truck was purring along at sixty-five miles an hour and the car was towing behind me without a problem in the world. About midmorning the play in the steering wheel became more noticeable. I had to constantly turn the wheel about a quarter turn back and forth to keep the truck on the road.

"What now?!" I said out loud to myself as I began looking for a service station that had U-Hauls for rent.

"Lord," I prayed. "You are going to have to help me out again with this!"

I was in the middle of nowhere and the map indicated the next town was *30 miles* away. Steering that truck was becoming more difficult with each passing mile. Then, like a mirage that seemed too good to be true I spied a service station in the distance. As I neared the turnoff to the station I noticed a billboard stuck behind the station that read, "U-Haul trailers and trucks for rent!"

"Incredible! What are the odds?!" I thought to myself as I prayed a little prayer of thanks and slowed the truck to turn off the road. I had to make a half a turn to engage the steering wheel and then another half turn the opposite direction to straighten the truck back on the road again. After repeated struggles with the wheel, I managed to pull the truck into the station and stopped. I hopped out, gave the door a slam, and ran to the station office.

The mechanic came out of one of the bays wiping his greasy hands on a rag. He spit a stream of tobacco juice that splattered on the pavement and wiped his mouth with the back of his hand. "Well son, what can I do for you?"

"There is some kind of problem with the steering on this truck. I was wondering if you might not take a look at it?"

"How about jumping into that old truck and pulling up here to the bay so I can check it out," He responded between another squirt of tobacco juice.

So, I ran back to the truck opened the door and climbed in and started the engine. I tried to turn the truck but the steering wheel just spun 360 degrees around and around in my hands. The wheels did not move. I was in shock. The steering was completely gone. What if the steering had gone out as I was hurtling down the highway at 65?

The mechanic discovered that two of the three bolts that controlled the steering had fallen out and that the third bolt had held things together just long enough for me to make it to the service station and no more.

I was now a new believer in U-Haul's slogan. It certainly had indeed been, "An Adventure in Moving!" I was just grateful that God sent extra angels with me along for the ride!

Hanging Out with the Boys

The Lord certainly does work in mysterious ways sometimes. After all, my very first call for a job after leaving medical school in Guadalajara, Mexico was to be a pastor of a district of three churches in northern Alabama. Faye had never been to "The South" before and had no idea what to expect from my new job.

She lamented, "I don't want to live there. They have no indoor plumbing and they eat all kinds of things like catfish and possum. I've also heard that the South is full of tuberculosis."

"Oh come now Faye!" I laughed, "The South actually has all the trappings of modern America. Trust me! You'll like the South. Folks there are downright friendly and the food is fantastic! You'll see!"

She wasn't so sure, but she finally relented and so we ended up accepting the call to Florence, Alabama.

Sure enough, as soon as we arrived, Faye began working in a *tuberculosis* clinic one day a week. Most of the people she dealt with were poor rural people who spoke with a very thick Southern accent. She would come home from work at the end of the day and tell me, "I just can understanding what they're saying! I mean, I got so frustrated trying to understand one particular lady today that I started talking to her in Spanish! Then, just the other day, a lady came into the clinic and told me, 'I is haven horrible troubles with flooden.'"

"Well," I asked her, "how bad is it?"

"Oh," she said, "it's plumb awful! I wuz up in me bed fur days and days!"

Faye went on, "I could just see her climbing into the bed to escape the rising water." So, trying to sympathize with her, I told her, "Oh that must have been just horrible! How long did the flooding last?"

"Oh, many days mam – many days!"

After the patient left, the nurse that was in the office with Faye, Edna, couldn't stand it any longer and broke out into peals of laughter. In between giggles she asked, "Do you know what that woman was talking about?"

Confused, Faye turned around and asked, "Wasn't she was talking about her house getting flooded out?"

"Oh no, my dear!" Edna could hardly breathe by now since she was laughing so hard, but valiantly explained, while gasping for air, "Let me translate this a bit for you. That lady was trying to tell you that she has been having problems with her *menstruation* and has been in bed for several days because of it."

Then Faye started laughing, "Really?! That's what she was saying?! Oh man, I don't know if I'll ever catch on?!"

Other patients came in with very unusual conditions like, "Smile Holy Jesus" (also known as spinal meningitis) or "roaches in the liver" (cirrhosis of the liver). However, it wasn't long before things settled down in the clinic as she started to learn the "language". Soon she grew to really love the people there and really enjoyed working with and for them.

Of course, back at home we had two growing and very energetic little boys. Usually, we split the job of taking care of Sean and Shannon with some help from babysitters on occasion. However, I'd never taken care of them all by myself for more than a day or so. One day, however, Faye came home from work and told me that she and several of the nurses were required to go to Birmingham for a three-day course in order to maintain their nursing certificates.

She looked up at me with a concerned look as she asked, "Do you think you can handle our two little boys while I am gone? It will be three whole days. Four if you include Friday morning."

"How could you question my ability to handle two *little* boys?!" How hard could it be?" I smiled down at her. "After all, I take care of them every Monday while you're at work without any problems at all. Why do women always think that men can't handle children? It's really no big deal. All it takes is a little organization and preparation. It will be a snap! You go on and have fun and don't worry about a thing!"

"Ok," she said as she smiled sweetly, but knowingly, back up at me. "Good luck!"

The first three days she was gone things ran pretty smoothly. However, the dishes were piling up at bit in the sink. Actually, things were becoming a little desperate since we were quickly running out of clean dishes. And, I hadn't emptied the trash, mowed the lawn or vacuumed the house yet – and the laundry wasn't done. Still, she wasn't due back until Friday afternoon, so I figured I'd put everything off until Friday morning – now tomorrow morning. I would save time and energy by doing everything in one shot. The house would be spick and span when she walked through the door.

Then she would be so impressed with my parenting and housekeeping abilities.

I woke up early Friday morning to a terrific rain storm that flooded part of our front yard near the street. Of course, that meant that mowing the lawn was out of the question even though the yard was beginning to look like a small rain forest by now – which meant more time for other things! So, since I had risen so early I decided to go back to bed for a few more minutes of sleep. It seemed like I had just closed my eyes when I was awakened by shrieks and screams coming from the backyard. I quickly glanced at my clock. I had overslept. I threw off the covers, struggled into my jeans and headed for the door. There, out in the flooded yard, were my two little boys (3 and 5 years old at the time). They were having the time of their lives playing in the pouring rain and muddy puddles! I enjoyed the site for a little while, but then it dawned on me that time was slipping away. There were many chores still yet to be done. So, I told the boys to strip off their clothes outside and then to go wash off in the bathtub. They were disappointed, but did as they were asked as I headed to the kitchen to start on the dishes. They took off their soaked muddy clothes and shoes that were now caked with Alabama clay, but forgot to take off their socks…

After a while, I headed to the bathroom to check up on them and saw two trackways of red clay footprints making their way across our lush pure-white carpet all the way to the bathroom. I ran to the washroom to look for some rags and cleaning detergent to try to clean the carpet. As I was searching around, I suddenly heard loud yells and shrieks coming from the bathroom. So, thinking the worst, I ran as fast as I could down the hall to the bathroom - and went sliding through the bathroom door and collapsed with my arms and legs hugging the toilet. My boys had emptied a whole bottle of bubble bath into the tub – which had overflowed the tub with masses of bubbles and spilled out onto the floor. They were throwing wash clothes at each other and the bathroom was covered in fluffy white bubbles and the floor was soaked and very slippery.

Finally, I got the boys out of the tube and quickly tried to dry them and the floor with some towels before getting some clean clothes on them. Then, I had them go around the house collecting all of the trash baskets to bring them to me. The rain had stopped by now so I decided that the quickest and best thing to do was to burn the trash in the brick barbecue that was in our backyard. After the fire was burning well, I told the boys to watch it and then come and tell me when it burned down enough so that I could put more trash onto the fire. Meanwhile, I headed back inside to try to finish cleaning the carpet and then finish the dishes.

"Finally, things were getting accomplished!" I thought to myself. However, not two minutes later I heard a blood-curdling scream from the direction of the barbecue. I dropped everything and rushed out the backdoor and I ran into Shannon, my three-year-old, who was yelling and screaming at the top of his lungs.

"Wha... What Happened?!" I yelled at him.

"Sh, Shhh, Sean hurt me in the back!" he managed to blurt out.

Quickly I looked at his back and saw the blistering and knew what had happened. My five-year-old, Sean, had stabbed Shannon in the back with a flaming red-hot stick from the fire. So, I took Sean into my bedroom to give him a "lecture" and some "correction" to his backside regarding the proper treatment of his little brother and the consequences for not doing so.

After that, I decided to try getting caught up on the dishes since I couldn't find anything that really worked on cleaning the footprints from the carpet. After washing two or three dishes, I noticed our German Shephard dog walking through the kitchen. Something was wrong with him. It looked like he had been run over by a lawn mower. Much of his hair looked like it had been butchered! As I went over to take a closer look, I saw the cat in the living room - in the same condition?!

"What on Earth happened to you guys?!" I asked them as they cocked their heads at me as if to say, "We don't know?!"

Back inside, I found that Sean was calmly looking at pictures in my study with my books spread out all over the floor, but Shannon was nowhere to be seen. So, I went to the boy's room. There was nobody there. But, as I turned to leave I heard something under the bed. As I bent over to look, I saw Shannon under there and pulled him out by his two little legs. As I turned him around and sat him up, I saw why he was hiding - and suddenly realized what happened to the cat and dog. His own hair in the front was also chopped off all the way up to his hairline, with scattered clumps missing from the rest of his head.

It turns out that, while I was dealing with Sean and working on the dishes, Shannon had gotten into Faye's sewing box and found her scissors and gone into the hair-cutting business. It seemed that his own hair, mingled with cat and dog hair, was scattered all over the entire house. At this point, there didn't seem to be one inch anywhere in the house that remained untouched by disaster!

I was in a near panic when the kitchen door opened and I heard Faye call out, "Come on in ladies. I want you to meet my husband and kids!"

At that moment I felt exactly like one of the foolish virgins mentioned in the Bible who were totally unprepared for the day of reckoning...

The Lost Snake

Most people don't like snakes because I think we have an inherited affinity against them, but Ruth Potts had a fascination for every living creature, even snakes. Her husband, Frank Potts, was a well-known attorney there in Florence, Alabama, and had a close relationship with then-Governor George Wallace. Frank and George had been classmates in law school, so Wallace had appointed Frank to the Alabama Alcohol and Beverage Commission - which surprised many since Frank, as a Seventh-day Adventist, did not drink. In return, Frank was a strong supporter of the Governor's presidential ambitions and campaigned vigorously for Wallace, putting Frank in the thick of things there for a while. In fact, some referred to Frank as the "political czar" of northern Alabama.

Ruth, on the other hand, while feeling very comfortable around her husband's sophisticated political friends, really enjoyed country living much more than politics. She enjoyed living in the country, having a large garden and lots and lots of animals – to include dogs, chickens, squirrels, birds of all kinds, snakes and ducks, and even a hermit crab that she kept in her sink. Frank was an animal lover too, but in a much more narrow range which was pretty much limited to his hunting dogs – especially one that he called "Nick". Now I may be wrong, but it seemed to me that Frank loved nick almost as much as he loved Ruth – and some days perhaps a little more than he loved Ruth. I first noticed it at church one Sabbath when Frank, one of the elders of the day on the platform with me, left several times to go to the pastor's office to phone the hospital.

"Is Ruth Ok?" I whispered over at him after several of these calls.

"As far as I know! Why do you ask?" he responded with a raised eyebrow.

"Well, you've been calling the hospital quite a lot and I was just hoping that she was Ok, or if I should go and visit her after church?"

"Oh no!" he grinned from ear-to-ear. "I ain't callin about Ruth! I'm callin the vet about my best bird dog Nick!"

Frank went on to explain that Nick had ripped a gash in his tail on a barbed wire fence chasing quail and had to have surgery to repair the damage.

So, I guess you could say that Frank loved his animals, but it was Ruth who really took it to the next level.

One year Faye was asked to take care of the kindergarten division at the camp meeting that was held every year in Lumberton, Mississippi on the campus of Bass Memorial Academy. She was trying to put together an interesting program for the kids and was brainstorming on what she might do one evening as she sat with me at the kitchen table cutting out paper figures for an illustration she was putting together when her face suddenly lit up.

"Say, wouldn't it be great if Ruth could attend camp meeting with some of her animals and come to the children's classes and give nature nuggets? We could call her the 'Nature Lady!'"

I set my book down and nodded my approval. Jumping up from her chair Faye headed for the phone. "I am going to go and call her right now."

"Nah, she'll never accept," I called after her.

I thought to myself, "There is just no way that someone as well connected and politically sophisticated as Ruth Potts is going to be "The Nature Lady" at our little camp meeting."

However, the next thing I knew Faye was on the phone talking excitedly to Ruth about her brilliant idea. I shook my head and was about to walk away when I heard Faye say, "You will?! Really?! That's Grrrrreat! Thank you so much! The kids are going to LOVE it!"

Ruth was true to her word. She arrived on the campus several days before camp meeting began with a pickup truck crammed with a very interesting assortment of animals. And, it became my job to find and appropriate place to keep all of these animals. Now that I look back on it, I think she would have given Noah a pretty good run for his money! – but I didn't have an ark! She had baby chickens, ducks, rabbits, a little goat, lizards, frogs, crabs, salamanders, and one very large black snake named "Festus".

"We need to take especially good care of Festus here," Ruth cautioned me as I was unloading all of her animals. "I borrowed him from my neighbor's son and he would be absolutely devastated if anything were to happen to him."

At this, I paused and turned around to get a better look at Festus. Ruth had him out of his cage all curled around her arm and waist.

"Wow, he must be at least six feet long!"

"He's just a tad short of it," she grinned. "You are not scared of snakes are you pastor?"

"N – No! Of course not," I said as casually as I could.

"Oh good! You'll really like Festus then. Why he's a real sweetie!" she crooned as she tenderly stroked his head.

After looking around a bit for the ideal spot, we found a place for Festus in an open patio right in the middle of the music building. Then, we borrowed a large aquarium from the biology lab and surrounded it with potted ferns and plants and placed Festus inside and securely fastened the lid.

"Oh, he'll be very happy in there all surrounded by nice plants and all," I said as I stood up and surveyed the situation.

"Yes, I think so," Ruth said with a grin.

During the week of camp meeting, Ruth made her rounds to all the children's departments. Each day she would introduce a different animal and talk to the children about the marvels of God's creation. The children were all excited about these animals, especially Festus. He was an instant celebrity.

Then on Thursday morning Ruth came running up to me with tears in her eyes.

"Festus is missing! He's missing and I can't find him anywhere! I went to get him out of the aquarium this morning and he was nowhere to be found! Can you please help me?!"

Well, a secret like that can't be kept for long. When the children found out that Festus was missing and saw the concern that Ruth had for this missing snake, hundreds of kids began to look all over campus for this lost snake. Yet, even after searching everywhere for the entire day no one found the snake. Ruth was beside herself with worry.

"What am I going to do?! What AM I going to do?! I simply *can't* go back home without that boy's pet! I promised him I would take very good care of Festus."

Some of the little children suggested that they pray that God would help them find the snake. So, many prayers went up to heaven on behalf of Festus that night. Yet, Friday arrived and *still* no snake was found. This was the day before camp meeting was to end. So, things were getting especially desperate for Ruth and the children were very much concerned. So, the kindergarten kids got a bright idea and asked that we adults pray for Festus during the morning meetings in the main auditorium. So, we did!

Still, Festus was not found all day Friday and late into the afternoon. Preparations were being made all over campus for the evening meeting. The music building was also bustling in preparation since the practice rooms housed the single senior ladies. Each room had been set up with a bed and a couple of chairs and these rooms were arranged around the central patio area – with shared bathrooms on one side of the building. During this time one of these little ladies shuffled her way into the bathroom and sat down on the commode. She was relaxing and humming a hymn when all of a sudden a big black snake pushed his way up between her knees and looked at her, flicking his tongue rapidly in and out of his mouth. Festus had been curled around the cool bottom of the toilet minding his own business when he was suddenly disturbed from his slumber and decided to take a much closer look. The poor lady though! She went into complete panic mode and starting screaming hysterically – and then passed out!

Dozens of people came running from all directions in response to all the commotion. Fortunately, the lady revived without injury, except perhaps for a bit of psychological trauma, and Festus was rescued, uninjured, from the sizable group of rather irate women who had gathered to save their poor friend from such a vicious beast! – all a clear answer to prayer as far as the kids on campus were concerned! and many adults too! – with the exception, of course, of the music building ladies who seemed to have real difficulty seeing the Divine Hand behind the whole thing.

Of course, Ruth was overjoyed to have Festus back again and continued to bring many animals to camp meetings year after year – but without Festus.

A Pigeon Named Charlie

We had just moved to my new church in Montgomery, Alabama and I was still getting settled into my new office when, one Friday afternoon as I was preparing my sermon, my concentration was broken by a light tap on my door.

"Yes, Come on in," I said as I put my pen down on the desk.

The door slowly opened and a thin little boy walked in and stood in front of me holding a cardboard box. His hair was scattered in all directions. His jeans looked like they hadn't been washed for several months and his tennis shoes were falling apart and untied. My eyes shifted from his small dirty face to the brown cardboard box that he held in his hands.

"What've you got there in the box Willie?"

"Just some birds," he said so softly I could hardly hear him. "Ya wanna see em?"

"Sure," I said as I smiled and motioned him to come around my desk so that I could have a better look.

He shuffled over to where I sat and shoved the box onto my lap. Curious, I peeked into the box and there, staring back at me, were two of the ugliest creatures I had seen in quite some time. They had big bulging eyes, huge heads and not a feather to be seen.

"What are they Willie?"

"Thems baby pigeons!" he said with a bit more animation as he started to grin up at me. "My mom says I can keep just one of um, sos I figured you'd want ta have the utter un seeins you got your boys and all."

I studied the birds for a moment or two.

"Where did you find them?"

"I gots um at the Conference office. Thar was fixing to kill um all cause they were messin all over the place all over evrathin. Sos I rode ma bike over thar and rescued sum of um."

"Well, I am proud of you Willie for being so kind to animals and I feel honored that you chose me to share with. Thank you Willie. I'll take one home with me and show the boys."

A big smile broke out on Willie's face. "I just knews you'd hep me out!"

I found a small box in the closet and set it down on my desk and said to the little boy, "Take your pick Willie and I'll take the one that's left."

Later that day I brought that ugly featherless pigeon home to Faye. When she first saw it she exclaimed, "What on Earth are we going to do with it? We don't know anything about raising a baby pigeon that's just hatched!"

I tried to sound reassuring. "We've managed to take care of about everything else I've brought home. I am sure it'll do fine!"

We decided on a formula of canned dog food mixed with raw eggs. "Charlie" was very hungry and from the moment we pried open his beak and dropped the mixture down his throat he became very animated, swallowed it down, and eagerly begged for more. He was constantly begging for food and was never full. So, Faye kept shoving it down his throat until his gullet got so full he toppled over face first – and couldn't get back up again. He just lay there like that. The boys and I were sure that he would never recover. I could stick my finger into his bloated neck and chest and it would leave an indentation.

"Oh, I've killed him!" Faye lamented.

"N- No you haven't," I said as I tried to comfort her, but I really thought she had.

After that, we didn't feed him for several days. We just gave him ground up egg shells and water. And, gradually, the food worked itself through and Charlie survived. In fact, he didn't just survive, he thrived on our formula of dog food and chicken eggs. It wasn't long before he started to put on a few feathers and, in a few weeks, he began to appear rather respectable. In a month he was a beautiful grayish blue pigeon who had a very independent streak. We placed a cardboard box on top of our chest freezer in the washroom for him and that box became his throne room. He did not allow you to go near his box without inflicting a peak or beating you with his wings.

The day finally arrived when we decided to let Charlie have his freedom. We opened the back door and watched to see if he would fly out. But, he didn't move. He just sat on his box craning his neck to look out the door, but he had no desire to leave the comfort of the washroom. So Faye and I decided to take the initiative and picked him up and carried him outside. At first, he was not at all happy with us, but once he actually got outside he began to walk around exploring all around the backyard. Gradually, he warmed up to the idea of being outside and seemed to enjoy it more and more. The boys taught him how to fly by tossing him up in the air and letting him flap back down. Fairly soon he actually learned how to fly around our house and around the neighborhood a bit, but he definitely preferred walking – perhaps because he viewed himself as "human" and walking was what humans did? In any case, when it came to socializing it always involved walking. He was the most curious bird alive and he was constantly walking around checking everything out.

For example, our next door neighbor Rusty liked to swim in his pool late in the afternoon right after he got home from work. When

Charlie saw him get in the pool, he would fly down to the side of the pool and pace Rusty as he swam his laps. He'd walk down to one end and then follow him back to the other end – back and forth, back and forth. And, Rusty grew to really like Charlie and would look out for him when he went swimming. This happened nearly every day until one day when Charlie was concentrating so intently on walking his laps and watching Rusty that he didn't realize that he was getting so close to the edge of the pool. To the surprise of everyone, including himself, he fell right into the pool! He'd never been in water that deep and so he panicked. Rusty had to swim over and fish him out. After giving himself a shake and preening his feathers Charlie flew up over the fence and into his own yard. After that, he still visited Rusty and would pace his laps, but he remained well away from the edge of the pool.

It was like this with many of our neighbors around the neighborhood. Charlie would make his rounds to each one of them during the day and they all grew fond of him and looked forward to his visits. He even made friends with our huge white tomcat that we official named "Napoleon" but almost always just called, "Cat". Even though Cat had been born as a tiny runt of the litter, he now had one of the largest heads I had ever seen on a house cat and he was a real fighter. His face carried the scars of innumerable battles that he'd experienced as he strived to maintain dominance in our neighborhood – and not just dominance over other cats. He would even walk along the top of our neighbors' fences and bait their *dogs* to attack him. It only took one encounter and the dogs knew they'd better leave him alone. Of course, this was all before Charlie came into his life. Generally, with new pets, like small birds or squirrels and the like, the boys would show the new pet to Cat and explain to Cat that this new pet was not to be harmed. And, Cat would dutifully examine the new pet, very carefully, and then leave it alone. The same thing had happened when we brought Charlie home – and so far Cat had left Charlie entirely alone and Charlie, for his part, had left Cat alone too.

Then came the day when Cat was sitting on the back porch cleaning himself after a night of courting and fighting. As he lay on the porch, his tail began to flick back and forth. Charlie was watching it all from his perch on the fence when, all of a sudden, he flew down straight at Cat and attacked his tail! Faye and I were looking out of the kitchen sliding door as it happened. We froze in fear, knowing that Charlie's days were now numbered.

"Our cat is going to kill that bird!" Faye stammered.

"It's too late." I groaned.

Charlie came in like a Kamikaze plane and made a direct hit on Napoleon's tail. I closed my eyes, not wanting to see the bloodbath. However, as I peeked through one eyelid I saw that Cat hardly flinched a muscle. He simply batted Charlie away with one paw while his claws were still sheathed. And, from that day onward, this sort of thing became like a game between the two of them. Every time, this game would continue until Cat would slowly get up, stretch himself, and amble over to the tree next to our tool shed. He would them climb the tree and gently drop himself down onto the shed roof and go fast asleep. Then, to our amazement when we saw it happen for the first time, Charlie would fly over to the shed, land next to Cat, and settle down next to Cat, often right between his paws. This is the way that they would spend most evenings together – like they truly enjoyed each other's company and friendship. It was one of the most unconventional, yet successful, relationships that I have ever witnessed.

Early mornings generally found Charlie checking out the neighborhood. He would fly to the top of the house and survey the land. If he saw something going on that was interesting he'd fly down to investigate. If any car in the neighborhood was pulling out of a driveway he would fly down and attach himself to the windshield wipers and ride to the end of the block and then fly back home. If something of interest was happening he'd fly down to the curb and then amble over to check out the activity. Sunday mornings moved slowly, but picked up momentum in the afternoon. Sunday afternoons were tough for Charlie because there was so much to get involved in. The neighbor's children would come over after church and play football with our boys. Of course, Charlie had to monitor every play and functioned as kind of a ball marker.

Sunday was also the day when our neighbors would wash their cars. Of course, Charlie had to be there to supervise. We had one neighbor who was very picky about his car. He had a red Corvette. Charlie would fly up on the hood and follow the rag as he cleaned and polished his car. Every once and awhile Charlie would stop following the rag and admire himself in the mirrored surface of the car. This seemed to be a Sunday afternoon ritual with them.

Then one crisp autumn Sunday afternoon Sean and Shannon were out playing football with the neighborhood boys and Charlie was carrying on his usual supervisory duties, walking along the curb of the road, marking the movements of the football during each down. Faye was cleaning the kitchen and I was sitting in the living room reading the Sunday paper. I was trying to decide whether to take a snooze or go out and join the football game. Suddenly I heard screaming and yelling. I had a horrible gut feeling about it.

"What's going on?" Faye called out from the kitchen.

"I don't know," I called back as I ran toward the front door.

However, I didn't make it through the door before the boys came storming in, followed by an assortment of neighborhood children. I looked at my boys. Tears were streaming down their dirty little cheeks.

"He killed Charlie! He killed Charlie!" Sean blurted out.

My glance lowered to the form of a dead bird lying in his grubby little hands.

"Who killed him?!" I angrily demanded.

"That big boy that lives three blocks over," Sean stammered. "Charlie had followed the ball into the street and that boy drove by in his car and swerved from one side of the street to the other to hit Charlie. He was driving so fast that Charlie didn't have a chance to get away."

Shannon choking back the tears added, "Charlie tried to fly but it was too late."

One little girl interrupted. "I know where that big boy lives. I'll show you where..."

Later that afternoon I paid that young man a visit. "I hear you ran over a pigeon this afternoon."

"Yea, I did," he responded. "It was just a bird. What's the big deal? I can get you another pigeon if you want. There are millions of them you know!"

I shook my head as I sadly stared down at my shoes.

"Charlie was a pet you know. He was irreplaceable. How could you ever replace a bird like Charlie?"

"Huh - Sorry," responded the young man with a smirk.

I just walked away. There seemed to be no use to say anything further to someone like that.

When I think of the loss of Charlie and the pain it brought to our family I begin to understand how God must feel about us and how unique each one of us is to Him. Each one of us is irreplaceable to a Father who takes notice when even a little sparrow falls wounded to the ground (Matthew 10:29).

The Kitten with a Bow

I liked Elmer Sanderson the moment I met him. He had a happy and positive personality. He was an elder in my church in Sheffield, Alabama and was enthusiastically involved in all of the activities of the church – especially when it came to working with young people. Kids just loved him and all the stories and jokes he would tell them. They especially loved his ventriloquist act with his "friend" Buzzy Blue Eyes. Although he worked full time at the Ford Motor plant in Sheffield, he always found time to entertain kids at camp meetings, summer camps and Pathfinder campouts. And Elmer's altered personality, Buzzy Blue Eyes, was particularly hilarious. In fact, Elmer was able to make Buzzy seem so alive that many of the kids truly believed that he *was* alive. It never dawned on many of them that Buzzy Blue Eyes wasn't really alive or that

Elmer was doing all of the talking. In any case, everyone just loved the man.

We kept in touch over the years as we moved on from church to church there in Alabama. Then, one day, I got a call that that Elmer had had a heart attack and died. Faye and I were living in Montgomery and the funeral was in northern Alabama, but I would have driven across the continent to attend his funeral. There was a very large crowd there, and as funerals go, it was a long one because everyone wanted to talk about their love for a man that had had such a positive influence in their lives.

There was one story, however, that stood out in my mind. Frankie Potts, the son of Frank and Ruth Potts, now a middle-aged lawyer, had been a teenager when I was the pastor in the Sheffield church. So, I was very interested to hear what he had to say about Elmer when he got up to say a few words.

"I want to tell you all a little story about how Uncle Elmer profoundly influenced me and impressed me with God's care for even the smallest things of life. One day a group of us kids, eight or nine years old at the time, were at Elmer's country home for a campout. Some of us were playing with a very small kitten when the kitten accidently fell into the uncovered well hole. Shocked, we all rushed over to where the kitten had disappeared and looked down the hole, but we couldn't see a thing – just darkness. However, we could hear the kitten meowing far below. All of us were very upset, wondering how on Earth we could get that kitten out of the hole? Then someone suggested that we go and get Uncle Elmer! So, we all ran together to the house. Uncle Elmer was there, sitting on the porch teaching another group of kids how to tie knots when we ran up to him and excitedly told him what had happened to the kitten.

'Good thing that well has been dry. Maybe we can lower a length of rope into the well and the kitten will grab it and then we can pull him up,' Elmer suggested.

Uncle Elmer went into the house and soon came back with a length of rope and then followed us as we showed him the way to the well. Hopefully, we all watched anxiously as Elmer lowered the rope into the well and then pulled it back out – but without any kitten hanging on.

After repeated attempts of lowering the rope into the well with no results, Elmer said, 'Why didn't we think of this before? Let's ask God to help us with this kitten!'

So Uncle Elmer gathered us around him and we all knelt by the well and he prayed a simple prayer.

'Lord, we have repeatedly tried to get this kitten out of the well without success. We can't do it, but you can!'

After praying we all got up and surrounded the well as Uncle Elmer tied a ribbon to the end of the rope and lowered the rope into the well again.

'Maybe the ribbon will attract the kitten,' he said with a chuckle.

After lowering the rope into the hole one more time, Elmer paused for a bit before he started pulling it back out again. Then, as he pulled up the rope a big smile broke out on his face.

'I think we have something on the line!'

Sure enough, there on the end of the rope was our kitten! And, the kitten wasn't just hanging onto the rope. There on the end of the rope the ribbon was securely tied around the kitten with a bow!"

At this point, Frankie paused and look up at the silent congregation before continuing.

"Now, there is no way that you can tell me that God does not perform miracles. All of those children there that day understood that God loves even the smallest of His creatures. Uncle Elmer's faith in God was amazing and this is something I will never forget for the rest of my life!"

After the funeral, Faye and I went up to Frankie and asked, "Was that story really true?"

"Oh yes! It really did happen just like I said!" he exclaimed. "There are eleven kids that will swear it was true because we witnessed it with our very own eyes!"

Crash Reynolds

Faye was in a hurry that day. There were too many things to get done. She also had an appointment at the church that morning and was running late. I had already taken the car to go visiting that morning and left our old Chevy pickup sitting in the driveway. Faye wasn't excited about driving the old pickup. She had torn out the transmission once when her foot slipped off the firm clutch peddle and was not eager to try it again. However, on this particular day, she was in a real bind and had no other option. It was either drive the truck or walk. So, she jumped into the truck and rammed it into reverse, peeled down the driveway, threw it into first and headed down the road. At the end of the block she made a right turn and crossed the railroad tracks at a good clip. Ahead of her were several cars parked on both sides of the narrow street, leaving only enough room for one lane of traffic. On the other side of this narrow passage she noticed another car approaching. Since it was a bit difficult for her to work the clutch and brake at the same time, she decided to try to beat the other car through the narrow passage. As she stepped on the gas and gained speed, the other car stopped on the other side of the parked cars to let Faye pass in her speeding Chevy truck. As she flew by, she didn't notice the police motorcycle parked in the driveway and the policeman writing tickets for all of the cars that he had pulled over that morning. Evidently, there had been complaints in the neighborhood of cars driving too fast through the residential area.

"Crash Reynolds", as he was affectionately known in his department for his tendency to regularly wreck patrol cars, had been sent to put a stop to these speedsters in our neighborhood. He was no longer in a patrol car, but had instead been given a motorcycle in the hopes that he would cause less damage.

So, when Faye flew by in her Chevy truck he raced to his motorcycle, flipped on his lights and siren and gave chase. Although Faye saw him right away as he flipped on his lights, she continued to drive a few blocks before pulling over to wait. A few seconds later he came blaring up behind her on his motorcycle, where he sat writing feverishly on his notepad. After several minutes, he finally got off his bike and walked up to her window. He was furious! His face was beet red and the veins on his neck were sticking out as he sternly asked to see Faye's driver's license and registration. After glancing them over, he abruptly handed Faye her ticket on which was written:

"1) Failure to stop for a police officer, 2) Reckless driving and 3) Going over fifty miles an hour in a 25 mile an hour zone!"

"Please sign the ticket," he demanded!

Faye looked at the ticket and questioned, "I've never had a ticket. Does signing mean an admission of guilt?"

"Lady! You can ask your questions in court!"

"Well," Faye continued, "There is no way I was going over fifty!"

"Lady, are you going to sign it or not?!"

"No, I'm not!" Faye said as she gave him a curt little smile.

He reached in the window and took the ticket away from her and wrote, "Refused to sign!" Then, he tore off a copy and handed it to her. "See you in court," he snarled as he wheeled around and stomped back to his motorcycle.

When I got home that evening Faye was in tears. "I got a ticket today and the cop threw the book at me. I've got to go to court in two weeks and I am probably going to have to pay a big fine, they are going to take my driver's license away from me and I will end up going to jail!" she sobbed. "And, I the mother of two small children! What am I going to do?!"

Of course, as the court date approached Faye's anxiety grew worse and worse. There was nothing I could say to make her feel better.

The day finally arrived. I dressed in my dark blue suit so as to look as official and dignified as possible as I sat with Faye before she was taken in front of the firing squad. There were many people in the courtroom that day. However, aside from the other attorneys, I was the only one wearing a suit. I don't remember who it was, but someone walked up to me and said that I looked like a lawyer for the mob.

Finally, after sitting there for quite some time, the judge came into the courtroom. He looked like he was in his seventies and had a very sour look on his face – and his demeanor matched his facial expression. We listened as case after case came before him. I thought that several defendants had excellent explanations for what seemed to be minor infractions. However, over and over again the judge banged his gavel and declared, "Guilty as charged!" and then proceeded to level a stiff fine. He had absolutely no mercy on anyone. Faye began to moan and squirm beside me, "I've had it! I am in really deep trouble this time for sure!"

After the judge had dispatched a dozen or so of his victims, it was getting close to our turn. The policeman who had written the ticket was supposed to be present for Faye's trial. However, he had not yet appeared. Then, he suddenly appeared in the doorway and stared intently at us – especially at me.

"That's him!" Faye whispered. "That's the cop who stopped me!"

I stared right back at him as intently as a laser locking into its target. He quickly turned and walked away.

"He must think you're my lawyer," Faye whispered again.

At that moment our case was announced and the judge asked for Mr. Reynolds. But, he was nowhere to be found. "He probably stepped out to get a cup of coffee," I said as I looked up at the judge. "He was just here a minute ago."

"I am postponing your case until next month," the judge declared with a growl as he hammered his gavel down. "Next case!"

All we could think about for the next few weeks was the pending traffic court appearance. During that month we found out that the judge in the traffic court had died. Evidently, he was suffering from cancer during the time we were there. No wonder he had acted like he did. He had been gravely ill. For us, however, we saw a ray of light. Faye was going to be assigned a *new* judge. Unfortunately, I was called away and could not make it to her trial that day. So, one of her friends went with her instead.

"I'll be praying for you," I said as I kissed her and said goodbye that morning. But I really wished I could be there in person.

Faye sat in front of the judge with a very sorrowful and concerned expression on her face. The new judge looked down at her and smiled and gently said, "It will be alright. Don't worry."

When Faye was called to the front to face the judge he asked her, "How do you plead; guilty or not guilty?"

"Not guilty!"

"Well," the judge continued, "You look familiar. What does your husband do and where do you work?"

"My husband is the pastor of the Seventh-day Adventist church on Atlanta highway and I work as a mid-surgery nurse in the Baptist hospital."

"That's interesting," he responded. "I knew I'd seen you before. I have talked to your husband several times. I buy fruit from your church all the time. I know it helps raise money for your church school. My wife loves the grapefruit."

Then, he adjusting his chair a bit, leaned over with his hands folded under his chin, and said, "Why don't you tell me what really happened?"

"Judge, there is no way I was going over fifty," Faye began.

"Why do you say that?"

"Because I went back there a few days ago and tried going fifty through that area and I almost wreck the pickup."

The whole courtroom erupted in laughter, including the judge, while the prosecuting attorney just shook his head in disbelief.

"Well then," interrupted the judge, "I am sure you will admit that you were going a tad over twenty-five."

"Not much over that," responded Faye.

"I'll tell you what I am going to do. How about you pay the minimum fine of twenty-five dollars, which will cover court cost, and we will let it go at that."

Faye was ecstatic when she got home. "You won't believe what happened in court today. The judge knows us!" she exclaimed as she gave me a big hug and lots of kisses and recounted the whole thing.

A few weeks later I was having trouble starting my motorcycle so I pushed it through the neighborhood to the main road, a couple miles away, where a motorcycle dealership was located. However, when I got there I found that the store was closed. It had been a tiring job pushing that bike so far so I began to check around the building to see if I could find anyone who might take a look at my bike, but no one was around. As I came back to the parking lot a police car pulled up with its lights flashing. The policeman jumped out of the car with his pistol drawn. I knew immediately who it was – Crash Reynolds.

"Put your hand up against the car and spread them!" he ordered.

After patting me down he asked me to sit down in the front seat of the cop car while he continued to question me. "What are you doing sneaking around this business establishment?"

"I wasn't sneaking," I responded. "I was looking for someone to leave my motorcycle with for repairs. I didn't realize the dealership was closed on Mondays."

Crash Reynolds pulled a sheet of paper from his clipboard and shoved it into my hands. "Who does this picture look like," he demanded?

I looked at the sheet of paper. "I have a vague resemblance, I suppose, but that's not me. I'm a preacher here in town at the Adventist church just down the road!"

"That fellow you see there has been involved in a dozen burglaries in the area."

Just then radio came on and announced that the thief had been apprehended at a coin and gun show a few blocks down the road.

"Wait here! I'll be back in a few minutes," he announced as I climbed out of the car.

He turned on his siren and peeled out of the parking lot leaving me standing alone wondering what had just happened. However, I was curious to see what would happen, so I stayed put. In a few minutes, he came roaring back.

"They got him," he declared with a big smile! "I guess you're free to go."

I cleared my throat. "Can you do me a big favor? I only live a short distance from here. Would you mind giving me a ride home? I've got a pickup and I can come back and get my bike."

"Sure," he grinned. "Be glad to help."

In a few minutes, we pulled up to our house. As Mr. Crash Reynolds looked at the blue Chevrolet pickup parked in our driveway his eyes widened.

"Is that *your* truck?!" he said with some alarm in his voice.

"It sure is," I smiled over at him.

"Do you have a feisty little wife with light brown hair?"

"Yes sir, I sure do!"

"I gave her a ticket a few months ago."

"I know you did," I said with another grin.

"You know," he said as he shook his head, "I've got one just like her. Last month she backed out of our driveway and hit the fire hydrant across the street. She knocked the whole things down! You should have seen it! It was like a geyser going off! – a complete mess! Water was everywhere!"

"Sounds familiar," I said as I shook his hand and thanked him for the ride. "But," I thought to myself, "No one is quite like Faye. She is special."

Then I smiled and laughed out loud as I thought, "It sure is good to personally know and have an understanding judge on your side." Then I thought how grateful I was that Jesus is a lot like the judge who helped Faye in her time of need (John 3:17).

Kenny, Sultan, and Bell's Palsy

Kenny Bowen ran a successful floral company in Hattiesburg, Mississippi and was one of the more affluent members of my church. As soon as we met, we struck up an immediate friendship. We shared so many common interests and hobbies, to include our love of flying. Even though my own father had died in an airplane crash, I loved flying and would go any chance I got. Kenny owned his own plane and every now and then he would invite me to go flying with him.

Another interest that we shared was a love for horses. Kenny had several beautiful horses that he kept on his farm. His newest addition was a half Arabian and half Tennessee-Walker colt by the name of Bo. They had driven their Cadillac to northern Alabama to pick the colt up and bring him back to Mississippi in the back seat of their car. Kenny's wife Zetra crawled into the back seat to calm him down and keep him happy during the trip. And, after they got him home, he became like the family pet, like a big spoiled dog. And, he learned all kinds of tricks that one might teach a pet dog. For example, Kenny would point his finger at him and say, "Bang, bang your dead!" and Bo would lie down and roll on his side. Bo would also play tag. In general, he was very mischievous and full of life. If you were wearing a hat he would take it off your head and run off with it. If you were working on the fence you had to be careful where you put your bag of nails or hammer because he would pick up any loose item and take off with it. He was a regular pest at times! And, as he grew bigger it became dangerous to play with him because he didn't know his own size and strength.

Kenny and I also liked to fish, and so Kenny would invite me and my boys to go down to the Gulf Coast to go fishing with him on occasion. We just became the best of friends.

Then, one day when Kenny called me on the phone, I knew something was wrong. He told me that he'd been diagnosed with leukemia, a form of blood cancer. In those days, chemotherapy wasn't what it is today. There wasn't a whole lot that could be done for him. So, as the weeks went by he grew weaker and weaker. The only treatment that made him feel better for a few days was to get an infusion of platelets. So, I volunteered to give him some of mine from time to time. It turned out that our blood was a great match and my platelets gave him a real boost. So, every two weeks I would go and give platelets for him.

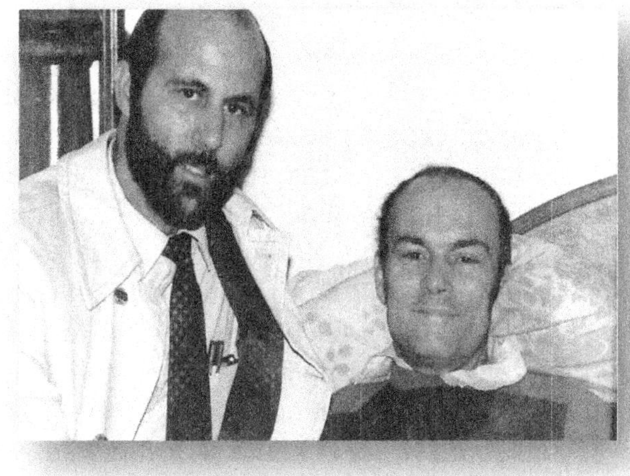

However, as his leukemia progressed my platelets had less and less of an effect. Instead of once every two weeks, I was asked to give platelets on a weekly basis. I tried it for a while, but after few weeks my body couldn't keep up and I was forced to cut back. I felt helpless. I could tell that Kenny was really struggling to stay alive and I hoped and prayed that something could be done – a miracle perhaps. But no miracles came.

One day, as I walked into his bedroom, he told me, "I don't think I have too much longer to live. I would like for you to do a couple things for me before I die."

I held his hand, "You know I'll do anything I can for you. What do you have in mind?"

Shortly before Kenny was diagnosed with leukemia, he had acquired a magnificent young pure-blood Arabian stallion named Sultan. Man, was this horse beautiful and full of life! Kenny had planned to break and train him, but his sickness prevented it. So, this beautiful stallion, who had never been ridden by anyone, was kept in a small barn at Kenny's dad's house. On occasion, when Kenny was feeling up to it, Sultan was let out of the stall on a lead rope. Kenny would walk him around for ten or fifteen minutes and then put back into his stall. I felt sorry for Sultan and went to see him and would take him out and exercise him myself on occasion.

Kenny knew that I liked Sultan, and he wanted to do something special for me. He gave me a weak smile as he continued.

"I noticed that you really care a lot for Sultan. I want to make a deal with you. I want to give the church about a thousand dollars of extra offering. I'll give you the ownership papers for Sultan - if you promise to pay the church that amount. Take as long as you want to pay it and don't let anyone know why you are doing it."

I laughed. "I do love that horse. I promise to take good care of him for you. And thank you. I know my boys and I will really enjoy him."

"That's not all," he continued as he patted my hand. "For my second request, I would like to go flying one more time. Will you go with me?"

"Oh, you bet I will!"

So, the next day we drove down to the airport. I pulled his plane out of the hanger and filled it with gas and checked the oil. I made a tour around the plane and did the inspection. Then I helped Kenny into the plane. He was very weak at first, but when he got behind the controls he seemed to come alive again. He cranked the plane and taxied to the end of the airstrip, checked the instruments, and then charged down the runway and into the air. We flew down to the coast and out into the Gulf. It was a beautiful day as we made our way over the islands off the coast before heading back. Kenny's eyes sparkled. He was his old self again.

However, as we neared the airport, Kenny suddenly closed his eyes and slumped over in seat – completely unconscious! I tried to arouse him but he would not respond. I could not believe this was happening! I started to panic just a little. I had flown planes myself when I was younger, but never one this complicated. For one thing, this plane had retractable landing gear, and I had no idea how to lower the landing system so that I could actually land at the airport. So, I tried again to rouse Kenny. Still no response! My mind was racing at this point. I had seen Kenny land this plane before so maybe I could do it. I had to think. How did he do it? The plane was flying fast. I had never flown such a fast plane before. I was used to flying the slow tail draggers, and the airport was coming up much faster than I expected. With my heart pounding, I prayed and said to myself, "Lord you are going to have to help me get this thing down."

I'd just lined the plane up for the final approach when I saw Kenny move out of the corner of my eye. I looked over at him and noticed that he was shaking up and down. Was he having some kind of seizure? No! He was laughing! He rolled over and tried to catch his breath as he said, "Scared you - - didn't I?"

"Man! This is no joke! You had me scared to death! I was sweatin bullets!"

"Now you know how I feel about dying!" he laughed as he slapped me on my shoulder.

The following week I went to see Kenny again. He looked at me from his bed and asked, "Is it wrong to give up? I am so tired of the struggle to stay alive."

I thought for a moment before asking, "How is it between you and God?"

"I have made my peace with God," he said as he looked up at me with a hopeful look in his eyes. He just wanted permission to leave.

"It's Ok then," I assured him. "Just let go and put your trust in God. It'll all be Ok."

Kenny died that afternoon, but I knew I'd see him again.

Several days later I went and got Sultan and brought him to my house. Like Bo, Sultan became more of a pet than a riding horse. Riding him was like being on top of a load of dynamite. You never knew when he was going to go off and explode under you. He spent many an hour in our back yard watching Faye through our sliding doors on the back porch. If she went to the kitchen he would walk over to the kitchen window and watch her from there. He also knew when I was coming home from work. The mufflers on my truck were pretty loud, and he could hear me start it up from two miles away and head in from the field to greet me as I drove into our driveway.

One Sunday morning I decided that the time had come to put shoes on Sultan. Unfortunately, Sultan did not want to be shoed. I managed to put two shoes on his two front hooves. But try as I might, I could not get them on his back hooves. After an hour I finally gave up. I was exhausted! I gained just enough energy by that evening so that I felt just up to going over to the school to play football with my team. I shouldn't have done it. It was cool and raining, but we played anyway. When I got home that night I was soaking wet and chilled to the bone. I also had a splitting headache and was so tired and sore I could hardly move. So, I went to bed.

The next morning I slept in a little. When I was finally able to drag myself out of bed I went to the bathroom to soak in the shower and shave. As I looked in the mirror, I was shocked at what I saw! The whole right side of my face was sagging and I couldn't move it. I tried to shut my right eye but I couldn't! I tried drinking some water, but the water just poured out of the right side of my mouth. The right side of my nose was pulled down at an odd angle. This didn't look good at all. Again, I started to panic a bit. I thought I had suffered a stroke at first, but I could walk with no problems and my arms seemed to work just fine.

Still, I had no idea what had happened to me. So, I got dressed and went to see our family practice doctor in Lumberton. He diagnosed me with "Bell's Palsy" and told me that giving all those platelets to Kenny and getting worn out trying to shoe my horse and then playing football in the cold and rain may have lowered my immune system and made me susceptible to something that inflamed my facial nerve.

"It is an infection of the cranial nerve of the face," he explained. "Most people get over the infection in a couple of weeks, but there is a certain percentage who suffer permanent damage because the nerve dies and doesn't regrow properly."

As the weeks and months went by I realized that I was in the percentage of those who suffered permanent damage. My facial nerve was dead and wasn't coming back. I had to sleep at night with my eye taped shut. I had a hard time drinking because I just couldn't keep my lips closed and whatever I was trying to drink would run out of my mouth and down the side of my chin. However, my worst problem, as far as I was concerned, was that I could not blow a single note on my saxophone – and I loved playing my saxophone. I'd been playing it since I was ten years old.

Three years later I was lying in bed one night talking to God during my private time with Him. "Lord," I said, "I sure would like to be able to play the saxophone again. It was a big part of my ministry and all. Do you think you could see yourself clear to make that happen? - to make it so that I can play again?"

Ten minutes later as I was laying there in the darkness I felt the paralysis start to move off my face. It did not completely go away but it moved just enough so that I could shut my eye and control the right side of my mouth again. That next morning I jumped out of bed, picked up my saxophone, and played for the first time in three years. Faye was so excited!

"What happened?!" she shouted as she came running in from the bedroom and gave me a big hug.

"God gave me a little miracle," I said. "I asked him if he would let me do this again last night, and he said yes!"

Why did God heal me so that I could play my saxophone again? Why did he answer that prayer, which was clearly a miracle of Divine power that I cannot explain any other way, and yet he did not heal my friend Kenny of his leukemia? I don't know. I just don't know. All I do know is that God is real and that he cares for us. I know that God dearly loved and cared for Kenny too – just as much as He loves and cares for me or anyone else. Every now and then I think that God gives us little gifts and answers to prayer that are just enough to know this and to understand that even in those difficult times, even in those cases where He says no to our requests, we can trust Him and understand that He who sees the end from the beginning knows what is best. While His actions may seem mysterious at times, I know that we would have it no other way if we could see things as He does. Now, this doesn't mean that I won't be asking Him a whole lot of questions once I see Him face-to-face one day. But, for now, I know, without a shadow of a doubt, that He loves and cares for me and my family.

About the Author

Tui DeVere Pitman has had a most interesting life - from his childhood living in South America with Missionary parents to his worldwide travels working as a scrub nurse, a probation officer, a dishwasher on a cargo ship, and a pastor in domestic and foreign lands, it hasn't been boring.

As a young newly-married pastor, Tui went back to South America for several years to follow in the footsteps of his missionary parents before returning to pastor in the southern United States. He has also been a principal of a boarding school and has worked many years as trust services director for the Seventh-day Adventist Church.

He is now retired and currently lives in Wetumpka, Alabama. He still loves to preach on occasion, play the saxophone, paint, fish, and visit with his five grandsons, telling them the stories of all his many adventures and of his love for God.

As far as his unique name, all of his friends call Pastor Pitman by his first name, Tui. He is often asked, by those who don't yet know him, if Tui is his real name. He used to smile and explain that Tui is, in fact, his real name and that he was named after an exotic bird from New Zealand. Of course, that was before he actually saw the Tui Bird, fairly recently, and was somewhat disappointed to discover that he was named after a crow-like bird with two white feathers on its chest...

Namesake: Tui Bird of New Zealand

CPSIA information can be obtained
at www.ICGtesting.com
Printed in the USA
LVOW13s2201110318
569491LV00023B/767/P

9 780692 828755